Security 101

Security 101

An Introduction to the Private Security Industry

Joseph J. Jaksa

CAROLINA ACADEMIC PRESS

Durham, North Carolina

Library of Congress Cataloging-in-Publication Data

Names: Jaksa, Joseph, author.
Title: Security 101 : an introduction to the private security industry /
    Joseph Jaksa.
Description: Durham, North Carolina : Carolina Academic Press, [2016] |
    Includes bibliographical references and index.
Identifiers: LCCN 2016024787 | ISBN 9781611637632 (alk. paper)
Subjects: LCSH: Private security services.
Classification: LCC HV8290 .J35 2016 | DDC 363.28/9--dc23
LC record available at https://lccn.loc.gov/2016024787

CAROLINA ACADEMIC PRESS
700 Kent Street
Durham, North Carolina 27701
Telephone (919) 489-7486
Fax (919) 493-5668
www.cap-press.com

Dedication

This introduction to security text is dedicated to the late Dr. Kenneth C. Christian, CPP. Ken Christian was a former law enforcement official who changed the focus of his career to the protection of lives and property in the private security field. He became a scholar and an expert in security theories, concepts, and practices.

Dr. Christian was highly influential in the development of my career. When I was an undergraduate student, Ken introduced to me the concepts and practices of the security industry and the protection of lives and property. Because of his teaching, I made the decision to pursue a career in the security industry. Upon graduation and as I entered the security field, Ken continued to guide me as a mentor and a friend. He motivated me to become a true security professional and to understand that lifelong learning is a vital means of remaining a professional. It was also Dr. Christian who first recommended that I consider teaching security classes to college and university students. He thought that I "connected" with the students in the classroom. He was able to see attributes in me that I was unable to notice.

Ken Christian was the cornerstone for my professional career and as a member of the academic community. This book is intended to honor his past and to continue his commitment to the private security industry and the education of college and university students.

Contents

Foreword

The world around us continues to evolve and change. Political mind-sets swing like a pendulum, from the right to the left, swaying public opinion and shifting policies. The private sector continues to use new methods and techniques to improve products, services, and profitability. New devices and communication mediums can change our society and how we view the world.

Through these various and at times overwhelming changes and advancements, a personal and professional need remains—the need to protect ourselves and our property. In our global society there are many individuals who desire to cause harm to our lives and property. Their motivations may vary, the techniques may differ, but in the end they wish to take advantage of others. They wish to harm the innocent and the indefensible. They want to take advantage of the unknowing or unaware. They want to harm others for their own personal gain.

Over three decades ago I made the personal decision to combat crime and protect lives and property. My education, military service, professional experiences, and contributions to academia have been and are intended to serve and protect. To protect the innocent, the unaware, the less fortunate, and those who cannot protect themselves or their belongings—this is my purpose in life, my mission, my passion, my calling.

As our world continues to evolve, either for better or for worse, we as a global society must always be aware of the perils around us and around those we love and respect. The battle against crime and those who intend to harm others is ongoing. Because of this ongoing battle, we must now recruit, train, and educate our next generation of protectors. This book is a contribution toward that effort. If we do not take time to learn from the past, understand the present, and plan for the future, the criminals and malcontents could gain an advantage with their illegal and immoral acts. We cannot allow this to happen. We must be strong. We must never give up. We must be always vigilant. Semper fidelis.

Joseph J. Jaksa, Ph.D., C.P.P.

Purpose of the Book

The intent of this textbook is to provide an academic-based instructional text for beginning college and university security students. This text (a primer) is written for first- or second-year students who have yet to enroll in an academic security course. The book discusses relevant theories and practices and offers topics for research and discussion questions, combining both academic theories and current security industry challenges.

The content of the book provides general security concepts, information, and examples, relevant for a 100-, 200-, or lower 300-level college course. It will be suitable for both community colleges and universities. The book is divided into 14 chapters to coincide with a typical academic semester. Each chapter will provide the basic academic building blocks needed to develop a solid foundation of knowledge and preparation for the study of advanced security concepts. With the complexity and depth of today's private security industry, great care has to be taken to offer the necessary knowledge and information intended to motivate a student to enroll into additional security courses and pursue a possible career in the private security industry.

Acknowledgments

There are many influential people who deserve acknowledgement for affording me knowledge, support, and friendship during my career and for this publication.

As a security professional, I was offered the opportunity to work in all major sectors of the security industry. These opportunities spanned over two decades and would not have been possible if not for the support of Mr. Steven H. Smith, CPP, Mr. Richard A. Daly, and Mr. Joseph R. Cozart, CST. In addition, I earned the trust and support of multiple security industry colleagues who offered me industry knowledge during my professional career. These individuals included Mr. R. James Benford, CPP, Mr. Allen L. Streu, and the late Mrs. Mary Anne Sumner, CPP.

With my transition from the security industry to being a member of the academic community, opportunities have been afforded allowing me to create and develop security-related courses. The support from Dr. Donald Bachand, Dr. Clifford Dorne, Dr. Joni Boye-Beaman, Dr. Avon Burns, and Dr. Eileen Johnson allowed me to enter into academia and work to prepare our future generations of security professionals.

Finally, I must thank my family for their love, support, and continual encouragement. This includes my parents, Mr. and Mrs. George and Esther Jaksa, my children, Ms. Jane Jaksa and Mr. Samuel Jaksa, my sister, Mrs. Mary Ann Johnson, and my fiancée, Dr. Anne Tapp (with an additional thank you to Anne Tapp and George Jaksa for their diligent editing of this book). Also, a thank you to my life-long friends who are more brothers than friends—Mr. James Block, Mr. John Dasky, and Mr. Gregory Kovel—for keeping me grounded and not allowing me to take myself and life too seriously.

I am truly a fortunate soul and it is in great part due to the people listed (as well as many others not listed) I have become the person I am today. Thank you to all.

Security 101

Chapter One

The Past Can Greatly Influence the Future: A Brief History of the Security Industry

Introduction

The private security industry has a long and sordid history. Security practices and devices have been in existence for hundreds of years. Human beings have taken great efforts to protect their lives and property throughout history. These devices and practices have developed and evolved over the years in order to adapt to potential threats to property and personal well-being. The study of the evolution of security and the security industry is important. By taking the time to understand the theories, practices, and devices used to protect lives and property, we can learn from the successes and errors of the past and continuously improve protective efforts for the future.

Learning Objectives

In this chapter, the reader will be introduced to a basic overview of the security industry. By the end of the chapter, the reader will have a working knowledge of the basic concepts of what security is, why there is a need to protect lives and property, and a historical overview of security dating back to 1500 B.C., concluding with the post-9/11 world that we now live in.

What Is Security?

When college students are asked the simple question "what is security?" many responses come to mind. To some, security means locking doors, lighting parking lots, or turning on an alarm. Others respond with security officers, armored car drivers, or private investigators. In addition, accurate answers to the question may include protecting computer data, information systems, or data on the Internet. All of these responses are correct. The security industry is a very large and vast field comprised of the protection of lives and property in many ways, shapes, and forms.

Private security is one of the multiple sectors within the criminal justice system. Unlike many of the publicly funded agencies, the security sector is primarily the protection of people and property paid for by private, personal funds. As the threat of crime continues to evolve, so does the stress and burden on our public law enforcement agencies. The reality of the protection issue is that there are simply not enough law enforcement personnel or public tax funding to pay for police or to protect everyone twenty-four hours a day, seven days a week. Since there is a tremendous imbalance in law enforcement versus criminal threats, people, companies, and organizations look to other methods and resources to protect their lives and property. The security industry has evolved as a method for the private individual to pay for additional protection to supplement public law enforcement efforts.

Private security is a hybrid between business and law enforcement. Security can also be defined as protection and enforcement for the private sector. The security industry develops, manufactures, and sells devices used to protect people, homes, businesses, and infrastructures. This can be as simple as a padlock or as complex as electronic security devices using biometric technology. Private security can include a security officer patrolling a parking facility or a risk manager surveying a corporation for possible security breaches and liabilities. The security industry is a multibillion dollar response from businesses to provide the protection needed outside the efforts of law enforcement. The private security industry is a series of for-profit businesses or departments within organizations and corporations charged with the protection of lives and property.

Another aspect of the security industry that sets itself apart from law enforcement is the **proactive** or preventative mind-set that operationally drives this sector on a daily basis. The overall goal of security is to prevent crimes and incidents from occurring. This differs from the law enforcement community, which spends a great deal of time reacting to crimes that have already taken place. In the security sector, the overall goal and practice is to prevent unwanted events from taking place. If or when a breach of security occurs, a tremendous amount of effort to review the event takes place. If crimes and unwanted incidents take place, the security device or system has potentially failed and must be possibly adjusted or replaced.

The Security Triad

With the evolution of the security industry through the centuries and all of the different businesses or departments that protect lives and property, the basic elements of security can be divided into three basic sections. These sections are known as the security triad. The first section of the triad is known as **physical security**. Physical security can be defined as any device used to protect lives or property. Physical security includes commonly used devices such as locks, safes, lighting, or fencing; intermediate devices like alarms, access control systems, or closed-circuit television systems (CCTV); and advanced technological devices including biometric identification devices, thermal recognition systems, body scanners, and computer network security servers. All of this equipment is designed, manufactured, and sold to physically protect lives or property.

The next segment of the security triad is **personnel security**. Defined as the protection of an individual or a group of people, personnel security can take many different forms or practices. The protection of people can include general crowd control and direction; protecting employees while in the workplace; or protecting executives, dignitaries, and citizens while traveling or working abroad. Also included in personnel security is working to avoid violence in the workplace, private investigations, and pre-employment investigations.

The final segment of the security triangle is **informational security**. Informational security can be defined as the protection of data, intellectual content, trade secrets, and proprietary information. Any information that is vital for a business or organization to operate can be categorized under informational security. Examples of the information can include future designs for products or devices, private or internal information vital for a business to operate, personal intellectual property, or copyright protected material such as movies, music, or software. The protection of information greatly changed with the public access to the Internet and the continued advancement of electronic equipment. In the past, the protection of information was limited to items on paper (hard copies) or the unwanted sharing of information verbally. With the incorporation of computer devices and the transmission of information on the Internet, informational security now includes the protection of computer infrastructures, data, and virtual networks.

When developing a strategy to protect lives and property, professionals will include, incorporate, or utilize one of the three primary areas of protection which together are known as the security triad.

The Number of Jobs in the Security Field

Many people are amazed as they learn about the private security industry and the different segments that account for all of the protective services available. In fact, the number of people working within the private security industry outnumbers other criminal justice employees in law enforcement, corrections, and parole and probation. Statistics from the United States Department of Labor reinforce this statement. As of May 2013, the United States Bureau of Labor Statistics estimated that there were 1,066,730 individuals categorized as "security guards." In the same month and year, individuals working as private detectives and investigators numbered 25,820 (United States Department of Labor, n.d.).

By comparison, in the same month and year, the Bureau of Labor Statistics reported that criminal justice employees working in law enforcement (police and sheriff's patrol officers) numbered 635,350; correctional officers and jailers accounted for 43,680; and probation officers and correctional treatment specialists numbered 86,810 (United States Department of Labor, n.d.). Of the 2,247,390 criminal justice employees listed in these statistics, almost half were employed in the private security sector.

This statistical review only illustrates security officers and private detectives. These numbers do not include those working in the electronic security field, cybersecurity, or professionals in supervisory and management positions. It also should be noted that even though security officers are the largest portion of this employment sample, the unfortunate reality is that they are paid the least amount of money. Compensation of security positions does greatly vary from entry-level positions to the senior management level, depending on experience and level of education. What can be drawn from this information is that many people work to protect lives and property in the private sector, based on supply and especially demand.

The Personal Need for Security

Many of us have experienced losing an item or having something taken from our personal possession. The experience of suffering a loss can leave us upset, depressed, confused, or feeling violated. As humans, we attempt to avoid or eliminate this suffering a loss by protecting ourselves. This emotional reaction is viewed as a human instinct to protect ourselves, our loved ones, or our possessions.

Although there are many theories or philosophies that attempt to explain human relations, one specific theory exemplifies why as humans we feel the need for security. In the 1940s psychologist Abraham Maslow developed a list of the "hierarchy of needs." Maslow believed that as humans, we are motivated to seek five basic human needs for our everyday lives. Of the five needs (four being physiological, affiliation, esteem, and self-actualization), Maslow theorized that humans also instinctively need security to achieve personal satisfaction. To Maslow, the concept of security drives humans to seek protection and security and avoid situations causing pain (Ortmeier, 2009). This need for security drives us to seek protection from harm, ensure protective stability in our lives, and avoid situations that may cause pain and suffering. This continual drive for safety and security is evident throughout history, from early primitive cultures to modern-day society.

SELF-ACTUALIZA-TION
morality, creativity, spontaneity, acceptance, experience purpose, meaning and inner potential

SELF-ESTEEM
confidence, achievement, respect of others, the need to be a unique individual

LOVE AND BELONGING
friendship, family, intimacy, sense of connection

SAFETY AND SECURITY
health, employment, property, family and social abilty

PHYSIOLOGICAL NEEDS
breathing, food, water, shelter, clothing, sleep

Maslow's Hierarchy of Needs pyramid © Elenarts via fotolia.com

Historical Evidence of Security

Based in part on Abraham Maslow's theory that humans seek security as well as safety, it can be debated that long before any formal law enforcement organizations existed, humans went to great efforts to develop and utilize security methods to protect lives and property. Because of the need to avoid loss and being violated, human beings found ways to avoid this pain caused by the forces of nature and other humans.

Evidence exists showing that ingenious cultures exercised their human need to protect lives and property. During the Neolithic Period (7000–3000 B.C.) groups developed basic rules to ensure order was maintained and possessions remained safe. These cultural norms were expected to be maintained by the group. Early bodyguards were deployed by the Sumerians, Greeks, and Egyptians to protect rulers or the general population (Collins, Ricks, & Van Meter, 2000).

During the Mycenaean Age (1500–1200 B.C.) cultures and populations formally built fortresses designed to fend off attacking groups, unwanted people, or wild animals. These fortresses were elevated, built of strong materials, and utilized natural resources to protect lives and property (Collins et al., 2000). The use of natural resources by these early cultures for protection and safety illustrates what is now referred to as "**Crime Prevention Through Environmental Design**" (**CPTED**). The concept of CPTED is based upon using the resources available when designing ways to protect lives and property. CPTED can utilize natural resources or man-made resources. The inhabitants during the Mycenaean Age used hills, mountains, or cliffs to build their dwellings upon or located their communities near water. By using these natural resources, the communities had extra protection to delay or deter any unwanted individuals or animals. Bridges, ladders, or passageways were needed to gain entrance over the natural terrain or geographic layout. This provided the communities methods to monitor and deny access into the protected areas.

Also during this time period, locking devices were developed and utilized by the Egyptians, Greeks, and Romans. These locks were the first evidence of formal physical security used to deter thieves from stealing articles or items. These locks were used for perimeter doors and placed on smaller items to keep them closed and secured. The designs for these early locking devices were used to eventually develop our modern-day padlock, pin-tumbler locks, and wafer-style locks (Collins et al., 2000).

Formal security personnel units were implemented by Greek and Roman societies from 700 B.C. to 100 A.D. These cultures utilized young and able-bodied men to protect cities, states, and the ruling class. These men would watch over the designated areas and intervene when conflict broke out, act as a neighbor-

Antique Locks © sergeka via fotolia.com

hood watch by alerting citizens to concerns or problems, be utilized as bodyguards to protect the ruling class, or act as quasi-military units enforcing rules and behavioral expectations. Specific examples include peltasts, men paid by Greek rulers to maintain order, as well as the formal unit developed by Augustus Caesar, known as the Praetorian Guard. Augustus Caesar used the Praetorian Guard as his personal bodyguards much in the same way our modern Secret Service protects the president of the United States. Caesar also developed a night watch system to deter unwanted acts such as assaults or burglaries (Collins et al., 2000).

During the Middle Ages changes in protection began to take place, shifting from a general security watch to the formal development of early police forces. One of the significant developments, pertaining to security, occurred during the time period from 300 A.D. to 600 A.D. In this period the Roman Empire collapsed, falling to barbarian rulers. These Anglo-Saxons migrated from what is today Germany up to England. These German descendants utilized a well-developed system of protecting towns and villages. The organizational approach used by the Anglo-Saxons focused on a communal effort to patrol and protect. The system, referred to as the "**frankenpledge**" required all adult men to be responsible to enforce positive behavior of all the citizens. If an offense took place, the group would pursue and investigate the occurrence. This concept of self-policing offered the basic principles for securing towns and villages (Collins, et al., 2000).

During the period of 700 A.D. to 1700 A.D. (known as the Feudalism and Norman Eras) the citizen patrols, developed by the Anglo-Saxons, became formally governed by landowners or an aristocracy. Even with the formalization of law and procedures, the local citizens were still involved with the protection of lives and property. Citizens were encouraged or expected to enact the process known as the "**hue and cry**" when they saw a problems occurring. In the event an unwanted or illegal act was witnessed by the citizen (the hue), they would call out for help (the cry) and alert the policing authorities (Collins et al., 2000). This basic patrol and notification process is still used by security services and employees today.

During the English Reform period between the years of 1200 A.D. to 1800 A.D., citizens were selected to act as a formal security force, paid from the citizen tax base. These groups, such as the Bow Street Runners, evolved into the organizational model for public policing departments. Formal criminal laws and punishments were developed and enforced by men selected and trained to secure the area. These protective groups began to gain more power and authority to arresting violators for formal prosecution, eventually becoming the formal law enforcement system.

Security in what became the American colonies reflected practices from other parts of the world. Early Native American cultures protected their communities through the concept of "Crime Prevention Through Environmental Design." Communities were built in high areas to form a natural barrier or established in clearings to provide a clear zone offering an unobstructed view of approaching threats. These communities were also patrolled by the men of the tribes.

As the Europeans migrated and settled in the "new world," they initiated the same basic security practices used in their homelands. As encampments became formalized, they were protected by a night watch comprised of the able-bodied men of the community. This Anglo-Saxon model of security also used the "hue and cry" system of calling for assistance in the event that an unwanted intruder entered their area. This basic format for security remained through the pre-colonial period, the colonial period, and into the 1700s. As the American colonies entered into armed conflicts, citizen military techniques and practices frequently replaced the citizen security approach protecting villages, towns, and cities. The practice of the "hue and cry" remained a primary system of notification in the event of a potential threat. This is exemplified by the famed ride of Paul Revere calling for the citizens to take arms as the British armed forces approached.

The development of security practices and formal law enforcement agencies mirrored the English and European practices of the time. With the formal defeat and independence from British rule, the American security and law enforcement systems and practices were derived from the European model. With the growth of the American states and expansion of the country to the west, the need for security remained. In each developing area, region, or territory, basic security practices were used to protect the lives and property of the settlers. As the populations grew, formal police officials were hired and paid to enforce the laws of the area. This system of security developing into law enforcement continued as the United States expanded into the western territories.

Even with the increasing development of formal police departments, it became evident in the 1800s that additional security measures would be needed to protect all lives and properties. With the unofficial practices of security enforcement and protection in place, opportunities arose for the creation of the security industry.

The mid-1800s became the period where entrepreneurial individuals created the first for-profit security businesses. During the Civil War, security businesses were established to protect the railroad system, the transportation of goods and services, and executives. These opportunist business owners laid the foundation for what is now a multibillion-dollar industry merging law enforcement and business.

The Security Pioneers

Allan Pinkerton

Allan Pinkerton became the cornerstone and the founding father of the contract security industry. Born in Glasgow, Scotland, in 1819, little is known about Pinkerton's early years. The son of a handloom weaver and jail guard, Pinkerton initially learned a trade in barrel making as an apprentice. It is also documented that Pinkerton was involved in what was considered a radical political group, known as the Chartists. The group supported many growing and popular "counter-cultural" ideologies of the time. These included the support of women's right to vote, the abolition of slavery, and the right for working-class employees to unionize (Jones, 2005). It is speculated that due to his radical political beliefs, Pinkerton left Scotland in 1842, traveling to Montreal, Canada, and then moving to Chicago, Illinois (Mackay, 1996). After a failed attempt with a barrel making business, Pinkerton accepted a job with the Cook County (Illinois) Sheriff's Department. He began to earn a reputation as a hard-nosed, honest, and smart police employee with a tireless work ethic. This reputation allowed him to become the first detective for the Chicago Police Department approximately one year later. Even though Pinkerton had a strong work ethic, his differing political beliefs and ideologies led the Chicago Police Department to terminate him in 1850 (Jones, 2005). He then took a job with the United States Postal Inspectors and began working personal investigative cases after hours. Pinkerton, along with his colleague Edward Rucker, opened what was the first known private investigative business in the United States in 1856 (Jones, 2005).

As a business owner, Pinkerton infused his strong and tireless work ethic into his business and his employees. Due to a lack of available or honest police employees, Pinkerton was called upon to investigate crimes and civil issues for his clients. He created and developed investigative techniques that were unheard of for the time. These techniques included the use of undercover informants and the creation of a data base (using a technique called daguerreotyping) to print the pictures of wanted criminals. This "rogue's gallery" of criminal pictures would later become the model used by a young J. Edgar Hoover at the U.S. Department of Investigations (later becoming the Federal Bureau of Investigation). In addition, Pinkerton was willing to take on investigative work across governmental jurisdictions. Most local law enforcement agencies did not have authority or the interest to track fleeing suspects (Jones, 2005). It was this willingness to track and apprehend criminals across jurisdictions that led Pinkerton to a job with the Illinois Union Railroad. Due to the large amount of crime that took place in and around the railroad, Pinkerton was tasked with the protection of the trains, cargo, rail lines, and passengers. From this work, Allan Pinkerton entered into working relationships with George McClellan and an attorney named Abraham Lincoln (Mackay, 1996). As the political life of Abraham Lincoln evolved into the United States presidency, Pinkerton personally took charge of keeping the new president safe. As the newly elected president of the United States was preparing to travel from Illinois to Washington, DC, Pinkerton's information network informed him of a potential assassination plot against Lincoln. The train's route would travel from

Illinois and eventually into Maryland, in route to the nation's capital. Many in the state of Maryland were sympathetic to the Confederate ideologies and considered Lincoln a threat to their well-being. Supporters of the emerging Confederacy planned to assassinate Lincoln as his train traveled through Baltimore, Maryland, approximately forty miles north of Washington, DC. Learning of the plan, Pinkerton planted plainclothes detectives on the train to keep Lincoln safe. He also shut down all telegraph communications along the train route, preventing the would-be assassins from having information on the train's location. Finally, the train quietly crept through Baltimore at night without notification or fanfare, thus avoiding any confrontation (Mackay, 1996).

As the Civil War emerged, Pinkerton and his agents were contracted by the Union Army to gather information and intelligence, sending the details to his former railroad colleague, General George McClellan. Using undercover techniques and aliases, Pinkerton and his agents would gather information on troop movements and numbers as well as infiltrate Confederate gatherings undercover to gain first-hand information the Southern war plans. Although this information was invaluable to the Union Army, it was often mismanaged by an inept General George McClelland. This lack of ability by McClelland to lead the Union Army eventually forced President Lincoln to relieve his one-time coworker of his duties. Loyal to both of his former railroad colleagues, Pinkerton continued to serve the Union Army while maintaining his personal fondness of McClelland (Mackay, 1996).

The assassination of Abraham Lincoln would be a difficult event for Allan Pinkerton. The protection of the president was the responsibility of the Washington, DC, Metropolitan Police. When learning of Lincoln's assassination and the failure of the Washington, DC, police to stop the murder, Pinkerton became distraught, believing that if he and his agents had been allowed to protect the president, the assassination attempt would have been discovered and stopped (Mackay, 1996).

After the Civil War, Pinkerton and his agents returned to serving the private sector. Pinkerton and his staff accepted work protecting the railroad from bandits and working to break up gangs intending to disrupt industrial production. Even with the apprehension and killing of train robbers such as Frank and Jesse James, the employees of the Pinkerton Detective Agency became known as a group of roughshod thugs and goons, doing the unscrupulous bidding of their corrupt clients. In the lawless states and territories, Pinkerton agents would track down the wanted criminals and kill them, beat them, and/or turn them over to law enforcement authorities. No example is greater of this abuse than that of the confrontation between Pinkerton agents with the Ireland-based Molly Maguires. The Irish labor activists were attempting to disrupt the work force used in the Pennsylvania coal mines. The Molly Maguires were using terrorist tactics and social propaganda to persuade the employees to form a labor union. The Pinkerton agents infiltrated the leadership of the Irish radical organization, uncovering their plans and sympathetic coal miners. The case ended with twenty Molly Maguires apprehended and hung. The hangings of the pro-union activists were blamed on Pinkerton and his agency, causing the organization to be labeled as an enemy of organized labor as well as further tarnishing the company as an out-of-control, lawless company (Jones, 2005). The organization referred to as "The eye that never sleeps," showed early both the positive practices of protecting lives and property in addition to the negative attributes of an unregulated security company.

Kate Warne

In 1856, Allan Pinkerton hired Kate Warne, who became the nation's first female detective. Born in 1833, Kate Warne was a young widow when she answered an advertisement for detectives placed by Pinkerton. When Warne arrived at Pinkerton's office, he made the assumption that she was there looking for a clerical job. Much to his surprise, Warne argued and stated the case that she was qualified to work as a detective, possessing an eye for detail and strong powers of observation. Pinkerton was willing to give Warne the opportunity she argued for and she became one of his most trusted employees (Niderost, 2009).

Kate Warne was an intricate part of Pinkerton's plan to protect president-elect Abraham Lincoln from being assassinated in Baltimore, Maryland. As part of the plan devised by Pinkerton, Warne played the part of Lincoln's sister, purchasing train tickets for both and helping to sneak the newly elected president onto the train undetected. During the trip from Illinois to Washington, Warne convinced the railroad employees to keep the door to her brother's sleeping car open so she could attend to her sick brother. This plan enabled the armed Warne to remain in close proximity to Lincoln and able to intervene in the event of an assassination attempt (Niderost, 2009).

During the Civil War, Warne was a key component to Pinkerton's gathering of intelligence against the Confederate Army. Posing as a widowed woman of means and influence, Warne was able to gather details of Confederate plans and activities by attending parties and social events. Posing under different aliases and wearing disguises, Warne was able to sway Southern officers and bureaucrats as well as their spouses into divulging the details of Confederate battle plans and activities (MacLean, 2011).

Rumors still remain of the relationship between Pinkerton and Warne. Some historians believe that the relationship between the two was strictly business related, while others speculate that Warne became Pinkerton's girlfriend. Kate Warne abruptly passed away from pneumonia in January of 1868 with Allan Pinkerton at her bedside. Warne was buried in Pinkerton's family plot in Chicago. When Pinkerton died in 1884, he was laid to rest next to her (MacLean, 2001).

Kate Warne was an early pioneer for women working in the criminal justice system. As a private sector employee, she blazed a trail for women to become detectives not only in the private investigations field but also for the law enforcement community.

The Railway Policing Act of 1865

The expansion of the rail system as a means to move travelers and commerce also opened up a viable target for criminals. As stated above, rogue criminals as well as organized gangs and politically motivated opposition saw the railroads as an easy target to rob travelers, disrupt the delivery of commerce, and create havoc to the transportation infrastructure. Since local law enforcement agencies only attended to incidents that took place in their specific jurisdictions, the railways became a "no man's land" for governmental authority or police intervention. Transportation across state and territorial lines failed to have a specific governmental body for enforcement and protection. Any protection of the rail system came from an over extended and undermanned United States Army.

Individual railroad companies hired their own security or deputies to protect the trains as they traveled. In those cases, most attacking criminals were wounded, killed, or scared off by the railroad security. These railroad security employees were early examples of proprietary security forces, working directly for the railroad and having no authority off railroad property.

In 1865, the state of Pennsylvania enacted the Railroad Policing Act. The act authorized the individuals acting as railroad security for the Pennsylvania based rail company as formal policing officers. While protecting the trains and the railroad's property, the newly authorized railroad police were given full law enforcement authority. Any individuals attempting to commit a crime on the railroad could be arrested and returned to Pennsylvania for prosecution (Campbell, 2001). The policing group had authority over all rail lines owned by the individual railroad company. This act blazed the trail for cross-jurisdictional enforcement of laws and also became an early example of private security personnel being granted limited law enforcement powers, while protecting their employer's property. This is a practice that continues today with proprietary security organizations and a limited amount of contact security agencies.

Edwin T. Holmes

Today, many people are familiar with alarm systems. They have the devices in their homes, places of work, vehicles, and as personal protection devices. What most people do not know is how long alarms and monitoring stations have been in our society.

In June of 1853, an inventor named August Pope purchased the first patent for a burglar alarm system he created. The alarm system, which was basic by today's standards, consisted of small magnetic devices placed on doors and windows. When the doors and windows opened, an electro-magnet current was send to a bell that began to ring (Abus, n.d.). This style of unmonitored alarm is today known as a local alarm. A local alarm is not monitored at a remote location and is only intended to deter the intruder from entering the facility.

In 1857, Pope sold his alarm patent to Edwin T. Holmes. A year later, Holmes opened up a business selling burglar alarms to upscale residential home owners. As a businessman, Holmes realized the limited amount of revenue that would be generated by the small number of wealthy residential owners who purchased alarm system. From that point, Holmes Protection, Inc. began to also sell alarms to at-risk businesses such as banks and jewelry stores. Holmes also developed what became the first central monitoring station for his alarm systems. With this system, the alarm signal would travel through local telegraph lines to the monitoring center. When the alarm signal came in, the proper authority was alerted (Lee, 2009). This is the same premise and format used by today's alarm companies.

Holmes began to see saturation in the Boston, Massachusetts, market (which had a limited number of possible alarm customers) and made the decision to open another office in the New York City area. Edwin Holmes continued with the same business model developed in Boston by offering alarm systems to wealthy home owners as well as at-risk organizations in the greater New York City area. Holmes again used the readily available telegraph lines for the transmission of his alarm signals, which ended in a monitoring facility. In New York, Holmes met Alexander Graham Bell, who was working on inventing the telephone system. Holmes allowed Bell to use his alarm stations as the first exchange points for the telephone lines. Holmes stayed in the alarm business until 1900, when he sold the company to an interested emerging competitor, American Telephone and Telegraph (Lee, 2009). Many today consider Edwin

T. Holmes as the "father of the alarm company," through the purchase and enhancement of the patent from August Pope.

Washington Perry Brink

As commerce and the industrialization of our country expanded, so too did a need to transport personal belongings, important documents, and money safely between locations. An entrepreneur in the greater Chicago area took advantage of this opportunity to create one of the oldest armored car and delivery services still in business today.

During the mid-1800s, Chicago, Illinois, was rapidly growing. Stockyards, the meat packing industry, shipping companies, and their supportive businesses were moving to the area. Chicago was becoming an emerging market and transportation hub to the western territories. With the business and industrial expansion also came banks, investment businesses, and other financially driven organizations profiting off this rapidly growing city. Washington Perry Brink detected a business opportunity to transport the luggage of wealthy individuals from the train station in downtown Chicago to their homes outside the city. In May of 1859, Brink's City Express was opened, consisting of one horse-drawn wagon. During the Republican National Convention of 1860, which was held in Chicago (where Abraham Lincoln was nominated as the Republican candidate for president), Brink delivered the luggage and convention parcels for the 50,000 plus delegates and convention attendees (Brinks.com, n.d.).

Brink continued to grow his delivery business up to the time of his death in 1874. By that time he had approximately twenty wagons making deliveries around the greater Chicago area. The economic distress in the 1880s and 1890s forced Washington's son Arthur Perry Brink to shift its business focus away from cargo transportation and toward the shipping of money. As Arthur Brink continued to grow his currency transportation efforts, he made a bold business move that paid dividends. In an effort to ease the uncertainty of customers that their money could be stolen, Brink formally bonded all of his employees. This bonding was in essence an insurance policy that provided the customers reimbursement if their money or property was lost, damaged, or stolen. During the early 1900s, Brink's began to expand its transportation services around the United States and is still in business to this day (Brinks.com, n.d.). From a basic concept of delivering luggage and parcels, Washington Perry Brink established a small company which turned into a multi-million-dollar armored car and secured transportation delivery industry.

American District Telegraph (ADT)

Another important occurrence in the history of the security industry is the creation of alarm company American District Telegraph, known today as ADT. In the 1800s and early 1900s, before the telephone and the Internet, the fastest way to deliver a message was through the telegraph. Using telegraph lines and electromagnetic pulses, a code was transmitted which was interpreted into letters and numbers. The message was then delivered by courier to the intended recipient. Companies such as Holmes Protection used the existing available infrastructure of the telegraph lines to transmit rudimentary alarm signals. The telegraph company Western Union purchased and consolidated numerous alarm companies and formed the new security company called American District Telegraph or ADT (Lee, 2009). The emerging alarm industry became an early opportunity for larger investors to expand electronic security services. As the need and popularity of alarm systems rose, larger companies purchased smaller competitors, either enhancing their market share or entering into the alarm industry. Both Western Union and their alarm entity American District Telegraph were purchased by American Telephone and Telegraph (AT&T). AT&T continued to invest money and resources into American District Telegraph and developed it into ADT Security Services (ADT, n.d.).

This is a small sample of the early security services and governmental acts that paved the way for our modern-day security industry. As this industry continues to grow and evolve, it is important to review and study the historical past. This security industry self-reflection cannot only provide motivation and insight for our modern-day policies and practices but also offer important examples of both the positive and negative lessons learned through the years. History is always a means to learn positive events and lessons as well as pitfalls and errors to avoid.

The Century of Professionalism

If the nineteenth century is known for the establishment of formal security companies and departments, the twentieth century could be known for the advancement of professionalism in the security industry. The security companies and departments started in the 1800s and 1900s often assimilated to the rough, lawless, and unsupervised business practices of the times. Security personnel were often used as draconian enforcers or "union-busters," and lacked professionalism. The lack of regulation, supervision, and positive business models gave the industry a poor and unscrupulous reputation. Even with successful attempts of some security businesses and organizations to work in a professional manner, far too many industry employees lacked the ethics and morals needed to be trusted by the public. The law enforcement community had a poor opinion of the security industry and the general public often feared security personnel as being corrupt. As the 1900s progressed, concerted efforts to professionalize this growing industry slowly became a driving force for the future of security businesses and organizations.

The Foundation of ASIS International

In the early to mid-1900s, leaders and executives in the security industry saw the glaring need for professionalism in both contract and proprietary protection services. These individuals agreed that leadership training and professionalism would be vital for the security industry to be respected and effective in the protection of lives and property. In 1955, the American Society for Industrial Security was formed. The mission of the non-profit organization was to provide training and educational opportunities for supervisors, managers, executives, and leaders involved in the security industry (ASIS, n.d.).

The organization of volunteer security professionals worked to establish recommended guidelines for security management practices, ethics, networking, and continued education. These standards and recommended practices worked to improve the overall respect toward the security industry, strengthen communication between the security and law enforcement sectors, and develop educational offerings to their membership. The society developed and created a professional designation for security management, known as the Certified Protection Professional (CPP). Candidates for the certification needed to have experience in security management, be educated, and pass a detailed and rigorous written examination on knowledge critical for security management.

With the global expansion of security into the late twentieth century, and a continued need for professionalism and education among security management, the organization changed their name to ASIS International. In addition, the society also expanded their professional certifications to include the Professional Certified Investigator (PCI) and the Physical Security Professional (PSP). Both of the recently created certifications also require past experience in the respective field, education, and passing a detailed and comprehensive examination (ASIS, n.d.). Today, ASIS International serves over 38,000 members in 234 local chapters on six continents. Headquartered in Alexandria, Virginia, the society continues to be one of the oldest and most respected security organizations in the world. The basic mission of the society when founded in 1955 still holds true today but has expanded to assist any professional affiliated in security management and operations, including those who work in law enforcement, business management, and government or political entities.

The Hallcrest Reports

Another significant event that took place during the twentieth century was the commissioning of the Hallcrest Reports through the Rand Corporation. The working and professional relationships between the security and law enforcement sectors historically was tepid and ripe with distain and distrust. Law enforcement did not respect security personnel and a large number of security employees did not trust law enforcement. With the rapid growth of the security industry and the continued strain in the relationship between the two entities of the criminal justice system, a formal review and study of the security industry was initiated to gain a better understanding of the rapidly growing security sector. In 1985, the initial Hallcrest Report was published (Cunningham, Strauchs, & Van Meter, 1990). The study was a three-year effort intended to analyze and better understand the various aspects of the security industry. The academic report offered great insights into the security industry, including the various professional entities that comprise the security industry, the mediocre relationship with the law enforcement sector, and recommendations for improving the shortcomings of security organizations and businesses. This report also gave a foundation for further academic study of the security industry.

In 1990, a second Hallcrest Report was released, building upon the research released five years earlier. The second report looked at trends within the security industry and possible future developments. One of the key components of the second report was in the continued recommendation of networking between the security and law enforcement communities. The study reiterated the initial findings of the first report stating the strained relationship and general lack of operational understanding between the two segments. The second report illustrated the numerous efforts of a "private/public" partnership to protect lives and property. Multiple efforts on the local, state, and national levels were offered, showing improved professional relations between the two segments. The report also offered ongoing concerns in the security industry such as ethical issues and mediocre public perceptions (Cunningham et al., 1990). The two Hallcrest Reports offered a formal examination of the security industry and identified areas for improvement and the need for continued expansion of security/law enforcement relations in the effort to protect lives and property.

The Continued Lack of Respect between Security and Law Enforcement

Why would two important entities of the criminal justice system have a long history of distrust and disrespect? Multiple reasons may be cited for this. First, the security industry also has an ongoing internal identity crisis not readily known to outsiders. Members of the contract and proprietary security segments of the industry have a mild history of distrust. Proprietary security organizations developed the opinion that their contract counterparts lacked training, supervision, and professionalism when compared to the proprietary security staffs. The contract security organizations believed that they were unfairly regulated by governmental and bureaucratic entities while their proprietary counterparts were not subject to the same level of scrutiny. Law enforcement officials respected many of the formal proprietary security organizations but not their contract counterparts. Second, even with the findings and recommendations of the Hallcrest Reports, encouraging cooperation between the private and public enforcement sectors, a general lack of understanding of duties and responsibilities still existed. Progress was made but full cooperation between the two segments in practice was not achieved. Finally, with emerging technology and newly created cybersecurity entities, the security industry as a whole continues to advance rapidly, according to need. This rapid growth hampers the efforts of law enforcement to fully understand what takes place in the security industry. To make matters worse, any needed attempts to regulate the companies (by law enforcement or bureaucratic organizations) are labeled as intrusive and unnecessary to security companies.

An immense amount of progress pertaining to the professionalism of the security industry occurred during the twentieth century. The constantly evolving efforts to proactively protect lives and property places a continuous strain on security companies and organizations: History shows that it can be difficult to maintain and balance between quality, innovation, and quantity and demand placed on the security sector to deter and prevent crime. The stresses and strains of everyday business takes time and effort away from communicating with the law enforcement community.

Security in the "Global World"

The term "global world" seems to be redundant but for today's global society, the phrase can be accurate. We now live in a world that is connected economically, politically, and culturally. Geographical borders appear to be dissolved as the global community shares all of its positive and negative attributes. These changes in our "global world" also have a direct impact on the security industry.

Post-9/11

After the horrific events of September 11, 2001, it was quickly learned that no place on our planet is safe from terrorist attacks. Even though crimes that can be classified as "domestic terrorism" have taken place for decades, the actions of rogue terrorist groups on American soil illustrated that no one is safe from these attacks. On September 11, 2001, our country was temporarily paralyzed. All flights were cancelled, businesses were closed, transportation systems shut down, and major events cancelled. The attacks on that day left people wondering what other landmarks were targeted and a mad scramble took place to protect lives and property. The criminal justice community was mourning the loss of colleagues, family, and friends while called upon to protect our citizenry. This one single day reinforced what academics, professionals, and experts had been advocating for years—that the private and public sectors need to work together in order to properly protect our homeland. Unselfish efforts of cooperation took place on that day in early September and set the tone for the future relationship between private security and public law enforcement. The two entities needed to put aside their differences and become a united front to protect American lives, property, and interests in this new "global world."

The 9/11 Commission Report

In 2004, the National Commission on Terrorist Attacks upon the United States published a detailed report reviewing the events of September 11, 2001, insights on the terrorist group responsible for the attack, the need for counterterrorism efforts to protect the homeland, and how this could be achieved (National Committee, 2004).

The 9/11 Commission Report recognized the importance of the positive working relationship between the private and public enforcement sectors. The commission called for advancements in physical security, specifically the use of biometric devices to help protect travelers both into and out of the country. Second, the commission recommended the use of a risk assessment model, used by the private sector, to review infrastructures and determine vulnerabilities. Next, a layered security system was proposed to establish the use of multiple security devices, providing redundancy and not relying solely on one type of security system or device for protection. This layered approach accurately stated that no one single security device can protect lives and property. Also, local, state, federal, and private agencies and groups were encouraged to share information and resources (National Committee, 2004). Through the combined efforts of the private and public sectors, the national infrastructure and American citizens can live in a safer country.

The Growth of the Electronic Security Industry

In the aftermath of the September 11, 2001, attacks and reinforced by the 9/11 Commission Report, the electronic security industry witnessed a tremendous increase in sales and funding for new and improved technologies. With subsequent attempts of terrorist attacks after 9/11, electronic security designers and companies were tasked not only provide advanced security systems but to work with the public sector to design equipment that may prevent new or emerging methods of attacks. This rush to develop and purchase security equipment provided an economic windfall for electronic security companies. This rapid growth and purchase of security equipment took place to protect the at-risk national infrastructure. Never in the history of the private security industry had one single event created such a monumental impact. Other segments of the private security industry also felt a shorter-term impact from the 9/11 attacks, but they were far less and far shorter in comparison to the rush for electronic security.

Moving forward, the threat of complacency can become a monumental detriment for the electronic security sector. Individuals and groups must properly maintain the equipment to ensure it is in working order. When new and improved technologies are designed, those with the purchasing authority must continue to look ahead for what type of attack may be in the future. Relying on the "status quo business model" where "if it isn't broke, don't fix it" could greatly expose new weaknesses that a terrorist group, foreign or domestic, could capitalize upon and exploit.

The Fear of Cybercrime

With the public access to the Internet and the surge in business and personal transactions taking place on computers every day, criminal activities quickly began to take advantage of the new medium. A new term arose defining the loss and grief to businesses and individuals. The term is **cybercrime**.

For the security industry, cybercrime presented a new venue and avenue of protection. The threat of a virtual attack, scam, or threat to lives and property now runs rampant. The public law enforcement sector has a limited amount of resources to fight cybercrime. The emphasis for protection again falls onto the private sector to combat this virtual threat. The birth of cybercrime should not surprise anyone. But the reality is that with the countless numbers of businesses, governmental entities, and individuals using the Internet every day, a cyber disaster could be just one click away. This threat greatly expanded the need for cybersecurity experts. These individuals are trained and highly astute in the electronic jungle that now exists. For the traditional or veteran security professional, this newly added virtual threat can be difficult to understand. Instead of working with alarms, cameras, and security officers an additional need for servers, network interfaces, and code writers was added to the norm. This computer and network technology created a new hybrid of security professional. The new security professional combines knowledge with information technology as well as security theories and practices. Frequently, the cybersecurity expert works outside the formal security department, instead being housed in an information technology (IT) department.

There will be a need for traditional security providers and employees to interface and work alongside the new IT security teams. Combined efforts for investigative techniques, the preservation of evidence, and the use of the information for possible civil or criminal actions are the new reality. Both of these security sectors can learn from and help one another in the protection of lives and property. Learning from the past lessons of security history, traditional security companies, departments, and organizations will need to work together with the new cybersecurity professionals when called upon in order to protect the greater good.

White-Collar Crime

The threat of white-collar crime will continue to plague the private security industry as well as the general public. Brought to the public's attention by criminologist Edwin Sutherland in 1939, white-collar crime is a continuous threat to the private and public sectors of our society (Friedrichs, 2007). Much like the ever-present threat of cybercrimes or street crimes, the peril of white-collar crime is vast and continuous. White-collar crimes come in various forms, may affect both the private and public sectors, and can have a detrimental impact on economies and personal finances. White-collar crimes may be categorized as corporate crimes (crimes against or committed by companies), financial crimes, crimes of professions (such as medical malpractice or unsafe labor practices), governmental/political crimes, or employee crimes (Friedrichs, 2007). This "silent killer" is different than the traditional street crimes. Often white-collar crimes are committed by individuals in a trusted position. These people take advantage of their power, understanding of the operational system, and a lack of oversight to steal money, property, and trust.

Public law enforcement agencies spend a majority of their time and efforts combating street crimes. When white-collar crimes occur, individual businesses or agencies are often forced to initially address the issue and then decide if the crime should be prosecuted in a criminal court or sent to civil court for possible financial recovery. The private security sector must be keenly aware of the threats of white-collar crimes, how to identify them, and how to address the issue.

White-collar crime directly affects the profits and losses of business, the gross domestic product (GDP), and the global economy. Losses from white-collar crimes can leave individuals bankrupt, force companies to suffer losses (potentially passing the cost along to the consumer), or even create an economic depression. It is only in extreme examples of white-collar offenses (such as the cases of the bankrupt company Enron or fraudulent investor Bernard Madoff) that the general public is made aware of the offenses. Frequently businesses privately address the issue through employee discipline or termination. Only in extreme events will civil recovery or criminal charges be filed. Individual victims who suffer losses due to white-collar crimes frequently face little hope of recovering lost finances. White-collar crime is a continuous plague that will never go away; therefore, proactive measures must be implemented by businesses and security professional to deflect, reduce, or avoid this "silent killer."

Conclusion

Human beings are internally equipped with a personal need for protection. Historically, societies and cultures developed practices and devices to protect personal lives and property. With the growth and expansion of civilized cultures and nations, the threat of crime has exceeded what public law enforcement agencies can address. Because of this unintended deficiency, the private security industry has become a viable and needed sector of the criminal justice community.

With the ever-evolving threat of crime and criminal activities, the private security sector must be able to adapt to new threats to lives and property while remaining vigilant against known dangers and perils that may affect the general population.

As the need for new security professionals exists and continues, remembering the lessons learned from the past and applying them to present day and future operational practices is essential. By recalling the past failures and successes, the private security industry will be able to evolve in an intelligent manner and apply all necessary knowledge and resources to combat the threat to lives and property.

Case Study—Allan Pinkerton: Hero or Villain?

The name Allan Pinkerton can invoke a wide range of emotions from different individuals. To some, Pinkerton was a great detective, an innovator of new crime fighting practices, and a business pioneer. To others, his name creates visions of violence, unethical business practices, and disdain by organized labor. After reading this chapter and better understanding the significance of the history of the security industry, contemplate and answer the following questions:

1. Do you think Allan Pinkerton was a positive or negative influence on the security industry?
2. How can the positive attributes of Pinkerton benefit today's security industry?
3. What can be done to ensure private security companies, departments, and organizations avoid illegal or unethical activities by their employees?

Discussion Topic—Police/Security Relations

In this chapter an underlying theme of the relationship between private security and public law enforcement was presented. Thinking about this information in the chapter, answer these questions:

1. Are there many ideological differences between law enforcement and security when it comes to the protection of lives and property? Why or why not?
2. What factors do you believe exist that may cause a lack of respect between police and security personnel?
3. You have been selected to lead an educational forum on police/security professional relations. Select three commonalities between the two groups that will help to enforce the similar goals and objectives of the different factions.

Research Focus—ASIS International

As one of the oldest security organizations in the world, ASIS International is considered a leader in the development of training and professional standards for the global security community. Visit the organization's website (asisonline.org) and research the following:

1. What is the closest ASIS chapter to your school or residence?
2. What are the qualifications to apply for the Certified Protection Professional (CPP) examination?
3. What is the monthly magazine published by ASIS International and what stories are listed on the cover of the latest issue?

Key Terms

Proactive	Physical security	Personnel security
Informational security	Hierarchy of needs	CPTED
Frankenpledge	Hue and cry	Allan Pinkerton
Kate Warne	The Railway Policing Act of 1865	Edwin T. Holmes
Washington Perry Brink	American District Telegraph	ASIS International
Hallcrest Reports	9/11 Commission Report	Cybercrime
White-collar crime		

Sources

Abus. (n.d.). *History of the alarm system*. Retrieved from http://www.abus.com/eng/Guide/Break-in-protection/Alarm-systems/History-of-the-alarm-system#alarmleit

American District Telegraph (ADT). (n.d.). *ADT Security—Company history*: 1874–1890. Retrieved from http://www.adt.com/about-adt/history

ASIS International. (n.d.). *Who we are*. Retrieved from https://www.asisonline.org/About-ASIS/Who-We-Are/Pages/default.aspx

Brink's, Inc. (n.d.). *Brink's history*. Retrieved from http://www.brinks.com/corporate/history.html

Collins, P. A., Ricks, T. A., & Van Meter, C. W. (2000). *Principles of security and crime prevention* (4th ed.). Cincinnati, OH: Anderson Publishing Company.

Cunningham, W. C., Strauchs, J. J., & Van Meter, C. W. (1990). *The Hallcrest Report II: Private security trends 1970–2000*. Stoneham, MA: Butterworth-Heinemann.

Friedrichs, D. O. (2007). *Trusted criminals: White collar crime in contemporary society* (3rd ed.). Belmont, CA: Thompson Wadsworth.

Jones, G. M. (2005). *Criminal justice pioneers in U.S. history*. Boston, MA: Pearson Education.

Lee, S. (2009). *The impact of home burglar alarm systems on residential burglaries*. Retrieved from Proquest Databases.

Mackay, J. A. (2007). *Allan Pinkerton: The first private eye*. Edison, NJ: Castle Books.

MacLean, M. (2011). "Kate Warne." Retrieved from http://civilwarwomenblog.com/kate-warne/

National Commission on Terrorist Attacks upon the United States. (2004). *9/11 Commission report: Final report of the National Commission on Terror*. New York, NY: Barnes and Noble Publishing, Inc.

Niderost, E. (2009). *Kate Warne: First female detective*. Retrieved from https://suite.io/eric-niderost/29tq2qd

Ortmeier, P. J. (2009). *Introduction to security: Operations and Management* (3rd ed.). Upper Saddle River, NJ: Pearson Prentice Hall.

The Railroad Police. (n.d.). *The early days of railroad policing to present*. Retrieved from http://www.therailroadpolice.com/history.htm

United States Department of Labor, Bureau of Labor Statistics. (2013). Occupational employment and wages, May 2013. *21-1092 Probation officers and correctional treatment specialists*. Retrieved from http://www.bls.gov/oes/current/oes211092.htm

United States Department of Labor, Bureau of Labor Statistics. (2013). Occupational employment and wages, May 2013. *33-3012 Correctional officers and jailers*. Retrieved from http://www.bls.gov/oes/current/oes333012.htm

United States Department of Labor, Bureau of Labor Statistics. (2013). Occupational employment and wages, May 2013. *33-3051 Police and sheriff's patrol officers*. Retrieved from http://www.bls.gov/oes/current/oes333051.htm

United States Department of Labor, Bureau of Labor Statistics. (2013). Occupational employment and wages, May 2013. *33-9021 Private Detectives and Investigators.* Retrieved from http://www.bls.gov/oes/current/oes339 021.htm

United States Department of Labor, Bureau of Labor Statistics. (2013). Occupational employment and wages, May 2013. 33-9032 Security Guards. Retrieved from http://www.bls.gov/oes/current/oes339032.htm

Chapter Two

Unnatural Partners: The Business of Private Security

Introduction

Frequently, when people are asked to say the first thing that comes to mind when they hear the word "security," many images and thoughts appear. These may include locks, alarms, cameras, and security "guards." The industry of security is very deep, detailed, and complex. It spans the private and public sectors, combined with civil, criminal, and contractual laws on local, regional, national, and international levels.

This chapter looks into the business of private security. Typically, most activities pertaining to security begin and thrive in the private sector. This can make understanding what security is a potentially confusing task. It is driven by profit and losses and governmental and private sector regulations, contracts, and agreements, as well as business practices and ethics.

Learning Objectives

By the end of this chapter, the reader will have a basic overview of the different business aspects of the security industry. This includes defining the primary business applications of the industry and specific sub-segments that help to drive the day-to-day operations pertaining to the protection of lives and property.

The Business of Protecting

Money is the ultimate driving factor in security. Finances come from generating business, requesting and justifying budgeting allocations, and showing a profit or a positive return on investment. **The financial mission of security** is a hybrid of protecting lives and property while generating profits or a justification in the investment. It can be a very difficult task to blend and justify actions and results in dollars and cents.

Profits and Losses

Looking at security as an industry rather than a segment in the criminal justice system may help put these concepts in focus. The **"business of security"** is similar to the corner store in your neighborhood. The local store has to purchase or rent property; pay utilities, taxes, and insurance to operate; invest in the goods or services to offer customers; and advertise and promote their product or services, as well as hire, train, and pay employees. In the end, if the corner store cannot bring in customers and make a profit, it will close and go out of business.

Many independent security companies are faced with similar challenges every day. They must treat their "business of protecting lives and property" the same way as any business owner. Instead of offering bread, milk, clothes, or shoes, they sell the ways and means to protect their customers. If they do not accomplish these basic business practices and theories, the business will fail to thrive and prosper.

Another way to look at security is as a department within a company or corporation. Companies and corporations are also reliant upon profits and earnings. They also strive to improve their operations and business practices to increase profitability (commonly known as the "bottom line"). Each department is responsible for a budget and showing overall productivity, which will assist in the overall profitability of the organization. If a department cannot show adequate productivity and production, the company or corporation may reduce their allocated funding, make personnel changes, or adjust expectations to change its unprofitable or unproductive outcomes.

This type of financial justification can be very difficult on a security department. In an industry where success is measured by a lack of incidents or problems, many corporate outsiders do not understand the **proactive** (i.e., anticipating future problems) nature of the security industry. This puts added stress on the security executive, director, or manager to justify and prove that their department's efforts do help to maintain the overall productivity and profitability of the company or corporation.

In the end, the person who is there to protect a customer, employee, or company must also be able to create a budget, prepare a business plan, and successfully manage employees. This is a downfall for many entering into the security industry. Many people coming into the industry know how to protect lives and property but they lack business knowledge and experience. The reality is that "the business of security" is as much about dollars and cents as protecting lives and property.

Training

Until the 1980s the practice and concept of properly training employees was looked upon as a possible deterrent from turning a profit. Many of the "old guard" security owners would avoid training employees because the company would have to absorb the cost of paying the employee while they were trained. This in turn would reduce profits.

This concept of the need to train security employees began to dramatically shift starting in the 1980s. This change was the result of many independent and at times non-related factors. First was the **liability of the untrained employee** and possible negligence of the company due to the lack of training. The increase of civil liability claims toward security employees who were not properly trained became a major concern. Our society began to adopt a litigious attitude (i.e., exhibiting a propensity to sue in court) pertaining to issues that were ignored in the past. Because of the threat of being sued for a negligent employee, security owners began to understand the need to train.

Another factor driving improved training for employees was **government intervention**. Individual states experienced unfortunate incidents at the hands of untrained security employees. The result was harm to individuals or damage to property. To help reduce these incidents, states adopted laws requiring certain security employees to receive minimal training. In some states, it became the responsibility of the individual employee to become trained (also known as certified or licensed). In these circumstances, unless a potential employee presented the credentials of the formal training, the employer is unable to hire them. This method of personal responsibility for training shifts the burden to the individual and not the company. If it is found that the employee is not properly trained, the individual as well as the company can face penalties. In other states, the company is responsible for providing basic training to the employee. This places the majority of the burden on the company to educate the employee and document the training. If employees are found who are not trained the company can face penalties.

The third primary factor in the acceptance of employee training was a **shift in professionalism** within the security industry. Under the leadership and encouragement of professional organizations such as ASIS International, headquartered in Alexandria, Virginia (2014), security owners were introduced to the benefits of training employees and the advantages for their organization.

As the security industry began to adopt the process of training and education, it forced all other companies to "keep up with the competition." The companies that trained their employees actively promoted their educational programs as a "value added service" to potential clients. In order for companies to maintain their client base, they too needed to develop and implement employee programs.

In the end, many security organizations now look at employee training as an accepted "cost of doing business." The practice of training employees, once viewed as a deterrent to profit, is now viewed as a standard business practice. This change in attitude has led to an increase in professionalism and reduced civil suits within the security industry.

Equipment, Sales, and Service

Another major segment of the security industry is the development, production, and sale of security devices. Within this sector of the security industry, two primary business areas have developed over the past three decades. First is the development and production of devices used to protect lives and property. These organizations' objectives are to research, develop, and engineer products within this now global industry. With the international need for protective devices, this segment of the security industry has also become highly competitive and must continually work to develop new product lines to stay viable, relevant, and competitive. Examples of these products include biometric equipment, computer servers, fire alarm and suppression systems, closed-circuit television systems (CCTV), access control systems, and alarms. In addition, devices such as locks, security doors and windows, fencing, and lighting can be included in this sector. Companies and corporations in this industry must stay competitive by the standard business practices stated above but also in the development and delivery of highly reliable and applicable devices.

The specific oversight of this industry comes from insurance providers and quality assurance organizations such as Underwriter's Laboratory (UL) and Factory Mutual (FM) (2014).

The second major segment is the security companies that sell, install, and service these devices. Some security device manufacturers will sell directly to the consumer, but a majority of companies produce the product and then sell it to an electronic security company. Examples of the reselling companies are local, regional, and national alarm, closed-circuit television (CCTV), and access control companies. Many of these businesses employ sales and customer service representatives, system engineers, installers, and service personnel in addition to employees to run the day-to-day business aspects of the organization.

Licensing, insurance, and manufacturer's approval do play a major role with these organizations. States and local governments will require regulation of the employees and the possible approval of the installation of many of the devices. In the case of fire alarm systems, fire codes (also known as "life safety codes") and approval are often needed before the completion of the installation. Business insurance is needed in the event of faulty design, installation, and service. The equipment manufacturers may also select specific companies to sell their products by granting a specific territory or region for sales and service. Other manufactures will sell products to as many companies for sales and service as they chose.

Finally, all businesses must adhere to all local, state, and federal laws as well as statues pertaining to the hiring and treatment of employees. These regulator and business factors illustrate how complicated the "business of security" has become.

Security Officers

Through the years, security officers have been fighting an identity crisis. Unlike many security officers in other countries, who are viewed as professionals and critical to safety, the American security officer is frequently looked down upon, the butt of irresponsible humor, and disrespected. This negative image does not portray the true effort of the many men and women who take the job seriously.

Still, a disparity exists with the security officer. Lower wages and less respect than many employees receive in the criminal justice field (and even within the security industry), immediately creates an unstable workforce. As the push for professionalism and training continues, the image of the security officer continues to improve.

The position of a security officer is not a one-size-fits-all occupation. The complexity of the security industry is again portrayed by the various categories of employment available, which may be classified as a security officer, agent, or professional.

Contract security officers are those individuals who are employed by a security company and then assigned to work for a client. These positions can range from basic security functions, such as observe and report, to complex security duties and responsibilities. The industry of contract security officers generally has a high employee turnover rate (i.e., employees frequently leaving and then new workers being hired). This can be attributed to factors such as low wages or limited promotional opportunities.

Proprietary security officers (commonly referred to as in-house officers) work directly for the company, organization, or corporation. Frequently, increased training along with an elevated level of duties and responsibilities accompany these positions. Their duties and responsibilities may be similar to those of their contract counterparts. These officers have a lower turnover employment rate based in part on stable working conditions, higher wages, and personal benefits offered to all employees of the company.

A growing trend in the security industry is combining both contract security officers and proprietary officers within the same department. The proprietary officers have greater roles and responsibilities than their contract counterparts. By hiring the contract officers to supplement the security staff, companies save money within budgetary aspects such as payroll taxes, insurance, and supplies for the contract officers.

Investigators are also utilized by both contract and proprietary security organizations. In the contract arena, the private investigator (commonly known as a P.I.) can be an independent business or part of a larger contracted agency. The proprietary investigator is employed directly by the department, company, or organization (much like the proprietary security officer).

The roles of investigators can vary depending on specialization or business need. The area of investigations may vary from domestic cases (divorces, domestic violence, or lost family members), to insurance claims (false workmen's compensation claims or false claims of property loss), to internal matters such as theft, harassment, or embezzlement.

Numerous contract investigators are former law enforcement or military employees who are investigating as a second career as well as non-law enforcement professionals with the proper training offered by the contract investigation agency or department. Unlike their contract counterpart, proprietary investigators may be hired for specific needs based on their education or experience. These individuals include forensic investigators (utilized for accounting purposes), information technology (IT) specialists (utilized for computer system crimes and breaches), and cases involving fraudulent products that may threaten the profitability of an organization.

Loss prevention (LP) specialists work primarily within the retail sector of society. Their mission is to reduce or eliminate the losses incurred within their assigned store, regional group of stores, or the entire company. The specific duties and responsibilities of these security industry employees will be explained in greater detail within chapter 8 of the text.

Risk Management is a complex field often entrusted to protect the business practices and operations of a company or corporation. Risk managers may be highly trained investigators or legal professionals. The duties and responsibilities of the risk management department may include investigating civil and criminal suits or insurance claims brought against their company, reviewing organizational policies and procedures for accuracy and consistency, reviewing potential contracts or agreements of potential suppliers or contactors, and conducting audits and surveys to ensure secure and sound business practices. This special sector of the security industry continues to grow as the need for internal protection and sound policies, procedures, and practices gains in importance.

A frequently overlooked aspect of the private security and investigation fields are those working as **bounty hunters or skip tracers**. When an accused person flees prosecution or trial, courts indirectly or directly turn to these individuals to find the suspect, return the individual for trial, or determine their location to initiate a penalty or judgment. Bounty hunters are granted rights and privileges outside the limits of law enforcement or the private citizen in order to return the accused for prosecution. Bounty hunters may work directly for a bail bonding agency or as private contractors. The employees of this industry must be highly trained in the appropriate legal aspects of the job and be proficient in self-defense and the use of necessary force. Those employed in skip tracing may not necessarily personally interact with the suspect; rather they seek, locate, and confirm where the individual is located. Upon the location of the suspect, the legal system can again impose or initiate the penalty or court order against the accused.

Another classification of security personnel which has been resurging over the past two decades is the field of **military operational specialist**. Formerly known as mercenaries or soldiers for hire, these highly trained individuals work in military combat conditions and are assigned to protect the lives and property of their contracted clients. Trained in both security and military tactics and techniques, these specialists are used to protect governmental and civilian interests within areas of conflict. Through the contracting of these individuals for protection, formal military personnel and resources can be used in other needed capacities. Regulation, supervision, and oversight of this security remains poorly understood, regulated, and defined. Personnel working in these assignments are private contractors, but the specialized area of operation and the geographic location (upon foreign soil) creates difficulties with supervision and legal standards. A collaborative effort between governments, the company's leadership, and security industry professionals continues to work on defining rules, regulations, and responsibilities.

Security Supervisors, Managers, and Executives

In any business and criminal justice personnel model, the employees working on the front lines are supervised and managed. The security sector combines both the business aspect of a company with the paramilitary structure of the criminal justice field. This combination of managerial factors helps to define and separate the security sector from the rest of the criminal justice community.

The **security supervisor** is the entry-level of security management. These individuals are often the immediate contact for the security officer. The supervisor's role may include the oversight of the security officers, conducting training and education for the security officers, initiating disciplinary and corrective action with the security officers, and acting as a liaison with the other personnel in the company while on duty. In addition, a supervisor may assume an active role in security procedures in the event an officer or their immediate manager is unable to carry out their duties or in the event an emergency.

The **security manager** is often the intermediary between the security staff and senior management. Depending on the organizational structure, the security manager may be actively involved with the development of training, human resource functions such as hiring or disciplining subordinate employees, conducting security and personnel audits, creating the department work schedule, oversight of department resources, and working on the development of the budget. The role of the middle manager is to supervise the general operations of the security staff and its well-being.

The **security executive** is the individual ultimately responsible for all activities of the organization or department. These executives may have the title of director, vice president, or owner depending on the organizational structure. The executive may be responsible for the development of training for the staff, the purchase of departmental supplies and equipment, and the oversight of investigations while acting as a company or corporate liaison within the organization, and ensuring adherence to all company, legal, or industry compliances. The organizational or business structure of the company will define the duties, responsibilities, and reporting capabilities of the executive. Not all organizations will have a member of the security department at a senior level, instead relying on the security manager for many of these responsibilities. For any security organization to be viable, relevant, and effective, a strong relationship must exist between the security department and senior management of a company or corporation.

Chain of Command and Span of Control

Two important organizational concepts for any security department are **chain of command** and **span of control**. Chain of command (often defined in an organizational chart) refers to reporting within the department or organization. To maintain a proper flow of communications and responsibility, all employees must report directly to their assigned individual, normally their immediate supervisor or manager. Span of control is the number of subordinates assigned to a supervisor or manager. To properly support employees, the number of individuals assigned to a specific supervisor should remain manageable. Since it is the responsibility of the supervisor to maintain the professional well-being of their subordinates, a clear chain of command and span of control is essential for day-to-day operations and imperative during times of crisis and emergency. Without these two personnel management concepts, the efficiency and effectiveness of the department or organization will be negatively impacted.

Formal Security Education and Careers

Historically, the educational process of security professionals mirrored our colleagues in the field of law enforcement. A security officer was hired by an organization or company then began to work their way up "the ladder" into supervisory and management positions. This style of practical education can be beneficial but can also limit the knowledge base and analytical skills of the ascending employee. The promoted employee relies on others within the department for knowledge and information, which can be a great benefit to "institutional knowledge" but very limiting toward a broader and well-balanced educational experience.

Recently, a number of retired law enforcement officials have committed to a second career in the private security sector. These new executives and leaders acquired excellent knowledge and skill sets in their former employment but are lacking in current day business practices and experiences. Some of these new security leaders find themselves struggling at the business practices of the security industry and need to expand their formal knowledge base to accommodate these organizational needs. Therefore, it is essential for today's security professional to be well versed in both criminal justice and business knowledge and practices.

Over the past three decades, formal security educational programs have developed at the community college and university levels. These programs are normally found within a criminal justice academic department. For individuals interested in a career in security management, a formal college education will provide a solid base of knowledge, theory, and skill sets that may be applied to the security industry. This education when combined with experience in a security department or company will offer a broad base of usable knowledge for the aspiring security supervisor or manager.

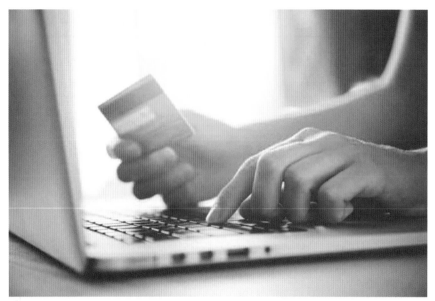

Laptop and Credit Card © Ivan Kruk via fotolia.com

As previously stated, the security industry is a combination of criminal justice and business practices. A formal education for prospective security supervisors and managers should include courses from both disciplines. Criminal justice classes should include courses such as investigative methods, civil law, criminal law, ethics, and research methods. Supplementary criminal justice courses can include studies in security practices and procedures, white-collar crime, domestic terrorism, organized crime, and cybercrime. Business courses can include personnel management, labor law, business ethics, accounting, and statistics, as well as marketing. These courses offer a solid base of knowledge for general application in the security industry.

For those who desire to work in a specialized field of security and security management, it is recommended that the student looks to specific courses for the area. For example, individuals who wish to work in cybersecurity need to take information technology (IT) and computer science courses. Individuals interested in a career in forensic accounting should take appropriate classes in math and business, especially accounting. These courses combined with security related criminal justice classes will help to build a solid knowledge base for these areas.

A growing trend today is the recommendation for aspiring senior security managers or executives to earn a graduate or master's degree. Depending on the organizational focus of the company or corporation, a graduate degree in security management, public administration, business administration, or information technology will be of benefit. Graduate programs promote deeper thought, advanced composition, and greater communication skills that are needed at the executive level.

Through the completion of a college and university degree, combined with experience in the security industry at any level, prospective security managers will be well equipped with the theoretical and practical knowledge needed to succeed as a leader in the security industry.

Issues in the Security Sector

The combination of the criminal justice and the private business sectors creates some unique issues for the security industry. Similarities in issues do exist between the two sectors, but the joining to the two areas can produce some challenging scenarios.

The first issue is the treatment and interdepartmental relationship of security as a corporate department. To many outsiders, security is a "necessary evil" that must be present for insurance and liability reasons. Another concern that may develop is the case where the security department is properly protecting lives and property; people begin to question why they have security because "nothing ever happens around here." This inaccurate attitude leads to the questioning of the need for security in part or as a whole. Security management and executives are forced to "sell the need" or justify the rationale for security. At times, this can be a thankless but necessary task for the survival of the department. The justification process must be able to relate the lack of crime and incidents to the effective operation of the security department.

This potential of losing budget and resources has also lead security to take on other customer service roles within the organization. This attitude creates a profit for service attitude to ensure the survival of the department. The security department could also be responsible for valet or parking services, receptionists and greeters, or phone systems operators. This shift to a customer service model has created new opportunities for security to remain viable in the eyes of corporate financial officers and senior management.

The next issue, brought on from the combination of criminal justice and business, is the regulation of the security industry. As stated earlier, the security sector is divided between contract and proprietary security. A large portion of governmental oversight, regulations, and licensing applies to the contract security segment. Because of prior poor professional practices within the contract security industry, many governmental and security industry leaders felt that the contract sector was out of control and lacking discipline and scruples. With the recent surge in training and professionalism instilled in the contract security sector, many of the owners and leaders now complain that their companies are being wrongly or unfairly regulated and their counterparts in the proprietary security sector are unregulated.

This debate is causing an unnecessary divide in the security industry. Many proprietary security executives argue that their departments have higher standards for training and supervision and do not need governmental oversight. Where these executives are accurate regarding the potential levels of training and professionalism, there is a segment of the proprietary security sector that is unregulated. A business or company can hire someone and call them "security," paying their wages directly. Entertainment venues, bars, and some retail stores are examples of organizations hiring "security" for the sole purpose of crowd control or the protection of property. At times these employees will use force, a dangerous or unethical practice that may go unsupervised and ignored. This reckless and unregulated attitude of these "proprietary security employees" creates a liability threat, a lack of respect, and a regulatory disparity in the security industry.

In addition, certain segments of the electronic security industry may also go unregulated due to an inaccurate or biased regulation. For example, companies that install and service burglar, hold-up, and fire alarm systems are commonly regulated and licensed. Conversely, companies that install access control systems or closed-circuit television systems (CCTV) are often categorized as an electronics businesses and do not need licensing or the same level of bureaucratic oversight. The emphasis of regulation is placed upon "alarm companies" while other electronic security companies are unregulated.

Without an open and honest dialog and lawmakers willing to take on the complexity of this issue, it will remain imbalanced, and a creator of tension within the private security sector. This lack of consistent regulation and governmental oversight has created a negative environment and lack of trust within the industry.

The final issue to be presented is the concern of potential illegal or unethical business practices forced upon the security staff. Unethical, unscrupulous, and illegal business decisions are made every day. Some of these poor actions can involve the security staff. This forces the security personnel to make an unwanted decision to support the negative actions or potentially be disciplined, ostracized, or terminated for not supporting their superiors. This scenario forces security to either support the negative activity or potentially lose their job.

For security personnel to be effective, respected, ethical, and maintain their professionalism, they must avoid these potentially poor decisions and situations. Supporting unethical or illegal business practices will discredit the individual, the organization, and the security industry in general. It is not always easy for security personnel to "do the right thing," but the long-term ramifications and consequences must be considered before making decisions. It is then, after a careful and thoughtful review of the circumstances, when making the moral and ethical decision will become evident as the right choice.

Conclusion

In today's criminal justice community, relatively few individuals understand the complexity of the security industry. Security personnel, equipment, loss prevention, risk management, and investigations can all be classified under this segment of the criminal justice system. In addition, the role of private security can be found at the local, regional, national, and international levels.

As training, education, and operational standards for the security sector continue to elevate, a balance must remain between free-market idealism and the paramilitary oversight needed to maintain professionalism and ethics. This is and will continue to be a great challenge for an industry that has grown exponentially over the past four decades. The hybrid between criminal justice and business is now a viable financial force in the protection of lives and property. As the world of crime and terrorism continues to evolve, so too must the security sector to remain proactive in the fight, while acknowledging collaborative efforts within the security industry and the criminal justice system as a whole.

Case Study — Security Officer Wages in the United States

According to the United States Department of Labor (2014), there are approximately 1,066,730 security officers in the U.S. (categorized as "security guards") as of May 2013. This number constitutes the largest employment sector in today's American criminal justice system as evidenced in the following table:

Employment Classification	Number of Employees (May 2013)
Security Guards	1,066,730
Police and Sheriff Patrol Officers	635,380
Corrections Officers and Jailers	432,680
Probation Officers and Correctional Treatment Specialists	90,300

Employment Classification	Median Hourly Wage
Police and Sheriff Patrol Officers	$26.99
Probation Officers and Correctional Treatment Specialists	$23.17
Corrections Officers and Jailers	$19.02
Security Guards	$11.57
National U.S. Hourly Wage (June 2014)	$24.45

This segment of the criminal justice system is also the lowest paid, with a median hourly wage of $11.57 per hour (as of May 2013). This number constitutes the lowest wage in the criminal justice sector as illustrated in the following table:

Simply stated, the largest segment of the American criminal justice system is the lowest compensated. Consider and answer the following questions pertaining to this topic:

1. Why do you think this wage discrepancy exists?
2. What can be done to increase wages for security officers?
3. How will the business sector react if wages for security officers increase?

Research Focus — European vs. American Security Officers

Security officers in the European Union (EU) are treated with a higher regard and respect than their counterparts in the United States. With this fact in mind, investigate the following questions:

1. How much are European security officers compensated?
2. Is this same wage applied in each European country?
3. Are there differences in duties and responsibilities between European security officers and their American counterparts?

Discussion Topic — The Fraudulent Employee

During the course of an administrative review, by a new contracted security company at a sizable job site, it was discovered that the former contract security supervisor, overseeing the security staff, was submitting fraudulent payroll records. The supervisor left employees on the payroll who no longer worked at the site. The checks were then cashed and dispersed to selected members of the security staff as addition pay. When the new security supervisor identified the payroll fraud, it was immediately confirmed that all of the employees involved in the payroll fraud no longer worked in the security department. A few of the employees involved in the scheme were hired by the organization in other non-security capacities.

When all the information was gathered and verified, the security supervisor presented the information to their contact within the organization. The organizational contact simply said; "Well that is in the past, you are here now and we do not have to worry about that type of thing anymore." The matter was dropped and never spoken of again.

With this scenario in mind, answer the following questions:

1. How do you think this payroll fraud could have been avoided?
2. If you were the new security supervisor, how would you react after being dismissed by their organizational contact?
3. What kind of consequences or ramifications could be experienced by the new security supervisor and the new contract security company if the matter were pursued, seeking justice and closure?

Key Terms

Business of security	Bounty hunters	Security executive
Contract security officer	Skip tracers	Chain of command
Proprietary security officer	Military operational specialist	Span of control
Investigators	Security supervisor	Proactive
Risk management	Security manager	

Sources

ASIS International. (n.d.). *Who we are*. Retrieved from https://www.asisonline. org/About-ASIS/Who-We-Are/Pages/default.aspx

FM Global. (n.d.) *About us*. Retrieved from http://www.fmglobal.com/page. aspx?id=01000000&utm_source=Google&utm_medium=cpc&utm_term= factory_mutual_g_Exact_&utm_content=FM_Global&utm_campaign= Q4_2012_Branded

Underwriters Laboratories (n.d.). Our mission: *Making for a safer world*. Retrieved from http://ul.com/aboutul/our-mission/

United States Department of Labor. (2013). *Occupational employment and wages, 3-3051 Police and sheriff's patrol officers*. (Data File). Retrieved from http://www.bls.gov/oes/current/oes333051.htm

United States Department of Labor. (2013). *Occupational employment and wages, 21-1092 Probation officers and Correctional Treatment Specialists*. (Data File). Retrieved from http://www.bls.gov/oes/current/oes211092.htm

United States Department of Labor. (2013). *Occupational employment and wages, 33-3012 Correctional officers and jailers. (Data File)*. Retrieved from http://www.bls.gov/oes/current/oes333012.htm

United States Department of Labor. (2013). *Occupational employment and wages, 33-9032 Security guards*. (Data File). Retrieved from https://owl.english. purdue.edu/owl/resource/560/10/

United States Department of Labor. (2014). *Table B-3. Average hourly and weekly earnings of all employees on private nonfarm payrolls by industry sector, seasonally adjusted* (Data File). Retrieved from http://www.bls.gov/ news.release/empsit.t19.htm

Chapter Three

Criminally Civil: Legal Aspects of Private Security

Introduction

It is essential for today's security leader to have a working understanding of legal aspects that influence their employment environment. As previously explained in the text, the private security industry is a hybrid of law enforcement and business. This intertwining of theories and practices leads to a potential conundrum pertaining to laws affecting day-to-day duties and responsibilities. This chapter will help differentiate and explain the legal authority and practices of the private security industry from other segments within the criminal justice community.

Learning Objectives

By the end of this chapter, the reader will have a basic working knowledge of the laws and legal responsibilities of the professionals working in the private security industry. These differences include the legal authority of security professionals, the concept of negligence, security's interaction in a courtroom environment, and the importance of reporting as it pertains to liability.

Defining Criminal and Civil Law

Security professionals are in a unique position with relation to legal aspects and laws while working to protect lives and property. Many of our colleagues in the criminal justice system need to be extremely well versed on the myriad of criminal laws that can vary between local, state, and federal jurisdictions.

Criminal law is defined as an illegal or unwanted act by an individual, resulting in a predetermined punishment or penalty by a governmental authority (Cole, Smith, & DeJong, 2014). Criminal laws are created by governmental bodies, and are designed to penalize acts determined to be wrongful against society as a whole. For every crime on the legal record, a punishment for the offense is also defined. For example, if a person commits murder, a predetermined and approved penalty of imprisonment or death may be imposed by the judge. Another example is the crime of assault. Depending on the severity of the circumstances, the person found guilty of the act could be faced with either **misdemeanor** charges (i.e., resulting in less than one year of imprisonment and/or damages under $1,000) or **felony** charges (i.e., resulting in more than one year of imprisonment and/or damages over $1,000). A conviction for the crime of assault could have a varying penalty of imprisonment as defined by the law. Laws for criminal offenses can and may vary depending on the jurisdiction where the crime took place. This includes the local, state, and federal levels.

As the protective arm of corporations or as formal businesses, the private security industry must understand and adhere to the civil law aspect of the legal system. Even though it is important for security professionals to have a basic working knowledge of criminal offenses and laws, the constant and overriding threat against the businesses and their practices comes from civil offenses. **Civil laws** govern the relationships between people. When there is a disagreement or if a person is "wronged," (believed to not be treated fairly and properly, or have been neglected) they can seek restitution or recuperation for their loss. This takes place in the civil court process. The individual bringing the charges into the civil court system (known as the **plaintiff**) files charges for damages, seeking restitution against the party or individual believed to have violated their well-being (known as the **defendant**). The complaint or civil suit then progresses through the court system and can either go to a formal trial in front of a judicial officer, or the parties can reach an agreeable settlement, ending the case. Unlike the criminal law process where a prosecutor brings about the charges against the accused (defendant), the civil law process is decided between individuals, companies, organizations, or corporations.

Variations of Civil Law

Like the criminal law system, where illegal acts may be classified as either misdemeanors or felonies, the civil court system has different variations and classifications. Civil law can also be referred to as **tort law**. A tort is formally defined as "A civil wrong, other than breach of contract, for which a remedy may be obtained, usually in the form of damages" (*Black's Law Dictionary*, 2009). Frequently the terms "civil law" and "tort law" are interchanged. For security professionals it is important to realize that torts address the relationships between individuals (parties) in cases other than contracts.

Another term used when addressing civil issues is that of "a relationship." Unlike a personal friendship or romance, a legal or professional relationship may include the interactions between an employee and supervisor, exchanges between coworkers, communications between employees and customers, and contact between an organizational representative and a vendor. Any interaction or communication between two or more people can become subject to civil court actions if harm or potential harm takes place between the parties.

Outside the realm of torts and tort law is **contractual law**. Formally defined, a contract is: "An agreement between two or more parties creating obligations that are enforceable or otherwise recognizable at law" (*Black's Law Dictionary*, 2009). Unlike a tort, contracts are specific documents that contain and detail information, duties, and obligations between the two parties. If the contract is not fulfilled or executed, the failed party may seek recovery (in the form of money, services, or products) in a civil court. Contracts can be a simple document, highlighting the parties, duties, obligations, services, and fees up to and including a complex list of duties, obligations, terms, penalties, and possible legal recourse. These documents may also be referred to as agreements, contractual agreements, customer agreements, or written agreements.

Contract security companies rely on written agreements as a way to retain clientele, define the scope of the goods or services to be sold or offered, and protect against the loss of business to a competing company. These written agreements are vital for contract security companies to remain viable and in business for a prolonged duration. Contract security companies need to take great care and effort, and pay attention to detail when developing customer agreements. The use of highly qualified legal professionals or attorneys to help develop, review, and revise the contractual language is imperative in today's business world. The contractual language is to be taken very seriously and strictly followed in order to avoid a possible civil suit for non-performance. Simply stated—the written agreement is the cornerstone for a contract security company to survive and prosper.

Written agreements are also imperative in the event that a contract security company sells their business (in part or as a whole) to a competitor. During the 1980s, 1990s, and into the 2000s, an acquisition frenzy took place in the contract security industry. Security companies and corporations took the approach that purchasing the competition is a way to increase business when standard sales and marketing techniques fell short. Larger companies purchased their competitor's contracts (or accounts) in addition to their resources and assets. Detailed reviews of the selling company's contractual agreements lead to the ultimate purchase price by the competitor. This practice of acquisitions took place in all areas of the contract security industry (electronic, personnel, hardware, and cyber) and continues to take place today. The result of the large number of acquisitions in the contract security industry led to fewer companies, market competition, and a smaller number of viable product or service options for the buyer.

Contractual knowledge is an important area for proprietary security departments as well. Frequently, the security department is responsible for selecting security goods and services to supplement and assist their efforts. As a proprietary security department receives sales proposals (commonly referred to as bids), the contract security company selected will request that a contract or service agreement be approved and signed. This is an example of not only one of the primary differences between the contract and proprietary security sectors, but also an example of how the two segments can co-exist and support one another. The proprietary security department must take great care to review the contractual agreement or defer the review and approval of the agreement to a senior manager, executive, legal representative, or risk manager.

Another area of civil law which security organizations may be affected by is the practice of **administrative law**. This is defined as: "The law governing the organization and operation of administrative agencies (including executive and independent agencies) and the relations of administrative agencies with the legislature, the executive, the judiciary, and the public" (*Black's Law Dictionary*, 2009). Security agencies and organizations may be affected by administrative law when interacting with government regulations and oversight, adhering to laws pertaining to operations, or entering into a contract to provide services with a governmental agency. Administrative laws may be able to impose penalties, civil charges, or criminal charges to security organizations that do not follow the law and regulations imposed by the governmental sector. It is important for security organizations and departments to know and understand these laws and guidelines as it pertains to their business practices, products, and services.

The final area of law to be addressed is **property law**. Simply stated, property law addresses ownership. This can be an important legal aspect for those working in both the contract and proprietary security industries. For contract companies, "ownership" may pertain to the protection of information and knowledge needed to operate the company. This information could include customer lists, pricing lists of goods and services, or information on the creation and operation of security devices. Also known as proprietary information, intellectual information, or trade secrets, these are specific areas of knowledge relevant to the operation of the company. Any information that could be beneficial to a competitor to acquire business from another company or information which could harm the business rival can be considered proprietary information or "property."

In today's cyber society, the fight against the loss of proprietary information is a continuous battle. The World Wide Web and the large amount of business conducted on the Internet opens companies to the potential loss of data and knowledge from the growing threat of cybercrime. Computer systems and networks are continuously under attack, which in part is caused by competitors looking to gain information on their rivals by illegal means. When and if the loss of information is detected, the most common way to seek restitution is to file a civil suit seeking monetary damages and restrictions. This form of cybercrime may go unpunished if the culprit is outside the United States and its judicial system. (More about the dilemma of cybercrimes will be discussed in chapter six.)

What Is Liability?

Responsibility is a concept that most people learn at an early age. We are told to "take responsibility for our actions" or be a "responsible person." When it comes to the business of security, the concept and practice of liability comes from responsibility (or a lack of it). Security companies and departments are responsible for their actions. They are responsible for the conduct of their employees while on duty. They are responsible to protect lives and property to the best of their abilities. The security company or security department is responsible or liable.

The term **liability** is defined as: "The state of being legally responsible for something," (*Merriam Webster Dictionary*, n.d.). This definition is the cornerstone for the actions of the security organizations, departments, and employees. When a security organization, department, or employee fails to perform the duties and responsibilities as assigned, the individual or the department may be found negligent.

Negligence is an unwanted act or a failure to act. This is formally defined as: "The failure to exercise the standard of care that a reasonably prudent person would have exercised in a similar situation; any conduct that falls below the legal standard established to protect others against unreasonable risk of harm, except for conduct that is intentionally, wantonly, or willfully disregardful of others' rights," (*Black's Law Dictionary*, 2009). When a security organization, department, or employee fails to follow the rules and regulations assigned, potential civil actions may be filed seeking restitution and compensation from the act or failure to act. It is imperative for security personnel to be properly educated in their duties and responsibilities as defined by their superiors. In this situation, the old axiom "an ounce of prevention is worth a pound of cure" readily applies. Security personnel must fully understand their duties and responsibilities as it pertains to the job. Time and care for training and education is needed in all security organizations and departments and then must be reinforced with proper supervision to ensure all employees are acting properly and legally. A failure to do so could end with catastrophic consequences for all involved, both directly and indirectly. Charges of negligence can occur for an unwanted action, a failure to act, or lack of knowledge and ignorance. Security personnel must be continuously "on guard" to ensure all duties, responsibilities, and products meet all standards and expectations.

Of the various subsets, or different types, of liability, two specific areas are important for the private security industry. First, is the legal concept of **strict liability**. Strict liability is defined as: "When a defendant is in legal jeopardy by virtue of a wrongful act, without any accompanying intent or mental state" (Cornell University Law School, n.d.). This civil violation is a continuous concern for security organizations and departments. In the event a security employee commits a violation of departmental or company policies, with or without realizing it, the individual may be personally held liable for the results of their actions.

For example, a security officer is on patrol and sees a physical altercation (a fight) between two employees. The officer decides to intervene by pulling the two parties apart. While this is happening, one of the parties strikes the other while the officer is holding onto him or her. This could result in a case of strict liability. Also for this example, if the security department has a strict "hands off" policy toward all employees and patrons, the officer has violated the approved departmental policy, creating additional issues and charges. This officer could face a civil suit for acting outside their policies and procedures, causing greater harm to one of the people involved in the altercation.

The second important legal concept is known as **vicarious liability**. This is formally defined as: "Liability that a supervisory party (such as an employer) bears for the actionable conduct of a subordinate or associate (such as an employee) based on the relationship between the two parties," (Cornell University Law School, n.d.). Vicarious liability may be simply explained as the responsibility of the organization for their employees' actions.

An example for this violation is if a hypothetical electronic security company is contracted to install a camera system (CCTV) in a corporate office building. During the installation, one of the male camera installers decides to place a wireless, covert Internet camera looking into the women's restroom. The hidden camera is placed solely for camera installer's personal use. Even though the wireless camera is not in the approved specifications for the camera system, the company will still be held vicariously liable for the actions of their employee. In this case, separate civil suits could be filed on both the employee responsible for the camera as well as the company responsible for the employee.

As policies, procedures, practices, and equipment advance, it will be imperative for all security organizations to understand what the company and their employees can and cannot do. Without continuous oversight and supervision, a civil suit can paralyze or destroy any security company or organization with a security department. Even in the event that a civil suit does not go to a formal trial, the security company or organization housing a security department must pay to investigate the matter, defend themselves, and possibly pay a settlement if agreed upon by all parties involved.

Criminal Law and Security

The rules and obligations set forth through criminal laws (including procedures) are concepts and actions that most security professionals need to know but are often not directly applicable to the private sector. Security personnel are not law enforcement officers or officials and should not be expected to act or portray our colleagues in the policing field. In fact, under most circumstances, security personnel have the same legal and law enforcement rights as a private citizen. In many cases, the role of security is to "observe and report." Yet, there are some aspects of criminal procedure that may have some applicability to the private security sector.

By definition, the act of an **arrest** is: "A seizure or forcible restraint, or the taking or keeping of a person in custody by legal authority, especially in response to a criminal charge" (*Black's Law Dictionary*, 2009). In most circumstances, private security personnel have no authority to formally arrest an individual. Some states and jurisdictions may permit what is known as a "citizen's arrest," which refers to detaining a person until the police arrive in the event of witnessing a felony or certain misdemeanor crimes or assisting a law enforcement officer to detain an individual upon request. By and large, most security companies or departments have a "hands off" policy, opting instead to observe and get a description of the person and then turning the information over to the police. As in many aspects of the private security industry, exceptions do exist, but only with high levels of formal training and education. These will be highlighted later in the chapter.

Another legal concept that has some applicability to the private security sector is the **gathering of evidence**. As with our colleagues in law enforcement, the gathering of evidence can be important to internal investigations. Evidence is defined as: "Something (including testimony, documents and tangible objects) that tends to prove or disprove the existence of an alleged fact" (*Black's Law Dictionary*, 2009). What the security professional needs to keep in mind is why or for what reason the evidence is being gathered. Is the evidence being obtained as part on an internal (company/corporate) investigation? Is it being gathered for a third party or client by a private investigator? Will it be used in a civil or criminal matter? Depending on the reason for the gathering of evidence and the purpose of its use, the individual must be properly trained and know the difference between gathering evidence that will be used in a civil lawsuit or evidence that will be used in a criminal case. If the gathering of evidence is for a civil case, then the policies and procedures of the company need to be followed. If the evidence being gathered is for a potential criminal case, it is then advised that law enforcement personnel be used to ensure the proper policies and procedures take place so the gathering is not illegal and "chain of evidence" is not broken. In either case, the security professional needs to have proper training on policies, procedures, and legalities for this action. An untrained security employee gathering evidence could lead to mistakes resulting in civil litigation or possible criminal charges.

Another area of legality that may occur in the private security sector is the **search and seizure** of evidence. In the law enforcement arena, searching and seizing evidence is normally conducted with a warrant approved by a judicial official. This concept can also be applied to the private security sector in the event the information is used for a criminal case. In a circumstance where the case may lead to criminal charges, it is best to allow properly trained law enforcement personnel to conduct the search and seize the evidence.

If the investigation is for company or private purposes, then the security professional must strictly adhere to the policies set forth by the organization. The searching of briefcases, backpacks, lunch boxes, lockers, and offices may take place in the private sector. The security professional must be properly trained as to the limitations of the searches and strictly follow the company policies to avoid or limit the threat of civil court action. The employer should have any and all policies regarding searches and seizure of property reviewed and approved by an attorney or legal expert. Unapproved or unauthorized actions taken to search employees or property could lead to violations of union agreements, company policies, or even civil rights, resulting in long and unnecessary lawsuits.

In general, since private security personnel are not law enforcement officials, great care must take place to understand the limits of the legal authority security employees actually have. Mistakes made pertaining to legal authority could have a massive negative impact on the employee, the security department, or the company as a whole.

Exceptions to the Legal Authority of Security Personnel

As previously stated in the chapter, the vast majority of security personnel have only the same legal authority as a private citizen. Yet, exceptions do take place depending on the need for protection within a specific environment. The first exception is when private security officers are **deputized** by a law enforcement authority. The deputizing will depend on factors such as the level of security needed at a specific location; the agreement between the specific location, its security staff, and law enforcement officials; the approved authority and areas of training for the security personnel; and the methods of supervision to avoid potential abuse of power. The specific deputized level of authority may vary, to include the issuing of parking or traffic citations or the detainment of individuals for suspected criminal actions, as well as the arrest of unauthorized individuals for trespassing on the property. Whatever the rationale may be for the issuing of deputized powers to private security personnel, detailed research must take place as to who, what, when, and why the authority will take place; the responsibility for formal and detailed training (including the documentation of those who underwent the approved training); the need for regular retraining ensuring proper adherence to policies and procedures; and the approval of all involved parties at a senior management level. Deputized powers may be authorized for groups such as retail center security, hospital or healthcare security, or educational institution security. In these cases, the private security officers must be trained as to when and why they may exercise their deputized powers, the proper documentation of the events after they take place, and the potential consequences for exceeding or abusing their powers. The increase of the power and authority of security personnel also increases exponentially the possibility for liability and civil issues. The deputizing of security personnel does not occur frequently because of these potential risks. Some security departments or organizations will refrain from this practice and instead rely on law enforcement personnel for assistance in these matters.

Another exception to the authority of private security personnel occurs in the field of retail security. In this environment, the concept and practice of **Merchant's Privilege** is used to protect the items being sold in the store. Also referred to as **Shopkeeper's Privilege**, this law allows the owners of a retail establishment (or their designated employee) to detain an individual suspected of stealing from the store. This process is used by loss prevention employees or store detectives while protecting the location of their employment. By definition, the merchant must have reasonable suspicion that the accused has stolen or has attempted to steal from their establishment, may only use non-lethal force to detain the suspect, and may hold the suspect only for a brief period of time to allow for questioning or the arrival of law enforcement authorities for formal arrest (USLegal.com, n.d.). Merchants and their employees must take great care not to exceed the limits set forth by this law. In the event a merchant or their employee exceeds the limits of their authority, they may sued by the accused individual or run the risk of being charged with a criminal act such as assault or false imprisonment. The development of formal policies and procedures as well as training for employees who will exercise this authority will be critical to avoid civil or criminal charges.

Reporting and Liability

One of the primary actions of security personnel is to observe and report information and incidents that take place on the property they are protecting. While this sounds like a simple act, great care, skill, and practice must take place to write a report. Written reports may be used in a number of organizational and legal situations. They can be used internally for disciplinary, investigatory, or civil matters, and when criminal charges are brought forth. Because of the potential importance of any security report (including activity reports/logs or incident reports) professionalism and care must be used when writing. Organizations should develop formal report writing classes, policies and procedures to ensure accuracy, and professional practices to avoid possible legal confrontations.

When writing a report, it is essential for the security employee to only write the facts that they personally witnessed. Basic reporting concepts pertaining to an incident such as "who, what, where, and when" can be easily documented in a professional manner. The writing concepts of "why and how" must only be documented if the security employee personally witnessed the act and clearly understands the rationale or cause for the act. With these final two concepts, security employees rarely understand or have the personal expertise to be considered an expert pertaining to the event. In addition, security personnel must also avoid speculation (guessing what happened when they did not personally witness the act) or embellishing the report (attempting to add words to make

Laptop Computer Display © Tomasz Zajda via fotolia.com

the event seem more important or of greater importance). These unnecessary practices may cause unwanted scrutiny in a court of law or possible civil charges against the writer of the report and their employer. A basic professional standard is to only report what is witnessed to the best of the employee's ability. All reports should be formally reviewed by a supervisor or manager upon completion to ensure all professional standards are being met.

In the event that non-factual, inaccurate, or personally harmful information is written in a security report, the person writing the report as well as the organization they work for could face civil charges. The first charge that could occur is known as **libel**. Libel is defined as: "A defamatory statement expressed in a fixed medium, especially writing but also a picture, sign, or electronic broadcast" (*Black's Law Dictionary*, 2009). When an inaccurate or harmful statement is written in any form of a report or communication (intentionally or accidentally) and is found and proven to be false, charges of libel can be filed by the defendant. The person accused of the false information can sue the organization and the employee for monetary damages to their character and well-being.

In addition, if the security professional states publically or formally testifies within a professional or legal environment that the false information is accurate or factual, charges of **slander** may also be brought forward. Slander is defined as: "A defamatory assertion expressed in a transitory form, especially speech" (*Black's Law Dictionary*, 2009). In this circumstance, a security employee could verbally state the false information to the organization, in a court proceeding, or to a member of the general public. The accused individual in the report can file slander charges, disprove the inaccurate statements, and then sue the organization or the security employee for monetary damages to their character and well-being. The bottom line is that security agencies need to be cognizant that any security report could be entered into a court or legal proceedings, with or without the author being present. The mind-set must be accepted by the company or organization that every report or activity log could, at any time, become evidence in a legal proceeding.

Rules, Regulations, and Directives of the Employer

Throughout this chapter, it has been stated that security employees must adhere to the policies and procedures of their employer. These written directives, also referred to as post orders, site instructions, directives, and policy guides, are the cornerstone for security rules, regulations, duties, and activities. The reasons why all activities and expectations need to be placed in writing is twofold. First, it allows security personnel the opportunity to review any procedure or directive as needed. Any activity that is required by the members of the security department needs to be placed in writing, reviewed by all employees on a regular basis, and updated or modified by management on a routine basis. The second reason for having this information in a readily available and written format is for liability reasons. Having the policies and procedures continuously updated and available can be of assistance to the security employee but can also potentially avoid an unwanted event or action. The document may also be a legal buffer for the security department, company, or the organization. In the unfortunate event that an employee acts inappropriately while on duty, the department, company, or organization can argue that the individual was trained to adhere to the rules and regulations but chose to act in free will and disregard the policies. This is not a guaranteed defense for inappropriate or unwanted employee behavior, but it may help with easing the burden placed on the company for potential liability.

The written rules and regulations should include everything that is necessary for a security employee to carry out their duties and responsibilities. Even small tasks such as checking in or off duty should be placed in writing. Other items for these documents can include directives for emergency situations, foot or vehicular patrolling guidelines, emergency notification lists, reporting procedures, service or installation guidelines, and access control procedures.

These guidelines need to be readily available as well as treated with care and professionalism, so they are not damaged, lost, or compromised. The directives can be general (for all security related activities) or specific (for a certain security post, position, or location). When the supervisory or management team updates the directives, any updates and when the review took place should be documented in all copies and initialed by the supervisor or manager.

Finally, it is recommended that senior management and also a legal representative review the policies and procedures on a regular basis. This review (also known as vetting) helps to ensure compliance with company or organizational policies and practices and appropriate legal concerns. The effort to develop and maintain a set of detailed, written instructions for security employees promotes a cohesive organizational unit, provides guidance in times of emergency, and potentially reduces unwanted mistakes and possible liability issues.

The Courtroom and Legal Process

The potential for a security employee to be called into a legal procedure is real and relevant to the job. Any security employee can be subpoenaed or requested to appear in a legal procedure during their employment. Security officers and managers can be called to testify for events that took place while on duty, private investigators can testify on events they recorded and documented while working for a client, and loss prevention associates can be called to inform and verify items the accused attempted to steal.

Although Hollywood has painted a fictional picture of how court proceedings are enacted, the fact is these media representations are often only partially accurate. Legal proceedings may include testimony in a formal court of law or an interview during an **interrogatory** or **deposition** that will be introduced as evidence, as well as a formal interview by a legal representative. A deposition or interrogatory is a series of questions taken outside the courthouse, normally in an agreed location such as a court reporter's office or an attorney's office. The witness will be asked a series of questions by one or both sides of the case and all the information will be recorded for potential use in a formal court proceeding. These proceedings can be very intense and grueling, lasting for a long period of time. This series of questions is part of the formal **testimony** process of the proceeding. The act of testimony can take place inside or outside of a formal courthouse but is still considered part of the case.

The security employee needs to be prepared for potential legal events that may take place as part of the job. These individuals must first understand that the American court system is designed to be an adversarial proceeding. This means that one side of the proceedings attempts to present evidence to support their case while the other side attempts to discredit the information. This can be a very stressful time and event for a security employee who has never been involved in this process. It takes calm and professionalism to properly endure the questioning and potential attempt to discredit the witness during this process.

Preparation for a legal proceeding is essential for all security employees. The employee needs to thoroughly review all of the appropriate documents or recorded material to have a solid grasp on the event that took place. The importance of the security employee writing a professional report, documenting the events in question as part of the legal proceeding, now becomes imperative and essential for the testimony. The report by the security employee can be admitted into evidence for the case with or without the security employee explaining the information. In either situation, the security employee should review all information pertinent or relevant to their involvement with the case.

The security employee may also be required to meet with their legal representative prior to the testimony. This meeting will allow the security employee to explain and educate the attorney as to what took place (also known as a pre-trial meeting). This meeting will help both parties to present the evidence or information and also to prepare for the potential cross examination by the opposing legal representative.

The security employee also needs to physically prepare for the legal proceeding. Professional attire should always be worn, either in the form of well-cleaned and pressed security uniform or professional personal attire. The employee needs to be well-groomed and project a calm and professional demeanor during these proceedings. A clean and professional appearance by the security employee will present a positive image to those involved in the legal proceeding. It is also recommended that a supervisor or manager meet with the employee offering testimony, prior to the legal proceeding, to ensure the needed professional appearance.

The personal testimony of a security employee needs to be treated with a great deal of thought, foresight, and preparation. Much like in the composition of a security report, the testifying employee needs to directly answer all questions from the legal representative to the best of their knowledge. The security employee needs to only testify to information with which they were directly involved or that is documented in their report. They are never to guess or speculate on any of the details in question—sticking only to the facts of the incident or report. All answers need to be accurate, brief, and professional.

After the initial questioning, the opposing legal counsel has the right to cross-examine the security employee. As stated above, this part of the legal process is intended to find factual errors in the information presented and to discredit the witness. This part of the legal process can be very stressful for the security employee. Calmness and professionalism must be maintained at all times during a cross-examination. Again, with this series of questions, all answers are to be accurate and brief. The employee should not inadvertently give more information than requested because it could become harmful to the case. In the event a question is asked where the security employee does not know the answer, a simple response of "I'm sorry, but I do not know" is recommended. Never guess or speculate when answering a question.

The importance of security's role in the legal system continues to increase exponentially. Detailed preparation and a high level of professionalism toward all participants involved in legal proceedings are essential for the security employee or investigator. Preparation and professionalism can help to de-escalate the stresses involved in interactions with the legal system.

Conclusion

As an ideological and practical hybrid of the business and criminal justice systems, the private security industry must be able to understand both the civil and criminal legal practices. In this chapter, a very broad-based portrayal of the legal interactions of the security industry was introduced. The intent of the information was to give the reader basic knowledge, ideologies, and practices pertaining to legalities and the private security sector. These basic building blocks were intended to show the different areas of knowledge and information needed for security personnel.

As the duties and responsibilities of the private security sector grow to meet the increasing supply and demand by those in need of protection, it is vital for all involved in protecting lives and property to be fluent in these and other essential areas of legality. Being vigilant in the current practices and changes to legal issues is essential for security professionals. The need for continuous education and review of the legalities affecting the security industry will remain a constant force driving security professionals, their departments, and organizations.

Case Study—The Case of the Dummy Camera

In the northeastern United States, a corporation wanted to protect its workers and visitors by installing a closed-circuit television system (CCTV). The images were recorded and viewed by the security department. The cameras were installed in many public areas of the facility, including common areas, entrances, parking lots, and parking ramps. Late one evening, a young, adult female was walking back to her car in a parking ramp. Before she reached her car, she was accosted by an individual and her purse was stolen. She contacted the security department immediately after the assault. Seeing a security camera in the ramp, she requested that the security department look at the footage of the assault in order to identify and potentially apprehend the assailant. Much to the victim's shock and dismay, she later found out that the camera installed in that section of the ramp was a "dummy camera." What the victim of the assault thought was a security camera was actually only the outside housing of a camera unit. There was no camera inside the housing unit; therefore, it was unable to record. This case brought national attention to the organization and spurred a debate over the use of "dummy cameras."

After reading this case study and the previous chapter, answer the following questions:

1. What do you think was the motivation by the organization to install "dummy cameras" around its facility?
2. Could this be considered a civil violation?
3. Does the victim have any recourse against the organization for the installation of the "dummy cameras"? Do you think the organization is liable for the assault or were they justified with the installation of the "dummy camera" as a deterrent?

Discussion Topic—The Conundrum of Moonlighting

In the past, security companies were in the practice of hiring off-duty police officers to work for their organizations. The practice is commonly known as "moonlighting," where a full-time employee of one job works a second job for additional financial support. Problems, issues, and complications began to arise when the moonlighting, full-time police officers began using their deputized powers to search, detain, and even arrest people breaking the law on the property. Frequently, the job of the security personnel is to strictly "observe and report," meaning that they are only to patrol and notify the authorities when problems occur. No proactive and physical intervention was to take place by the security officers while on duty.

Take a moment to contemplate this scenario, and then answer these questions:

1. When is a police officer not a police officer?
2. Does a police officer step outside his or her boundaries as a security officer if he or she enforces public law?
3. Do you believe a security company could be held liable for the actions of the off-duty police officer?
4. Should a security company continue to hire off-duty police officers? Why or why not?

Research Focus—Civil Court: Cases vs. Settlement

For this research exercise, take some time to search for the civil court systems for your individual state through the Internet. Once found, look to see how many civil cases were filed in the past reporting year, the number of cases still pending, and how many cases were settled between the parties prior to going to trail.

With this data readily available, consider the following questions:

1. Is there a difference between the numbers of civil cases pending versus the number of cases settled by the parties involved?
2. Why do you think parties would settle a case and not proceed to a formal trial?
3. Why do you believe that people file civil lawsuits? What could be their motivation for filing a lawsuit and then settling without a formal trail?

Key Terms

Criminal law	Felonies	Misdemeanors
Plaintiff	Defendant	Tort law
Administrative law	Liability	Negligence
Strict liability	Vicarious liability	Arrest
Gathering of evidence	Search and seizure	Deputized
Merchant's Privilege	Libel	Slander
Testimony	Civil laws	

Sources

Administrative law. (2009). In *Black's Law Dictionary online*. Retrieved from
   https://vmail.svsu.edu/service/home/~/?auth=co&loc=en_US&id=134
   260&part=2&view=html

Arrest. (2009). In *Black's Law Dictionary online*. Retrieved from https://vmail.
   svsu.edu/service/home/~/?auth=co&loc=en_US&id=134198&part=2&
   view=html

Cole, G. F., Smith, C. E., & DeJong, C. (2014). *Criminal justice in America*
   (7th ed.). Belmont, CA: Wadworth.

Contract. (2009). In *Black's Law Dictionary online*. Retrieved from https://
   vmail.svsu.edu/service/home/~/?auth=co&loc=en_US&id=134203&part=
   2&view=html

Evidence. (2009). In *Black's Law Dictionary online*. Retrieved from https://
   vmail.svsu.edu/service/home/~/?auth=co&loc=en_US&id=134204&part=
   2&view=html

Liability. (n.d.). In *Merriam-Webster Dictionary online*. Retrieved from http://
   www.merriam-webster.com/dictionary/liability

Libel. (2009). In *Black's Law Dictionary online*. Retrieved from https://vmail.
   svsu.edu/service/home/~/?auth=co&loc=en_US&id=134200&part=2&
   view=html

Negligence. (2009). In *Black's Law Dictionary online*. Retrieved from https://
   vmail.svsu.edu/service/home/~/?auth=co&loc=en_US&id=134197&part=
   2&view=html

Search and seizure. (2009). In *Black's Law Dictionary online*. Retrieved from https://
   vmail.svsu.edu/service/home/~/?auth=co&loc=en_US&id=134201&part=
   2&view=html

Shopkeeper's Privilege. (n.d.). In *USLaw.com online*. Retrieved from http://
   definitions.uslegal.com/s/shopkeepers-privilege/

Slander. (2009). In *Black's Law Dictionary online*. Retrieved from https://vmail.
   svsu.edu/service/home/~/?auth=co&loc=en_US&id=134199&part=2&
   view=html

Strict liability. (n.d.). In *Cornell University Law School online*. Retrieved from
   http://www.law.cornell.edu/wex/strict_liability

Tort. (2009). In *Black's Law Dictionary online*. Retrieved from https://vmail.svsu.
   edu/service/home/~/?auth=co&loc=en_US&id=134202&part=2&view=html

Vicarious liability. (n.d.). In *Cornell University Law School online*. Retrieved
   from http://www.law.cornell.edu/wex/vicarious_liability

Chapter Four

Fortifying the Facility: The Concept of Physical Security

Introduction

Every day we see and use different types of physical security measures or devices. In chapter one, it was presented that physical security measures have been used for centuries. For modern day security professionals, it is vital to know when to use physical security, where it should be utilized, and which devices are appropriate. This process takes great planning and attention to detail to implement.

Physical security is not "fool proof." A single security device cannot be expected to keep 100% of intruders away from the target. Security should be "layered," using multiple devices to act as an effective deterrent. Many people already use this methodology to protect lives and property. A security device can be as simple as a padlock or as complex as a biometric access control system. The decision to determine what devices will be utilized depends primarily on need and budget. Any room, building, or complex can be turned into a fortress but many decisions will dictate exactly what devices will be used and to what extent.

Learning Objectives

In this chapter the reader will be introduced to concepts of designing and utilizing physical security systems, the basic devices commonly used to protect lives and property, and how the devices work. These systems include locks, fences, lighting, alarms, camera systems, and access control devices, as well as fire detection and suppression systems.

Designing a Security System

Designing a security system takes time, attention to detail, and an understanding of your objective. This process cannot be underestimated or treated as a necessary evil. The planning and design of the security system is a worthy and needed investment of time and energy. Proper planning and design of the security system will make the difference between an effective security system or a waste of time, resources, and money.

For this planning and design process, some important questions need to be addressed. The questions can seem basic but they are important for the success of the security system. The first question is: *what is to be protected?* Knowing the value or importance of the object, room, or building will give insight as to what types of devices will be needed to impede intruders. Second is: *why does the object, room, or building need to be protected?* Talk with the owner or manager and get details on this question. *Why is this important to your client or manager?* It is helpful to get a solid understanding of the importance of this question through their eyes. This knowledge can give the system designer an idea as to which devices may be needed.

The next question is for the system designer. Specifically, *how can someone break in and take, destroy, or corrupt what you are trying to protect?* This is a concept that many people have difficulty grasping. To simply state the question: *how can someone break in?* The designer needs to put themselves into the shoes of the would-be criminal. This is a skill that takes time to develop. You need to understand not only what you are trying to protect but also what are you protecting against. *Where could someone gain unwanted access? How could they do it? What could they effectively use to gain access?* Asking these questions can greatly assist in the design of the system and deterring unwanted access.

The fourth question can create some uncomfortable emotions but is necessary for the process. The designer needs to understand the budget for the project or simply, *how much does the individual want to spend?* Most individuals or organizations do not have a bottomless pot of money. Tactfully inquiring about the project budget is vital to the design. Knowing this financial information will help the designer create a physical security solution that is appropriate for what is to be protected as well as cost effective. Designing a system that is too extravagant for the need and the available budget is a waste of time and effort. Conversely, under protecting the area or object when additional resources could be budged may lead to an insignificant effort and possible liability concerns. If the client does not wish to share their budget, the designer should come up with multiple options with varying prices to protect the object, room, or facility. The client can then be presented with the multiple options and different levels of protection due to the price. They then will select the design that best fits their budget. Some system designers will offer multiple options based on price whether the budget is or is not known. This method of design inclusion with the client may help to relive possible anxiety or potential concerns with the system.

The final primary question is: *which resources are available to assist with the design?* This can mean simple things, such as *where is or what is the power source*, as well as complex questions such as *what type of building or construction obstacles will the installation crew encounter when installing the system?* Questions about the available resources may also include: *which devices are appropriate, available, and applicable to protect the object, room, or facility?* Knowing not only what the client wants protected but also how the home or facility is constructed will be a great benefit to the overall effort of installing the system. If the designer takes the time to think about these potential obstacles then time, effort, and money could be saved.

The planning phase of security system design is vital for success. No two security systems are the same. Knowing the background information as to what is to be protected, the reason for the protection, the possible budget, and the resources available can greatly improve design, effectiveness, and client satisfaction. If the designer fails to take the proper time with the system development and then underestimates the importance of this process, the system or protective measures may be inappropriate and ineffective.

Crime Prevention through Environmental Design (CPTED)

In 1974, the formal term of Crime Prevention Through Environmental Design (**CPTED**) was introduced by the National Institute of Law Enforcement and Criminal Justice (Collins, Ricks, & Van Meter, 2000). As described in chapter one, the practice of CPTED is used when local resources are incorporated into the protection of lives and property. These resources can be natural (as explained in chapter one) or man-made, created, or available for protection. This concept is very important when determining the use of physical security devices or designing physical security systems.

These natural or man-made barriers can impact physical security in two primary ways. First, natural or man-made barriers may be able to reduce the need for physical security. For example, a solid wall that reaches from floor to ceiling may not need to be protected due to its design. If the wall cannot be easily penetrated or compromised above or below then a lesser amount of physical security protection may be needed. If a complex is built on a higher elevation, the side that faces the drop-off may not be as susceptible to unwanted entry as the other sides of the building. More resources could be used in the flat areas instead of where the natural barrier is located. In addition, the construction of a building can provide protection as well. Traditionally, vaults used in banks are constructed under the surface of the facility. Since there is no open access to outside the building in a vault, the natural barrier of the ground also protects the contents. Finally, if a room intended to be secured is located deep within the interior of the building, the constructed wall, floors, and ceilings may add additional physical protection against unwanted entry.

Conversely, some barriers may actually hurt the protection of a facility. For example, the interior walls along a corridor or hallway become a risk if the walls do not meet the actual ceiling (as opposed to a false or drop ceiling), are constructed of thin or hollow materials, and could be compromised by a would-be intruder. It would be easier for an intruder to go up and over a partial wall (with a dropped or false ceiling), cut through a thin wall, or break a window and enter into the adjoining space. Another example is if trees or shrubs are too close to the exterior of a building. These natural barricades could prevent anyone from seeing activity around the building or allow someone to climb up and enter through an opening on an upper story or the roof. These barriers are detrimental to the protection of the building and may merit the installation of additional security devices in the building to protect from unwanted entry into the facility.

Something important for those who may be designing a physical security system is to perform a detailed survey (also known as a risk assessment) of the protected area. In addition, the designer needs to ensure all natural and man-made barriers are noted and taken into account with the planning of the security system. Some barriers may be able to assist with protection, while others may pose a threat.

Target Hardening

The concept of **target hardening** may ultimately lead to the installation or use of physical security devices. The term target hardening can be defined as defending or protecting an item or a location in order to deter or prevent intrusion or loss. The design or selection of the physical security devices should ultimately lead to making the protected area difficult to enter and deter or deflect a possible attack. For example, if a priceless painting is stored in a room and concern exists that it could be stolen or damaged, the proactive steps to secure the room from possible unauthorized entry is a form of target hardening. Another example could be that if a VIP is traveling in an area and the threat of harm exists, the vehicle in which the VIP is riding in can be fitted with armor plating or bullet resistant glass to reduce the threat of harm.

The designer of a security system must always be aware and cognizant of what needs to be protected and what the potential threats may be, and then work to protect the room, facility, or complex. Target hardening will take place as the area becomes secure and the threats of intrusion or damage are reduced through the use of CPTED, thoughtful design of the security system, and proper use of security devices.

Exterior Protection

Taking the time to review, plan, and develop exterior protection for any facility is literally the first line of defense from unwanted entry and intrusion. The devices utilized to protect may be either simple or highly complex. The key for the individual developing the protection is to know and fully understand what is to be protected, what the potential risks may be (as well as the likelihood of the potential risk), and how the protective devices work, as well as their positive and negative attributes. Using multiple security devices or systems, known as **layering**, provides multiple levels of security devices working in conjunction to protect lives and property. This redundancy with security devices will help to fortify and defend the facility, its contents, and its occupants.

The exterior of the facility is defined as the property that leads up to the physical building. The exterior may include parking lots as well as open fields or green spaces. Designers of the security system must be keenly aware of property lines and property ownership. As a general rule, the installation of protective systems should only affect the property owned by the company, organization, or corporation. In this section, three preventative methods for the protection of a building's exterior will be introduced. They are lighting, fencing, and clear zones.

Lighting

The proper use of lighting can be a solid defense against unwanted activity or intrusion. Lights have been found to prevent criminal or unwanted activities because the person may be easily viewed. This can be a strong deterrent and method to protect lives and property.

Protective lighting should be installed to offer overlapping areas of illumination and provide light down to the ground level. The specific amount of illumination needs to be determined by the facility and security management and ensure that any and all applicable industry guidelines or regulations are followed.

Lighting may be classified in multiple groups or classifications. The basic classifications of lighting styles are stationary, portable, stand-by, and emergency (Post & Kingsbury, 1977). **Stationary lighting** is normally affixed to a pole or a building. Commonly referred to as streetlights, lighting attached to poles is commonly used in parking areas, walkways, or the property leading up to the facility. Stationary lighting may also be affixed to the building and shine on the building and the immediate property leading up to the facility. This style of lighting has a permanent power supply and may be activated by a timer or light sensor. Environmental considerations must also be taken into consideration with the powering of exterior lights. Light timers provide the user with a set time to activate and deactivate the lights. The use of a light timer may impede illumination during times of inclement weather conditions. Timers may also offer the facility with the ability to light certain areas of the property during specific times of the day and night. This selected distribution of lighting allows for energy conservation but should never deter from the protection of the facility or its occupants. Permanent lighting may also be powered by sensors detecting the amount of natural light available. As daylight fades, the detector senses the lack of natural light available and activates the street light or light attached to the building. Exterior light sensors are commonly and effectively used to help to illuminate the property as natural lighting wanes during the evening hours, dense fog, or storms.

Portable lighting is any form of illumination that can be moved or relocated to provide temporary lighting as needed or required. Temporary lights are powered through a portable generator or electrical cords attached to a permanent power supply. Portable lighting is commonly used for evening events or an occasion when permanent lighting is unavailable or is inadequate. These lights may be connected to an extendable pole and can be elevated to any necessary and appropriate height. The use of portable lighting can help reduce the cost of lighting operations (or a lighting operation) because they are only utilized in time of specific need. They should not be used as an alternative method to permanent lighting.

Stand-by lighting is a device that activate in times of emergency or power outage. Through the use of an independent, temporary, or rechargeable power source, the stand-by lights are designed to illuminate when the permanent lighting fails due to natural or man-made events. They are typically mounted on walls near openings such as pedestrian doors, hallways, or stairwells. Stand-by lights are intended for temporary use until the permanent lights become operable. They do not emit the same amount of illumination due to their smaller design but can be extremely helpful during a time of crisis, emergency, or inclement weather.

Emergency lighting is often a portable style of light used for brief periods of time during abnormal circumstances. Emergency lighting can be mounted to a structure, moved with a vehicle, or even handheld. Commonly referred to as "spotlights," this form of light is manually activated and offers the user with a bright and narrow beam of illumination. Emergency lighting is used very infrequently but can be a great asset when portable and short-term lighting is needed.

Equally important with the design of lighting is to understand the types of light available and the amount of illumination produced. Unlike interior lighting that may use incandescent, florescent, or compact florescent light bulbs (CFLs), the exterior of the building and the natural elements must be taken into account when selecting the type of light. Traditionally sodium vapor or mercury vapor lights were used for external illumination. These styles of lights produced a yellow cast (sodium) or a blue cast (mercury) with their illumination. The color cast can aid or hamper illumination during natural weather events such as fog, mist, or snow. Another detriment of these traditional styles of lighting is the amount of time needed to begin emitting light. As the sensor or timer activates, the traditional styles of lights may take two to five minutes for the light to "warm up" and begin working. This is due to time needed for the gases inside the bulb to generate the light needed. With the advancement in lighting technology, many newer exterior lights are being produced with **LED** (light emitting diode) bulbs (Cast Lighting, n.d.). Unlike the color cast by the sodium or mercury vapor lights, LED bulbs offer a stronger, condensed, and white glow when illuminated. The LED light provides a compromise for both the protection of the property and concerns for environmental conservation. This style of light offers adequate lighting for external protection while using less energy to operate. With the installation of any external lighting, it is imperative to understand the product specifications of the lights used and the expectations of the property management as to what is to be illuminated and for what purpose. Having too much lighting can be a waste of money and energy, while having too little lighting can lead to unwanted acts, crime, or civil threats.

Fencing

Fencing is another method to protect the exterior of a facility. Fencing is a barrier with the intended purpose of keeping unwanted intruders from coming onto the property as well as keeping unauthorized individuals or property from leaving the grounds. Fencing is normally placed near the outer edge of the property line. It is essential that the owner or manager of the property determines the legal property line to avoid unwanted disputes over the fence location. It is also important to research and review any governmental or institutional regulations and requirement on the selection, installation, and use of fences. Governmental bodies may have defined statutes on the type of fencing that may be installed and its location. In addition, certain industries may also have requirements for the installation and maintenance for fencing. Prior to any selection or installation of fencing, proper research must be conducted to determine if any regulations or requirements exist.

The most common style of fencing is **chain-link**. This type of fencing is a very cost effective style because of its relative ease of installation and overall low level of maintenance. Chain-link fencing also allows clear vision of all activities taking place both outside and inside the fence line. Adequate time and research must take place to determine the style of chain-link fence needed to keep people or items both in and out. The gauge (strength) of the fence will directly affect its pliability and possible manipulation to get an item through. The size of the opening in the fencing is also critical to deter items or object from passing through. Chain-link fencing must be properly attached to well-grounded poles to prevent unwanted compromise. For added security, the bottom of the fencing may also be buried to avoid objects or individuals from sliding under. The height and length of the fence also needs to be determined for use and regulatory purposes. If a fence is too low, it can be easily jumped over. If it is too high, it can be unstable and easily compromised. In addition, if a fence does not completely cover the property line, someone can easily walk around it or slide through an opening, defeating the purpose of the protection.

In addition to the chain-link fencing, **barbed wire** can be added to the top or bottom of the fence line for added protection. As with the regulations for the installation and use of chain-link fencing, it is also equally important to know the guidelines for the use of barbed wire. These guidelines may include how the barbed wire may be installed, what type of barbed wire may be used, and where geographically it may be allowed.

Barbed wire can come in the form of barbed tape, barbed strands, or in rolls or spools. Sharp and small welded sections of wire (barbs) are attached onto the primary wiring (the strands) with the intent to cut anything that attempts to go over or through it. Barbed wire is typically used in two or three separate strands, connected to metal extensions on top of the chain-link fence. The fence extension with the barbed wire (known as the parapet) must be securely attached to the chain-link fencing at a 45-degree angle either facing outward, inward, or both. The angled strands of the barbed wire need to be facing the direction where the threat may be coming from. For example, if the threat to the property is solely on the outside, then the 45-degree angle should be facing outward. Barbed wire in the form or a roll or spool (also known as concertina wire) may be used at the bottom or the top of the fence. This wire can be produced in narrow rolls or can be as high as three feet. Much like the installation of barbed wire, concertina wire must be properly secured in a stationary position so it cannot be moved or pushed away.

One of the primary criticisms with chain-link fencing is that it offers what is called an "institutional look" to the facility. Chain-link fencing, with or without barbed wire, may be viewed not only as a visual deterrent to possible crime but also to potential business. Depending on the specific business conducted on the property, chain-link fencing may be detrimental to the aesthetics (image) the organization wants to portray. Although cost effective and useful, chain-link fencing and barbed wire could be offensive to potential business and illegal for the specific geographic location.

An alternative style of exterior barrier is a **wrought iron fence**. The design of the wrought iron fence allows for solid visibility of the area, sturdy construction, and a lesser degree of an institutional appearance. Comprised of either steel or iron, sections of horizontal poles (or rails) are attached at the top and bottom to vertical poles. The wrought iron fence offers a solid fence line which can be difficult to climb.

The distance between the vertical poles (rails) can vary depending on the degree of security needed. The closer the vertical rails are together, the higher the difficulty to slide anything in between. The property owner or management must decide how low and high the fence line should be constructed. For additional protection, the top of the vertical poles may come to a point (also called a spike). To many professionals, wrought iron fencing may offer a "dignified" but more expensive alternative to chain-link fencing.

Privacy fencing provides yet another alternative for the protection of a property's exterior. Privacy fencing can be constructed of concrete, metal, wood, or plastic. The intent is to provide a solid wall of protection from an outsider. The concern with the use of privacy fencing is the inability to see what is taking place on either side of the fence. This lack of vision can create a major risk to those both entering and exiting the property. Privacy fencing is fairly uncommon in commercial use but can be used in specific industrial or residential settings.

The same primary design, construction, and installation concerns are also applicable with privacy fences. The owner or manager must ensure the fence is constructed with the appropriate materials, installed properly, and maintained to safeguard against deterioration. In addition, governmental and industrial regulations must be reviewed to verify the proper use and construction of the privacy fence.

Another key component with fencing is the use of gates and openings. Even with the proper installation of the fence line to deter unwanted access onto the property, some type of gate or opening must be considered for vehicular and pedestrian entry and exit. Gates are typically constructed of the same material, style, and height as the surrounding fence line. The gates can be movable on a hinge or rollers. They may be opened manually or automatically, depending on the amount of use and what is entering or exiting the facility. In some cases a horizontal gate arm or a turnstile is used to regulate traffic flow. Gates may also incorporate access control systems and closed-circuit televisions systems to help with the authorized entrance and exit (these systems will be discussed later in the chapter).

Clear Zones

The final practice for the protection for the exterior of a building is the use of **clear zones**. A clear zone is preferably a flat stretch of land on either side of the property line that is unimpeded by obstructions. In basic terms, a clear zone allows people to see what is taking place on either side of a property line. Clear zones can vary in depth according to the amount of land available, natural vegetation, man-made obstacles, and the preferences of the property owner or facility management staff. Clear zones can also be used at building entry and exit points, sidewalks, and vehicular drives. Under ideal conditions for security purposes, no natural or man-made obstructions should be in the clear zone. In reality, many properties will have trees, shrubbery, statues, signs, or other obstacles in place. Even with the intent to beautify or allow the property to be identified (with a sign), any obstacle is a potential hiding spot for a would-be attacker or someone or something that could hurt, injure, or damage lives and property. The ability to freely monitor all activity near the property line, close to the building and in any other open area, is not only a solid method to deter crime but it also gives employees and visitors the peace of mind that they are being protected.

As simple and cost effective as this method of exterior protection seems, it can also become a highly contested debate between those who want an aesthetically pleasing external environment and those trying to protect lives and property. When these differences take place, a compromise between the parties may become the solution. A limited number of trees and greenery may be placed in the clear zone as long as they are well maintained and trimmed to offer the best view possible. The security staff will also have to take additional measures to personally patrol these areas to ensure against unwanted activity.

Often ignored or forgotten, the exterior of the property is a vital area for protection against unwanted activity or intrusion. Through the development of a solid exterior security system, the threat of unauthorized outside entry can be greatly reduced. Taking the time and effort to begin the security design from the outside may greatly assist with the goal of protecting lives and property.

Facility Protection

As the layering of security devices continues to protect lives and property, the next primary area to focus upon is the facility itself. The amount of security necessary to defend against unwanted attacks will be determined by numerous factors. They include the location of the facility, the work or production taking place within the facility, and the budget afforded for protection. As with the design of the exterior protection, thought and pre-planning should take place to determine possible threats, the likelihood of dangers, and the level of security desired by the property owners or management. The following categories of protection can be found in facilities of various size and activity.

Locks

As described in chapter one, the lock is one of the oldest forms of physical security protection used. Locks come in different forms, sizes, and capabilities. Before the use or installation of a lock or locking system, a review of the goals and objectives of the protection must be addressed. If it is determined that locking devices will benefit the protection of the facility, the proper lock can then be selected and installed.

One of the most common locking devices today is the **warded lock**. First developed during the Mycenaean Age by the Egyptians (Collins, Ricks, & Van Meter, 2000), the padlock is used to protect single points against intrusion. The warded locking system involves the use of a key to be inserted into the lock and allowing the internal components to rotate and release or open the lock. Examples of warded locks include padlocks on door locks (also known as pin-tumbler locks). This style of lock is very cost effective and can deter a minimal to moderate attempt to gain entry. In the event the key for the warded lock is lost or damaged, duplicate keys may be used or in the case of the pin-tumbler lock, the locking cylinder within the door can be replaced and new keys may be issued.

Wafer locks are another example of basic locking devices. Similar to a warded, pin-tumbler lock, wafer locks are activated with the use of a key. Under this circumstance, when the key is inserted into the lock, the internal unit rotates as one whole unit, opening the device. As with the warded lock, the wafer lock provides basic to moderate protection against unwanted intrusion.

Lever locks also afford basic to moderate protection against intrusion. Through the use of a key or a switch, the lever lock operates by allowing the internal components (tumblers) to rotate and open or close. Lever locks can be found in dead bolt locks, door knob locks, or padlocks.

From the basic locking devices listed above, different styles of locks or locking systems have been developed and used to protect lives and property. An example is a **combination lock**. Combination locks can be simplistic, as in the case of a padlock, or more intricate in the case of a manual or electronic door lock. The combination lock requires that a series of numbers or characters be dialed or pressed in a predetermined order. When the proper code is applied, the locking device releases. Combination locks can offer a medium to higher degree of safety than basic lock devices. The amount of protection from the lock depends on their design and the application in which they are used. With the advanced style of these locking devices, the combination may be changed according to need. The practice of regularly changing the combination gives an added layer of protection against unwanted intrusion.

The **electronic strike lock** and **electromagnetic lock** offer a higher amount of protection against unwanted intrusion. In the case of electronic strike locks, the locking device is found within the actual door and door frame. When the lock is deactivated, the internal device releases the locking mechanism and allows the door to open. The electromagnetic lock is normally found on the outside of the door and door frame. When the door is properly deactivated, the electric hold on the magnet is released and the door can be opened. Electronic strike and electromagnetic locks may be activated through the use of a combination lock or a card key.

The use of card keys continues to increase in today's society. **Card keys** can be very cost effective due to the lesser price per card than a standard key (when the product and the cost of labor for replacement are considered). In addition, card keys may be easily replaced, and a new card may be reprogrammed for that specific lock or series of locks. The cards are programmed through small recording and programing devices and can be recorded into computerized software systems. Card keys are normally produced with either an outwardly visible magnetic strip or an internal computer chip. Cards with a magnetic strip on the outside must be inserted into a reading device for the lock to operate. The **magnetic strip cards** (commonly referred to as mag-strip cards) require the proper insertion into the reading device. If the card is swiped

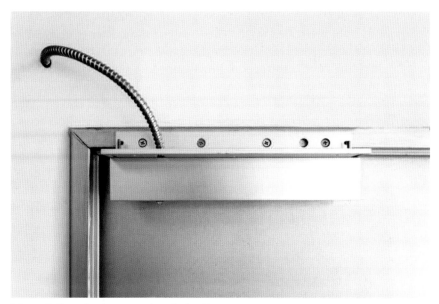

Magnetic Door Lock © cunaplus via fotolia.com

or inserted incorrectly, the lock will fail to deactivate. Cards with a computer chip inside the actual card are often referred to as **proximity cards**. With this style of card key, when the card is within the required proximity for the reading device to recognize the internal computer chip, the lock is released. In addition, the distance in which the card reader can recognize the key card can be adjusted (for example: 3 inches, 6 inches, or 12 inches) allowing for faster deactivation of the lock and entry past the door. The development and use of locking devices can be an effective way to protect openings when they are properly incorporated with an appropriate entry device.

Doors, Windows, and Openings

The protection of exterior points of entry into a facility is imperative to prevent unwanted intrusion. The unfortunate reality is that property owners and managers can easily overlook an entry point and fail to consider it as a viable way to enter into the structure.

The use of properly designed exterior doors can greatly defend the structure against unauthorized entry. Not all doors are constructed alike. Interior doors tend to be produced of lighter weight materials and may be hollow on the inside. This type of door is completely inappropriate for exterior protection. Exterior doors should be constructed of heavy and solid materials, typically metal or certain styles of pretreated wood. These materials can deter or delay entry into the facility simply based on the solid material with which they are constructed. In addition to the door construction, heavy-duty door hinges should also be used and installed to be accessible only from the inside of the building. This prevents an unwanted intruder from dissembling the hinge and removing the door. Also, a solid (preferably steel) door frame must be securely attached to the building. Using a lighter or solid door frame or not property attaching it to the building could allow an unwanted intruder to pry, pull, or push the frame away from the wall. When this occurs, entry is easily gained. Finally, proper locking devices need to be installed on the doors (as previously stated) to prevent unwanted entry but allow for easy exit in the case of an emergency.

Overhead doors (also known as bay doors) also need to be properly constructed and protected against the threat of intrusion. The doors should be constructed of metal with the locks and tracks for the rollers on the inside. The doors may be opened with automatic or manual devices with all the controls on the interior of the building.

Windows can be overlooked as a viable method of unwanted entry. The construction of the window within a commercial setting should be researched and considered when designing the facility protection. Unlike the common double-hung and double-paned glass windows used for residences, commercial windows need to be constructed of stronger materials such as Plexiglas or an approved plastic or acrylic material. All windows on the first and second floors need to be considered as viable points of unwanted entry. In the event trees or ladder wells are adjacent to the building, additional security precautions may be needed to prevent window entry. If the existing windows can be opened, proper locks should be installed to prevent outside access but not to deter from emergency exit. If the window is non-opening, then consideration must be taken for protection to deter or prevent entry.

With proper consideration taken with the selection of doors and windows as well as the protection of any viable spot of entry, the protection of the physical exterior of the building or facility will work to deter unwanted entry. This second line of building defense is vitally important to prevent an incident and may save lives and property.

Other areas of concern, which may be overlooked, are openings that may lead into the building. Air intake vents or grates that lead into a sewer system or roof hatches or doors also require ways to lock and secure against unwanted entry. Depending on the type of entry, consideration and devices need to be researched to either disallow any entry or exit or prevent external entry while permitting exit for life safety situations.

Alarm Systems

The basic and rudimentary alarm system developed by Edwin T. Holmes in the 1860s has become a multifaceted notification system. Today's alarm systems can protect against unwanted entry, hold-ups, environmental concerns, and medical emergencies, and may now be connected to activate lights and other household appliances. They can be interfaced with closed-circuit television systems, access control systems, fire systems, and a multitude of computer systems.

Alarm systems are primarily monitored by either a proprietary security force or a central monitoring station, through a contracted entity. A very small percentage of alarm systems are for "local" annunciation purposes only. This means that the alarm will activate and sound but only at the specific location. No monitoring of the alarm signal takes place with a local alarm.

False Alarms

Alarms are becoming common and can be an effective way to protect lives and property. The commonness and popularity of alarm systems also creates concerns that have a direct impact on the law enforcement community. Faulty installation of alarm systems and user error can create false alarms and deter the effectiveness of the electronic protection system. When alarms are poorly installed or maintained and inaccurately operated, false alarms are generated. These unintentional alarms must be investigated and verified by proprietary security departments, property management, or home owners, or by law enforcement, fire, or emergency medical technicians. The high rate of false alarms, due to equipment or human error, places an unnecessary burden on the departments and agencies responding to the signal. The high rate of false alarms can cause a desensitization to the importance of the alarm by the responding agencies. In cases of a large amount of false alarms, fines can be imposed by local governmental authorities. This may assist in the perpetration of actual crimes committed due to the delayed or ignored response. False alarms continue to plague the industry and dilute the effectiveness of the alarm device. Proper installation, maintenance, and use of the systems are imperative for the necessary protection intended by these devices.

System Design

The design of the alarm system is highly important to the success and reliability of the devices. Careful thought and consideration must be used for the development of the alarm system. These questions or the following questions should be asked that pertain to the need for an alarm:

- *What problems or concerns are motivating the installation of a system?*
- *What natural or man-made obstacles are present that would impede the proper use of the alarm?*
- *What alarm devices would be appropriate for the system?*

Alarm systems are not a one-size-fits-all security solution and must be properly investigated, analyzed, and designed for effective use. The system designer must know all of this information as well as how the alarm and its components work to protect lives and property.

Alarm Components

Alarm components come in different sizes and shapes and can perform different functions. The alarm system can be broken down into three primary categories: the **triggering mechanism** (alarm device), the **actuator** (control unit), and the **annunciator**. Triggering mechanisms for alarm systems can be designed to protect specific items or general areas. The specific triggering mechanism is hardwired or programmed to send a signal when the circuit has been broken or disrupted. For example, if a door has an alarm contact on it, when the door is opened and the alarm is activated, a signal is sent because the connection has been broken. Another example is if a passive infrared motion detector is placed in a hallway and someone crosses the path of the motion detector while the alarm is on. At that moment, the system is alerted that the beam has been broken by something that is large enough and has enough heat (passive infrared motions detectors activate through movement and heat). The final example is when someone physically pushes a hold-up alarm button. At that point, a signal (frequently silent) is sent that the button or device has been depressed or activated.

When the triggering mechanism or device is activated, the signal is sent via wire or wireless transmission to the actuator or control unit. Commonly referred to as the CPU (central processing unit), the actuator is comprised of a circuit board that is programmed to identify the specific alarm device activated and its location. The size and capability of the circuit board will vary depending on the number of triggering units programmed into it and the specific type of alarm system. Some control units are small and are only used for one specific type of alarm (burglar, hold-up, or supervisory) or can be complex, containing multiple triggering devices for different styles of alarms. The alarm system is commonly controlled (turned on/off or cleared) by an electronic keypad, or in cases of older alarms, a simple on/off switch.

When the information from the triggering mechanism is received by the control unit, an annunciator is triggered and can be viewed at the alarm's keypad (used to turn the system on or off), or into an alarm signal receiver mon-itored by a proprietary security force or contract alarm company. Annuncia-tors may also be programmed to activate a stand-alone siren, a warning sound on the system keypad, a bell (in some older units), or a strobe light. These local alarm annunciators are designed to deter an intruder from further entry, notify occupants inside of a possible intrusion, or assist to notify the author-ities of the specific location of the incident. In the event the alarm is moni-tored by a proprietary force or a contract alarm company, alarm signals may be transmitted through telephone lines or wireless transmission signals. In ad-dition, alarm signals may be received on smart phones, personal computers, or other electronic devices.

With humble beginnings in the mid-nineteenth century, alarm systems can now be used detect entry, signal for assistance, activate household appliances, or detect an environmental concern. The common use of alarm systems by residential and commercial customers drives the alarm industry to properly install and maintain systems; instruct the customer on the proper use of the devices; and collaborate with law enforcement, fire, and emergency response authorities to uphold standards intended to reduce the threat of false alarms.

Closed-Circuit Television Systems (CCTV)

The use of closed-circuit television systems (CCTV) has taken place for decades. Unlike public television, which provides broad, open, and public ac-cess to the transmissions, the closed-circuit systems offer a narrow viewing ca-pability to those with appropriate access. Older CCTV systems included images on 35 mm film and VHS tapes. The vast majority of systems in use today are digitized. The new digital systems provide ease of access to the images and eas-ier storage of the "digital tapes." Whereas the 35 mm and VHS tapes needed to be categorized and physically housed in a secure area, today's digital images can be recorded and maintained within a secure computer system.

Closed-circuit television systems may either be watched by a human or recorded for later use. Many CCTV systems are recorded and in the event of a problem, reviewed to find the desired events. This creates a practice which differs from the overall goal of security. As stated earlier, the goal of security is to be proactive and prevent unwanted events from occurring. Even though the use of CCTV systems can be a visual deterrent against unwanted activities, the current common use of the devices is more of a reactive method. When an even occurs, the images are searched and then used after the fact. This reac-tive use of a CCTV system is understandable because the cost of the needed man-power to continuously observe the cameras images. It should also be stated that many security departments will use CCTV systems as a "real time" way to protect lives and property. In the event the images are transmitted into a base of operations, the security professionals can control the camera system and view live events as they are taking place. These events are viewed on monitors and the camera can be switched to view a specific image while all the cameras are being digitally recorded for later use, as needed.

CCTV System Design

The design of a CCTV system also takes time and attention, like the design of alarm systems. For this style of protection, one simple question can be asked: *what do we want to see?* This simple question is essential to determine the camera and components needed. The system designer must emphasize to the customer or user that CCTV cameras do not have the same peripheral vision of the human eye. The camera will view a much narrower image. Different lenses can be used to widen, narrow, lengthen, or shorten the view of the camera, but it will never have the same peripheral vision as the human eye. In addition to determining what is to be viewed, additional preparatory questions include:

- *Will the camera be inside or outside?*
- *Will the images be viewed in "real time"?*
- *Will the images be recorded?*

These basic questions will begin to help with the process of hardware selection and determine the proper equipment needed to view the desired activities or images.

CCTV Basic Components

As stated above, the camera lens is one of the primary components for a CCTV system. The type of lens will vary, depending on what is going to be viewed. Lenses can offer a narrow image, a wide image, or be manually controlled to zoom in and out. Lenses can also include an "auto iris" which allows the lens to adjust to different levels of lighting. Lenses for night vision may also be used for appropriate needs. The cameras themselves may either transmit a color or black and white image. Cameras need to have a power source for operation and can transmit the images either via a cable or a transmission signal, also known as a wireless system. The images can be viewed on commercial monitors, specifically designed for closed-circuit imagery, and can also be recorded simultaneously on a proper digital recording device. The mounting hardware and potential enclosures for the cameras are equally important. Some camera systems are mobile, allowing for frequent location adjustment or they may be permanently mounted in one specific spot. Cameras may also be integrated and programed to activate when alarm systems are activated. The cameras may be enclosed in a casing to protect from vandalism or shield the camera from inclement weather. In addition, the mounting hardware and selected enclosure may allow the specific camera to rotate and move up or down (referred to as a "pan, tilt, zoom" camera). In addition, the cameras can be wired to also record sound and can be small enough to hide (using "pin hole" lenses) for investigative operations.

Closed-circuit television systems can be a great asset in the protection of lives and property. Great care and planning must take place to ensure the system is properly designed, installed, and maintained. In addition, the proper use of the system must be ensured to protect against any civil or criminal violations. The professional closed-circuit television system is a great tool that may be used as a proactive or reactive device as determined by the owner of the system. In either case, the CCTV system is a sound investment and helpful in the effort to protect people and their working or home environments.

Access Control Systems

The need to control "who goes where and when" is the primary goal of access control systems. These security systems can combine alarm and CCTV technologies in addition to allowing authorized individuals access into specific areas. Today's access control systems are computerized, which greatly assists in the programming of the system as well as recording all activities that take place. When properly designed and implemented, access control systems can be a tremendous asset in the protection of lives and property.

System Design

Typically, access control systems are used to allow or disallow access into protected areas. The systems can be installed on the exterior entrances of buildings and/or inside facilities, permitting various degrees of entry and exit into designated areas. When designing the system, what should be determined is what is to be protected, who can have access, when they can have access, and how critical the area to be protected is. These questions will help the system designer determine which equipment to use, under what circumstances it is to be utilized, and how intricate the system needs to be. Engineering and building construction must also be considered, especially if the system is being installed into a preexisting facility. The vast majority of access control systems are "hardwired" and need ample power as well as back-up power supplies. These factors will assist with the selection of hardware and software, and ultimately the cost for the system.

Access Control Basic Components

The level of security and protection needed will determine how intricate the access control system needs to be. In most cases, access control systems are comprised of a locking device, the keypad or reader to initiate the system, and an appropriate computer with the necessary software to operate and record the activities. Locking devices utilized include an electronic lock or an electromagnetic lock that will open or release when properly activated. Access control systems can be tied into pedestrian doors or turnstiles, overhead doors, and vehicle gates. The keypad or reading device varies depending on the level of security needed and the amount of money available for the project. Push-button combination locks or number pads can be incorporated into the access control system. These can be used for smaller or limited access control systems, which may work independently from one another. Card readers are also common with access control systems. This style of reader (magnetic strip or proximity) will allow for programing the cards for specific individuals. This programming can limit the area of access as well as the time frame the cards will work. With the advancement of technology, biometric readers can be used in higher security areas. Biometric readers work like card readers or keypads but require advanced and individualized specifications for activation. Biometric readers may include fingerprint, voice, hand, facial, or iris recognition for activation. In addition biometric systems can also incorporate a card keys or a numeric codes for an additional layer of security.

The proper recording and storage of the activities is a critical component of the system. A major advantage of access control systems is the data that can be recorded from personal use and activity. Cards and biometric engineering can record who attempted or gained entry, the location, and time. The name of the person as well as their photograph can be entered and monitored. With the incorporation of CCTV technology, the recording of the actual person accessing the secured point can be compared and recorded with the name, photo, and personal data stored in the system. In addition, the system may also be used to allow entry and exit into the protected area. If the access control system is being monitored by security personnel, "real time" and instantaneous changes could be used to override the access and disallow entry or exit from the protected area.

When combined with proper doors, gates, and locking devices, access control systems are a solid and systemic way to protect areas. The proper selection of the devices, training of the employee on system usage, and maintenance of the system all have a bearing on this advanced style of security system. From a basic control system up to an intricate and recorded structure, access control systems provide a solid tool in the protection of lives and property.

Fire Systems

Fire alarm systems have similar structural design as burglar alarms. There are protection devices, a primary control panel, and an annunciation unit. For residential fire alarms, they may be stand-alone and battery operated or part of the burglar alarm system. For the majority of commercial applications, these systems are separated from burglar alarms. In addition, the design and up-keep of fire systems may be the responsibility of the safety department or safety manager. Safety personnel will work and at times rely on security personnel for the review of the status of the system (maintaining it in working order) as well as act as the contact point with fire departments when they come onto the site in the event of an alarm. If an organization does not have a formal safety manager or department, the facilities (maintenance) department may have responsibility over the fire alarm and/or fire suppression system.

System Design

The design, installation, and upkeep of a fire alarm or suppression system is a very detailed and important process. Formal specifications for the design and installation of the fire system may have to be approved by local or state fire marshals as required by law (also known as fire codes). The laws may also dictate which style of device is to be used and where or under what conditions it can be used. This acceptance may be dictated through accepted industrial organizations such as The National Fire Protection Association (NFPA). Organizations such as the NFPA and their life safety guidelines may also be required by insurance organizations to ensure the proper installation, maintenance, and use of the devices.

Fire Alarm Basic Components

Fire detection and suppression systems vary according to need. As previously stated, fire alarm systems have similarities with burglar alarms. The systems have a main control system, keypads or switches to activate or deactivate, and annunciators such as sirens and strobe lights. The triggering devices may include smoke and heat detectors as well as fire suppression components such as dry or wet pipes with sprinkler heads. Commercial-grade smoke detectors may use either ionic or photoelectric technologies to detect the threat of fire while it is in the beginning stages. These smoke detectors will activate when the basic properties of smoke begin to form or may have advanced to a smoldering state. When the smoldering or smoke particles reach the detector, a beam inside the detector is interrupted or broken, triggering the sensing device, and the alarm is sounded. Heat detectors may also be used for fire safety when the environment will not permit the use of a smoke detector. In areas where there is dust or high humidity, smoke detectors may create a false alarm because they cannot distinguish between the environmental particles and smoke. In these cases heat detectors may provide proper coverage. A standard heat detector activates when the triggering device melts and degenerates as the temperature rises. A fixed heat detector activates the fire alarm system when the temperature reaches the predetermined temperature inside the device. The rate-of-rise heat detector activates when the temperature increases a predetermined number of degrees. Smoke and heat detectors are commonplace in a great number of commercial and industrial facilities.

Fire suppression systems work in conjunction with or in place of smoke or heat detectors. Fire suppression systems can be categorized as wet or dry pipe systems. In a wet pipe system, pressurized water exists throughout the suppression system. In the event the system is activated, water immediately begins to cascade out to suppress the fire. In a dry pipe system, the water is held back by pressurized air and levers (or paddles). When the system is activated, the air first comes out and releases the water to suppress the fire. In some circumstances when the use of water could damage valuable property, pressurized chemical agents are used to suppress the fire when activated.

In the water suppression systems, sprinkler heads are used to not only detect the fire but also distribute the water below. Some sprinkler heads are designed with heat detectors in them. With these units, when the heat detector activates, the water begins to flow from that specific sprinkler head. This style of sprinkler head allows for localized water distribution and begins to fight the fire where needed. Other sprinkler heads are activated by fire systems and can either distribute water in the specific area of the alarm or activate the entire sprinkler system.

Conclusion

Physical security devices are an important part of protecting lives and property. The selection, installation, and upkeep of physical security devices may be regulated by governmental, bureaucratic, or industry authorities. Some companies will invest in physical security to reduce security personnel costs as required by insurance agencies. It is critically important to remember that any single security device can be defeated or compromised. A sound physical security plan will incorporate multiple styles of devices that are layered and overlap, providing redundant protection to deter, disrupt, and potentially apprehend any and all unwanted activities.

Case Study—Quality vs. Price

A store owner contacted an electronic security company requesting a price quote on a closed-circuit television system. The security representative met with the owner and asked for the rationale for the cameras, surveyed the premises, and composed a price quote for the system. The store owner said the price for the system was too high. The security representative explained that the quote was for a complete "small business" camera system that included three interior cameras, a monitor, a recording device, and the labor to install the items. The owner said that the camera system was too expensive and he would purchase a less expensive system at a local retail outlet. Two weeks later, the store owner called back and asked the security representative if the price quotation offered earlier was still valid and if he could purchase the camera system. The owner explained that the less expensive camera system purchased at the retail outlet did not provide the same number of items as the commercial camera system quoted by the security representative. In fact, the owner's store was robbed, and the less expensive camera system from the retail outlet did not record the event. The cameras were only projecting the images on a small monitor. After reading this case, answer the following questions:

1. What steps should the store owner have taken to ensure that the camera system first purchased was adequate for the store's security needs?
2. When the security representative was told that the CCTV system proposed was too expensive and the store owner was going to select a lesser quality model, what could the security representative have said to the owner to explain the differences in the systems?
3. Is it necessary for the security representative to educate the store owner on the different styles of camera systems available to be used in the store, even if they are models their company does not sell, install, or service?

Discussion Topic—When Does "Aesthetically Pleasing" Become a Risk?

During the chapter, the reader was introduced to the term "aesthetically pleasing." Formally define the term and answer the following questions:

1. What does aesthetically pleasing mean?
2. Can this be a detriment to the goals and objectives of security, and if so, how?
3. What kind of potential compromises could be developed to allow for aesthetics and still provide a safe and secure environment?

Research Focus—Commercial and Residential Smoke Detectors

Access the Internet and research residential smoke detectors and commercial smoke detectors. With the information at hand, answer the following questions:

1. How much is the price for the residential and commercial smoke detectors?
2. How are both of the devices powered?
3. What are the differences between the two in the way they detect smoke and annunciate?

Key Terms

CPTED	Target hardening	Stationary lighting
Portable lighting	Stand-by lighting	Emergency lighting
LED bulbs	Chain-link fencing	Barbed wire
Wrought iron fence	Privacy fencing	Clear zones
Warded locks	Wafer locks	Lever locks
Electronic strike locks	Electromagnetic locks	Card keys
Magnetic strip cards	Proximity cards	Triggering mechanism
Actuator	Annunciator	CCTV

Sources

Cast Lighting, (N.D). *Products*. Retrieved from http://www.cast-lighting.com/
    products/

Collins, P. A., Ricks, T. A., & Van Meter, C. W. (2000). *Principles of security
    and crime prevention* (4th ed.). Cincinnati, OH: Anderson Publishing
    Company.

Post, R. S., & Kingsbury, A. A. (1977). *Security administration: An introduc-
    tion* (3rd ed.). Springfield, IL: Charles C. Thomas.

Chapter Five

The Human Element: The Concept of Personnel Security

Introduction

The human element of security can be very difficult and dangerous. Human beings are motivated and driven by countless internal and external factors. The end result is the total unpredictability of humans. This unpredictability creates a silent tension and continual threat in the workplace. Examples exist of people who are seemingly calm and composed changing unknowingly and becoming a threat to those around them. These individuals include employees, former employees, or employee family members entering a workplace and assaulting or killing workers. These stressed individuals can also create a negative work environment due to their threatening actions or outbursts of anger.

In addition to violent employees, examples exist where individuals who appear to be honest are actually capable of defrauding their employers, friends, and family. Due to personal circumstances, employees may feel the need to steal from their employers and their fellow co-workers. These acts can be relatively small and petty, or they can be highly detrimental to the well-being of their co-workers and the company as a whole. Because of this unpredictability, securing the human element in the workplace takes consistency and continual vigilance.

Learning Objectives

In this chapter the reader will be introduced to basic elements of protecting people from harm as well as protecting organizations against possible harm from their employees, suppliers, or patrons. Pre-employment background investigations will be addressed as well as legal considerations when protecting organizations from unwanted acts or potential liabilities caused by errant em-

Biometric Finger Print Reader © wittybear via fotolia.com

ployees. The chapter will also address the threats that employees face while in the workplace, including violent acts, kidnapping, and the threat of terrorism.

The Need for Pre-Employment Searches

Why do we conduct background checks or pre-employment searches on perspective employees? There are three primary reasons why there is a viable need to conduct these searches on potential new employees. The first reason why these checks are important is the need to protect current employees from harm and loss. This harm and loss can include violent acts or harassment by a coworker or someone in their circle of friends and family. Second, is the need to protect the company and its assets from loss or damage by a malcontent employee. The background check can help to avoid possible theft from the company as well as a loss to the company in the form of physical damages or a civil suit. It also serves to protect the integrity and reputation of the organization. The final reason why there is a need for solid background checks is, simply, that people lie. People submit inaccurate information on their personal background and experiences. This can be in the form of emitting information that could be detrimental to their hiring, offering inaccurate information on their past, or submitting falsified documents needed to fulfill the requirements of the job.

It is vital for organizations to develop solid human resource policies and procedures on the hiring of new employees. These guidelines need to be well developed and then reviewed and approved by legal counsel as well as included in written policies and procedures and carried out by all the designated employees who take part in the hiring process.

Authorization for permitting pre-employment investigations should take place at the initial application phase of the hiring process. Information needs to be presented to the applicant stating that the organization has the right to conduct a pre-employment investigation, during which aspects of the applicant's background will be checked, and require the approval of the individual to conduct the checks. This approval from the applicant can come from their actual signature on a paper form or the checking of a box acknowledging they understand and agree to the investigation within an electronic form. Also, the depth of the investigation should be determined by the duties and responsibilities of the position for which the individual is applying. For example, the higher the level of authority required for the position, the more in-depth the pre-employment check should be. This may include the verification of college degrees, investigation of both civil and criminal records, and the candidate's personal financial history. Any and all of the pre-employment verification process must be vetted by the qualified individuals and strictly followed.

Organizations should also consider establishing policies and procedures to routinely check the appropriate information on the employee, which could have a bearing or impact on their employment responsibilities. This type of ongoing investigation mirrors a pre-employment verification but is often not implemented by organizations. If an organization deems it appropriate to continue checking certain aspects of an employee's professional or personal life, then which aspects are to be investigated must be approved by management and proper legal counsel as well as acknowledged by the employee. Employers must be very careful not to violate any laws, policies and procedures, or labor agreements. If the axiom, "information is power" is true and accurate, then employers must ensure the materials gathered are legitimate, justifiable, and legally obtainable.

Sources of Information for Pre-Employment Checks

Information on prospective employees comes from a multitude of different sources. Before the emergence of electronic databases and the Internet, pre-employment checks were a slow and often tedious series of phone calls, written requests, and personal visits to courthouses or residential communities. Today, pre-employment investigations can be completed faster than in previous years but the person conducting the investigation must remain diligent to ensure the information sources are legitimate and accurate.

Governmental agencies are excellent sources for information. These agencies may include local assets such as county clerks, state agencies such as departments of corrections or prisons, public colleges and universities, as well as national agencies such as the Federal Bureau of Investigation (FBI) or the branches of the United States military. Legally accessing these agencies can provide detailed information on an applicant's past activities.

Contacting prior employers can be an important component in a background check, depending on the information the prior employer is willing to offer. In many cases today, larger organizations are only willing to release basic information on the past employee. This information may include the date of hire, job title, and the date the employment ended. Due to the litigious nature of the American population, many employers now protect themselves against a possible civil suit from the previous employee. In the event the information released could be deemed as detrimental to the former employee's well-being, legal action may be taken. These possible threats of a "defamation of character" civil suit now limit the information some organizations may offer. It should be noted that even a confirmation of past employment can be helpful with the background investigation. In the event an applicant uses a former employer, supervisor, or coworker as a personal reference, additional details may be obtained that could be helpful in the pre-employment investigatory process.

Finally, the use of legitimate electronic databases and background services may permit access to large amounts of information. Today, much of the necessary information needed or wanted for a background check can be accessed through digital archives and databases. Some of this information or detailed information cannot be obtained by the general public. In these circumstances, companies and organizations that provide this information have earned and achieved the proper authorization needed to access these records. It is the responsibility of the organization potentially hiring the employee to verify that the electronic database organization is providing accurate and legal information needed for the search. All national, state, and local employment laws and procedures must be followed by both parties (the organization hiring the individual and the company providing the information). In the event illegal information is obtained (or obtained by illegal means), both parties can be held liable for damages against the applicant.

With the multitude of information existing on potential and current employees, it is vital for organizations to develop sound policies and practices on obtaining this data. The hiring organization also must have policies and procedures in place as to how to respond when detrimental information is discovered that may have a negative bearing on the potential employee. Great care is needed to ensure all policies and practices for pre-employment screening steps are legal, moral, and ethical. Organizations have a right to protect their employees and business interests from harm as long as the process is deemed acceptable by the legal and bureaucratic organizations involved with the process.

Legal Considerations

The process of pre-employment investigations and hiring employees is a very serious process that requires time, effort, and knowledge of the hiring process. For those who are tasked with searching out the information during a pre-employment check, their role may be one of an adviser and presenting the details uncovered for another member of management to make the hiring decision. In the case of security departments or for contract security companies, they may be or will be directly responsible for the entire hiring process. There are a multitude of laws which dictate what hiring entities can or cannot do while selecting potential employees. The numerous laws and regulations can and will change according to need and changes within laws and statues. For that reason alone, having a trained representative within the organization responsible for staying abreast of these laws is essential. These laws can be amended, added to, and discontinued according to need and changes to legislative bodies. This "human resources or hiring expert" can be tasked to stay educated and current on laws pertaining to hiring, firing, and disciplining employees. In addition, companies or organizations may have potential employees sign authorizing statements which give permission to check their background information. This could be a general statement of intent by the organization or list the specific information that will be accessed as a part of the pre-employment investigation. This authorization process can also be used for employees to allow future investigations of personal information as needed. As with any policy or procedure, the organization needs to have all verbiage and potential practices vetted by a qualified legal authority.

The following are United States federal laws which can have an impact on pre-employment investigations as well as the human resources oversight process.

The **Civil Rights Act of 1964** worked to change discriminatory or unfair hiring practices for all American citizens. The concept of the law is to provide "equal protection of the law" to all United States citizens (Archives.gov, n.d.).

Specifically, the act created legal standards for hiring, terminating, compensation, and workplace treatment of employees. Under the Civil Rights Act of 1964, employers are not allowed to discriminate against employees or potential employees for the reasons of "race, color, religion, sex, or national origin." The act also created the Equal Employment Opportunity Commission (EEOC) to enforce and regulate these laws and practices (Archives.gov, n.d.). Additional amendments to the law have taken place to expand the list of non-discriminatory groups to include creed, age, and disability. Also added to the act were changes prohibiting discriminatory acts pertaining to setting wages; determining promotions; and establishing employee testing, training, or apprenticeships as well as creating or implementing any additional conditions of employment (Archives.gov, n.d.).

The **Fair Credit Reporting Act** (FCRA) works to protect people by promoting "the accuracy, fairness, and privacy of information in the files of consumer reporting agencies" (FTC.gov, n.d.). With the continuous threat of unauthorized access into personal financial information, the FCRA works to set standards to deter unwanted access to financial information and requires notification (in the individual's credit file) if one's credit record has been accessed. The act also requires the following:

- The individual is to be told if information in their credit file has been used against them.
- The individual has the right to know what is in their credit report and have access to it.
- The individual has the right to know if someone has taken harmful, negative, or adverse action against them because of the information in their credit report.
- A "fraud alert" can be placed in the individual's credit file if they have been the victim of identity theft.
- Notification if the individual's credit file contains inaccurate information due to fraud.
- No negative financial action can be taken against the person if they are on public assistance.
- No negative financial can be taken against the person if the individual is unemployed but expects to apply for unemployment benefits within 60 days.

(FTC.gov, n.d.)

As of September of 2005, every consumer has the right to obtain one personal report on their credit information each year. These reports can be obtained through "each nationwide credit bureau and from nationwide specialty consumer reporting agency," (FTC.gov, n.d.). Also added at that time were the following conditions:

- Individuals have the right to ask for their credit score
- Individuals can dispute inaccurate information on their credit reports
- The credit reporting agencies must make corrections to credit reports when errors are discovered and verified within 30 days

(FTC.gov, n.d.)

Organizations seeking credit information for pre-employment investigations or for ongoing employment reasons must ensure that the rationale for obtaining the data is necessary, ethical, and legal. As previously stated, all policies and practices pertaining to the accessing of applicant or current employee information should be properly reviewed and approved by a qualified legal authority.

In 1996, the **Health Insurance Portability and Accountability Act** (HIPAA) was created to protect patient's medical records and health information from inaccurate reporting and unwanted or harmful use. The law requires organizations and agencies that may create or access personal healthcare information to safeguard the details to protect the patient from harm. This includes limits and conditions on possible disclosure on the information and the potential use of the data without the patients' knowledge (HHS.gov, n.d.).

Security organizations and departments working within the healthcare arena must be continuously cognizant to protect this information. Any unauthorized or accidental release of medical information can be extremely detrimental to the security department, organization, or agency.

In the event a security organization or department has concerns about an applicant's or employee's medical condition, immediate notification with a qualified member of management or legal counsel is needed to review the laws and limitations set forth through HIPAA. Asking an applicant or employee for personal medical information may be a severe mistake and a violation of this act.

The **Family Educational Rights and Privacy Act of 1974** (FERPA) protects the academic records of students from unwanted or unnecessary disclosure. This law deters those performing a pre-employment investigation from viewing the actual course grades or other academic information when a child is in the K-12, publically funded educational system or an adult attending a publically funded college or university. The act deters the educational institution from giving the information out to an unauthorized or unapproved third party (U.S. Department of Education, n.d.). Because of the safeguards set forth by law, agencies performing pre-employment investigations will not be allowed to see grades while the applicant is an active student. Upon the student's graduation, the confirmation or verification of degrees and transcripts can be requested if deemed appropriate and necessary.

As part of the **National Labor Relations Act** (NLRA), the concept of **Unfair Labor Practices** (ULPs) is defined and explained. The focus of the legislation is to protect workers who wish to form or join a labor union or protect those belonging to a union from unfair and unethical treatment by the employer (Cornell Law, n.d.). For those conducting pre-employment investigations, any previous union involvement or membership by an applicant cannot be used to discriminate against hiring the individual. If the pre-employment investigation is being conducted for a company or organization that is currently unionized, all policies and practices within the union agreement pertaining to the hiring process must also be strictly followed.

The laws and legal processes given are just a small portion of the rules and regulations that are faced by those conducting investigations on potential or current employees. Additional laws and guidelines may also be present at the federal, state, and local levels. It is imperative that any plan for pre-employment or employee investigations be well thought out and properly vetted by both senior management and a qualified legal authority. Any violation of law or statute while conducting employee or potential employees investigations can be enforced by the governing body and potentially harm the company or organization. For this reason alone, only properly trained individuals should be authorized to conduct pre-employment investigations or follow-up investigatory checks on current employees.

Elements of a Pre-Employment Investigation

Taking the time and effort to investigate a job applicant's background can pay dividends to the organization in the future. As stated earlier, many applicants send outdated or fraudulent information to potential employers with the hope that the hiring agent will be impressed or not take the time to verify the information. In the event an employee is hired with unverified and false information, the organization could be held liable for any problems that the fraudulent employee causes. It should be noted that many applicants do offer accurate information on their resumes and applications. Even in cases where the applicant is honest, having a company or corporate policy in place to verify all applicants' information prior to offering employment is strongly recommended. The following are areas that may be checked by the hiring agent prior to offering formal employment. The specific areas to investigate and the depth of the investigation need to be researched, developed, and approved by senior management as well as a qualified legal professional.

Criminal and Civil Court Records

Many governmental agencies require that those working in a security capacity must have a criminal record investigation conducted. These checks can reveal criminal offenses, both felony and misdemeanor, within the United States. If offenses are discovered, the hiring agent must verify the law to see if that employee is eligible to work in a security capacity. The same laws and regulations may apply to those working in other non-security jobs. Depending on the practices for that particular position, checking the court records for all employees may be extremely beneficial to the organization.

Equally as important and often overlooked is conducting civil record checks on the applicant. The information discovered in this particular court search may reveal patterns of civil actions by the applicant. These civil actions could be against former employers, insurance companies, corporations, or personal acquaintances. Unlike criminal offenses that may automatically disqualify a person from employment, information found in a civil court search needs to be vetted and determined if the applicant is a risk for employment. Any decision of possible employment determined from the details discovered in a civil court search needs to be approved by senior management and the appropriate legal professional.

Residential History

A review of an applicant's residential history can reveal inaccurate records and create concerns of possible illegal or unethical activities in those emitted geographic areas. With the authorization of the applicant for the background check and supplying their Social Security number, a search can be performed showing the applicant's residential rental or home ownership history. If the information on the investigative report does not match the personal history offered by the applicant, then additional scrutiny must be afforded by the organization and verified by the potential employee.

Employment History

As previously stated, many employers today only give those conducting pre-employment investigations limited information on their past employee. Often the information offered is the employment start date, the end date, and the position they held. The investigator may not be able to determine what the rationale was for the person's departure but the simple confirmation of employment can be helpful. Investigators need to be concerned with long and unexplained gaps in the applicant's work history or working for numerous employers in a short period of time. When these situations are discovered, additional scrutiny on the applicant's information must take place, including asking the applicant to explain the employment gaps or numerous employers in a short period of time.

Educational Records

The level of education an applicant has could have a bearing on their possible employment with an organization. Either governmental agencies or the employers can set the standards for the appropriate level of education for the job position. The levels of education could vary from a high school diploma or a general education degree (GED) to completion of post-secondary education in the form of a degree from a community college, trade school, or university. Applicants may offer fraudulent information on their education with the hope that the hiring agency may not take the time to verify the data. In addition, hiring agencies must still verify educational degrees even if the applicant supplies copies of the actual degree or formal transcripts. The rationale for this is due to a number of "novelty degree" companies that print bogus educational degrees or transcripts from non-existent institutions or from legitimate schools that the applicant never attended. These novelty degrees and transcripts appear authentic but have no educational quality.

Military Records

Another area where an applicant could produce false information or a falsified document is with military discharge records. American military records offered upon discharge are referred to as a DD-214. This information provides a synopsis of the individual's military activities, promotions, commendations or awards, and discharge status. With the advancement of current computer technologies, fraudulent military documents can be produced and fraudulently provided as accurate. By contacting the appropriate branch of the military, the potential employer can verify items such as enlistment and discharge date, military duties (occupations) performed, and the discharge status (honorable, general, other than honorable, or dishonorable). The hiring organization must determine which types of military discharge are appropriate for their vacant position. For some agencies, only veterans with an honorable discharge will be granted employment, while other agencies may allow certain discharge statuses, depending on the reason for the separation and the type of employment they are seeking to fill.

Personal References

There is a procedural debate ongoing between those who conduct pre-employment searches on the validity of the information uncovered by checking an applicant's personal references. For some investigators, checking personal references can be a waste of time, money, and resources because most applicants offer individuals who give solid reports on the potential employee. Even with this as the case, situations may occur when the applicant is not careful with their references and negative information is uncovered by the investigator. Often, many hiring organizations may ask for references who are not personal friends or family members. In these cases, applicants may offer former supervisors or managers who do not abide by their organization's policy for releasing information. These personal references could give positive or negative insights of their former employee (or student), which can have a bearing on the pre-employment investigation. Verifying personal references does take time and patience but can offer important information about the applicant.

Professional Licenses or Certification

The importance of verifying professional licenses and certifications is equally as significant as the confirmation of educational degrees. False documents may be produced stating the applicant holds the distinction listed on the document. Professional licenses can include documents to legally practice medicine or law and to be qualified as a Certified Public Accountant (CPA). In addition, specific industries may have professional certifications showing expertise in a specific area of interest or discipline. All of these licenses and certifications must be verified to prevent a fraudulent claim by the applicant.

Financial History

Hiring agencies must take great care and effort to legally and ethically check the financial history of an applicant. As stated earlier in the chapter, the review and verification of an applicant's financial history is protected by law and must follow the specific process for checking a financial history. The hiring organization must pre-determine which employment positions would require a review of a financial history and obtaining the proper approval of the applicant to verify these records. These practices must also be scrutinized by senior management as well as a qualified legal authority.

The time, effort, and investment needed to conduct a proper pre-employment check must be formalized in policy and approved at the senior level within the organization. Proper applications must be used or developed to obtain the necessary information and approval of the applicant. The actual investigative process must be conducted by trained and qualified staff or outsourced to a reputable investigative agency. In the end, the time, effort, and investment will be rewarded through the hiring of quality employees who can become an asset to the organization.

Testing for Alcohol or Illegal Substances

Thousands of hours of productive work time are lost every year due to the abuse of alcohol and prescription drugs, and the use of illegal drugs. According to the U.S. Department of Labor, it is estimated that problems due to alcohol and drug abuse cost American economy 246 billion dollars in 1992, when the last data on the topic was available. Those employees who abuse alcohol and drugs are more likely to leave work early, call in sick, take extended periods of time off, be involved in a workplace accident, or file workmen's compensation claims for injuries sustained on the job (U.S. Department of Labor, n.d.). For these reasons many companies, organizations, and corporations will test for alcohol and drug abuse as part of the pre-employment background check. Prior to any practice of testing prospective employees for alcohol or drug abuse, research must be conducted on the legalities of substance testing and sound policies must be developed and approved by senior management, as well as reviewed by a qualified legal entity.

Testing methods have various results in regard to accuracy and the duration of time the specific substances can be detected in the body. The following are a sampling of the most common methods for detecting alcohol and drugs.

Breath analyzing is a common method to detect recent alcohol use and consequent abuse. This test, known as a breathalyzer test, can measure the current level of alcohol in the system as compared to the legal limit for alcohol consumption while driving a motor vehicle. Since alcohol purges from the body faster than drugs, testing for alcohol with by breath can only detect immediate or recent use.

Urine testing is a common method to detect the use of illegal drugs. These tests are designed to detect specific substances by placing a small sample of urine in a testing unit then and waiting for the result. This style of testing can give initial results in a matter of minutes. Many organizations will train specific employees to administer these tests at the work site and then send the sample to a formal laboratory if there are questions about the validity of the results. These tests come in different "panels" or groupings of substances detected. These tests can be in 5-panel, 8-panel, or 10-panel increments. The tests can detect substances such as amphetamines (meth, speed, crank, and ecstasy), THC (cannabinoids, marijuana, and hash), cocaine (coke and crack), opiates (heroin, opium, codeine, and morphine) and phencyclidines (PCP and angel dust). The larger panel test can also search for substances such as hallucinogens (LSD, mushrooms, mescaline, and peyote), inhalants (paint, glue, hairspray, and aerosol), hydrocodone (Lortab, Vicodin, and Oxycodone), and anabolic steroids (U.S. Department of Labor, n.d.).

Blood testing is another method to detect alcohol or drugs in the human body. Typically, the potential employee is sent to a lab to have blood drawn and analyzed. Unlike a urine test, which simply detects the substance in the body, blood tests can determine actually how much of a substance is in the body. This can be determined for recent drug and alcohol consumption.

Hair analysis provides a larger "window" for the detection of drugs in the system. For the test, the individual is sent to a lab for the removal of a small amount of hair somewhere on the body. The hair is then analyzed and can determine the specific drugs used for approximately 90 days prior to the test. This testing offers an excellent evaluation of drug use but is not effective in the detection of alcohol abuse (U.S. Department of Labor, n.d.).

With the increased use and abuse of prescription medicines, employers must also have a policy in place to determine if the prescription medicines found during drug testing are legal or illegal. In many cases, prior to the drug test, the potential employee must list all prescription medicines they are currently taking, the dosage, as well as the prescribing physician. In some cases, the potential employee may be asked to also list any over-the-counter medicines taken as well as vitamin supplements. When traces of prescription drugs are found, the potential employee may be asked for additional information for verification of legal use of the drug. The reality is that the abuse of prescription drugs is on the rise and must be addressed by employers. If the employer fails to create policy for the testing of abused prescription drugs, they may face the same dangers and liabilities as employees who use illegal drugs.

The proper policies and practices by the employer must be in place to detect and address the potential of drug and alcohol abuse. Employers must be proactive to test and deter the use of drugs and alcohol or being under the influence of the substance while in the work place. The investment into this testing may prove highly valuable in the future.

The Debate for Continued Verification of Employees

Many organizations grapple with the concept of continued testing of employees for drug or alcohol abuse and checking for legal changes in the employee's personal lives. This is a practice of employee verification that can be continued in all organizational settings, as long as proper policies and guidelines are written, vetted, and followed. For some organizations or companies, the continued efforts to test or check employees can be viewed as burdensome and a possible disruption to productivity or morale. In the case of continued drug testing, the employee must take time away from work to be tested either in the workplace or at a clinic. This causes a lack of production in the eyes of some employers. Another problem is when there is a lack of confidentiality during the testing process. Employees or their managers can inadvertently or intentionally say they are going for testing and make light of the procedure. This can result in inaccurate assumptions by co-workers or create unwanted attitudinal changes toward the employee being tested. In some cases, verbal outbursts and lack of professionalism can lead to civil suits filed by the employee for defamation of character. For these reasons, some employers will avoid ongoing drug testing. The continued verification of employees' records is also potentially viewed in a negative context because of cost and possible infringement on their personal lives.

In some cases, employers exercise testing and checking records on an as needed basis. Policies are composed and approved by management and acknowledged by the employee that in the event of a workplace accident or verified incident, the employer will require the employee to be tested for drug or alcohol in their system. For example, if a driver of a company vehicle gets into an accident, the company may require the person to immediately report to a nearby clinic for drug and alcohol testing. This policy of testing or checking employees on an as needed basis must be clearly defined and vetted as well as comply with all applicable labor laws and union contracts.

The final debate is centered on the continued testing and checking of certain legal aspects of an employee's personal life. With this scenario, the employer believes that they want to protect their investment in the employee and protect the company from unwanted risk or harm. In addition to continued testing for drug or alcohol use, some companies may want to ensure their employees are abiding by all relevant laws, see whether they are involved in a civil suit that may be harmful to the company, or know if employees continue to maintain the necessary professional licenses or credentials required for the job.

As with conducting continued employee checks on an as-needed basis, employers must ensure that these continuing verifications are required for the job, compose a detailed policy defining the checks and testing procedure, follow all applicable labor laws, and receive verification from senior management and a qualified legal representative.

Protecting the Employee

Working to protect employees is a continuous task that requires diligences and a keen sense of observation. Not only does security need to protect the employee but also vendors and visitors while they are on company property. The following is an overview of issues, situations, and challenges that face security personnel every day while attempting to protect those who work for or visit the company.

Violence in the Workplace

Violence in the workplace is not a new problem or phenomenon. These unwanted acts which harm employees or disrupt productivity include verbal harassment, bullying, inappropriate physical contact, or violent acts. During the 1980s a rash of violent acts and massacres took place within the job setting. Disgruntled or emotionally distraught employees or relatives of employees came into the workplace with firearms and began shooting and killing workers. These acts immediately forced the increased awareness of stressful workplace conditions, the recognition of stressed or potentially violent acting employees, the entry of current or former family members attempting to harm someone, or the return of terminated employees seeking revenge or harm. For the security departments and their personnel, the key objective is to be the "eyes and ears" for the organization to potentially deflect or deter a violent act and to notify management of threats. In addition, security personnel can be directly affected by these human threats as they maintain access into the facility, escort terminated employees from the property, or encounter these unwanted acts while patrolling the facility.

The protection against violent acts in the workplace can be a difficult task. Appropriate policies, procedures, and training must be developed to teach all employees what unwanted or inappropriate acts are, the recognition of potential problems or issues with employees, how to report concerns to the proper individual or department, and what procedures will take place upon the notification. Security must be aware of all these policies and procedures and remain vigilant in the attempt to address or avoid these acts. In the event of a violent act in the workplace, security may need to assist in the evacuation of the building, track and identify the offender, and be the liaison with local law enforcement.

Since human beings can be very unpredictable, security personnel can never assume that someone is not capable committing an unwanted or violent act in the workplace. Security must always keep a continuous and professional "watchful eye" on all employees, visitors, and patrons in the workplace. These unwanted acts can happen suddenly and without notice or indication of their occurring. In a matter of seconds lives can be lost, individuals can be injured, and productivity can be disrupted.

Kidnapping

With today's global business society, increased travel around the world for business purposes is a growing practice. With this travel as well as working at subsidiaries on foreign soil, the threat of kidnapping is real and ever-present. Foreign criminals and malcontents look upon outsiders as an opportunity to make some money, promote a specific cause or ideology, or to disrupt company operations and productivity. For some higher-ranking company officials, executive protection teams may also accompany the executive on the trip for continued protection. Unfortunately for the majority of foreign business travelers, they are not afforded the luxury of personal protection. These employees are at a greater risk of kidnapping. Kidnappers may be operating to secure a quick cash payout (also known as an express kidnapping), looking to hold onto their captive for a prolonged period of time to promote a social or political cause, or be part of an organized crime ring or rogue militia group. Whatever the case or cause, company employees or their family members traveling with them may become the targets of a kidnapping.

The responsibility to educate employees on the threat of kidnapping and what to do in the event of an abduction may fall upon the corporate security staff, risk managers, or the human resources department. Any of these entities should have the advance travel plans of the employee, monitor the activities in the geographic area for possible threats, and have a contingency plan in place if an abduction occurs.

To protect these travelers, organizations and corporations may use governmental websites to monitor global issues and travel warnings, establish liaisons and communications with embassy officials and local law enforcement agencies, and invest in insurance policies to possibly pay a ransom if a kidnapping occurs.

The security staff may be the first to receive a possible communication from a kidnapper or the organization perpetrating the abduction. Policies and practices must be written directing employees to gain as much information from the caller as possible, the proper notification process of company personnel about the event, and the possible contact of governmental law enforcement agencies. From that point, an emergency response team within the company may take charge of the incident and work to secure the safe release of the employee or their family member.

The Threat of Terrorism

Organizations and corporations must be continuously on guard against the threat of a terrorist act intended to harm employees or company assets. The threats or violent acts may come from either foreign or domestic sources intending to promote an ideology or cause at the expense of harming the lives of employees. It is vitally important for all companies, organizations, and corporations to develop safeguards and plans in the event of a terrorist act. No company, organization, or corporation is immune from a possible terrorist attack. A major problem in the protection against terrorism is simple complacency. Companies, organizations, and corporations need to avoid the mind-set that their company would never be the target of a terrorist attack because of the type of organization they are or their geographic location. For many, the threat of terrorism is one that occurs in large metropolitan areas or for larger corporations or governmental entities. This ill-advised mind-set needs to be avoided and replaced with a proactive plan to watch for potential harmful acts to lives and property as well as an appropriate response to a specific act.

For many security departments and organizations, the detailed policies and procedures for the everyday protection of lives and property will suffice to counteract a terrorist attack. Proper access control, the monitoring of the property, development of incident response protocols, and evacuation plans will assist in protection against a terrorist act. The plan to prevent or detect terrorism must also include policies and procedures to interact with and notify the appropriate law enforcement agency to share the information. As highlighted previously in this book, the 9/11 Commission Report emphasized the need for the private sector and law enforcement to interact and better communicate to avoid and deter acts of terrorism (National Committee, 2004). The former self-imposed boundaries and lack of trust between the public and private sectors need to be abolished and replaced with an attitude of trust and protecting the well-being of the public. Each side of this effort (public and private) has resources and knowledge that can help with the deterrence of terrorism and the apprehension of terrorists after the event. Private security personnel must understand that continued cooperation and professional interactions with law enforcement agencies is a "win/win" scenario. Through this cooperation and sharing of information and resources, the company's employees and assets will be better protected but so too will the general public. These acts of protective solidarity are promoted and encouraged for the protection of all.

Schools and Educational Institutions

Over the past decade, the protection of schools, colleges, and universities has become a very important topic. Even though chapter eleven of this text formally addresses the protection of the individuals within these buildings and institutions, it is worth noting here the growing concern about dangerous acts taking place within the educational system. In previous generations, K-12 schools and to an extent colleges and universities were viewed as safe havens from crime and violence. This concept of naivety regarding these academic buildings and institutions can no longer be accepted or tolerated. The unfortunate truth today is that any school or academic building can be victimized by a violent act. Much like the ill-advised mind-set held by some companies or organizations that "terrorist attacks would never happen here," schools, colleges, and universities everywhere must be on guard and observant of a possible violent act. These acts may occur from internal and external threats. Violent acts by students, and teachers, are a continuous threat, as is the possibility of violent acts from parents, volunteers, educational vendors or suppliers, and members of the general public. The days of schools, colleges, and universities being considered a safe haven have ended. Security personnel, campus police officers, faculty, teachers, staff, and administrators must accept that a potential violent act in their facility may be "right around the corner" all day and every day. Please see chapter eleven for additional information on this ever-growing threat to lives and property.

Conclusion

Protecting company personnel (and protecting the company from personnel) is a very fluid and never ending challenge. In this chapter there has been a common denominator: there is a continuous need for detailed and approved policies and procedures when dealing with the various aspects of personnel security. It is imperative for organizations to take the time to research and develop policies and procedures for the myriad of personnel security issues. Only with great thought, foresight, and planning will a security department have the necessary guidance and authorization to protect the employees, visitors, and vendors on the organization's property or while the staff is out on company business. In this world where people act "consistently inconsistent," the clearly defined roles and responsibilities of the security department when interacting with personnel are vital for the ultimate goal of protecting lives and property.

Case Study—Hostility in the Workforce

Recently, within a large metropolitan city's thriving and busy business and shopping district, a man shot his former supervisor. The assault occurred on the sidewalk outside an iconic landmark building where the company offices were located. The shooter was a disgruntled former employee who was upset about being fired. Instead of attempting to enter the building to seek out his former supervisor, he waited on the busy sidewalk outside to commit this shooting. After reading and contemplating this scenario, answer the following questions:

1. Why do you think the shooter waited for his former supervisor to come out of the building instead of going in and finding him?
2. Was the security staff responsible for protecting the supervisor outside the building?
3. How could the security staff have prevented this shooting?

Discussion Topic—Background Investigations

There is a fine line between investigating an applicant's background and violating their personal or legal rights to privacy. Contemplating the importance of "knowing who you are hiring," what kind of problems or events could a potential applicant try to hide on their application or resume and what could their motivation be for not being honest or forthright?

Research Topic—Violence in the Workplace

Take some time and go onto the Internet and search the topic "Violence in the Workplace." Look at three or four actual events that took place over the past few years on this topic and then answer the following questions:

1. In what type of workplace environment did these events take place?
2. How did the perpetrators carry out the violent acts?
3. What was the motive of the perpetrators for the violence?
4. What could the organization and/or the security department have done to prevent the violence from occurring?

Key Terms

Pre-employment checks	Civil Rights Act of 1964	Fair Credit Reporting Act
Health Insurance Portability and Accountability Act	Family Educational Rights and Privacy Act of 1974	National Labor Relations Act
Violence in the workplace	Kidnapping	Terrorism

Sources

National Commission on Terrorist Attacks upon the United States. (2004). *9/11 Commission report: Final report of the National Commission on Terror.* New York, NY: Barnes and Noble Publishing, Inc.

United States Department of Labor. (n.d.). *How does substance abuse impact the workplace?* Retrieved from http://www.dol.gov/elaws/asp/drugfree/benefits.htm

United States Department of Labor. (n.d.). *Workplace Drug Testing.* Retrieved from http://www.dol.gov/elaws/asp/drugfree/drugs/dt.asp#q2

Chapter Six

Protection in the Black Hole: Cybersecurity in Our Society

Introduction

Our modern society now continuously relies on the Internet and computer technology for all aspects of our lives. We use this technology for communication, entertainment, and business matters. The unfortunate reality is that the development of the Internet and computer technologies also spawned a new breeding ground for criminal activities and conspiracies. These deviant individuals take advantage of unsuspecting individuals, a lack of governmental oversight, and poor regulation to perpetrate both traditional and newly developed criminal acts. Every time a person accesses the Internet with their electronic device, they risk becoming exploited or ending up as a victim of an unwanted or illegal act. Because of this constant and very real threat of crime and exploitation, a war is under way to protect the innocent users of this electronic medium from the parasites trolling cyberspace in search of their next victim. The World Wide Web has now become "a black hole" of deceit, lies, and criminal maleficence.

Learning Objectives

In this chapter, the reader will be introduced to a general overview of what the Internet is, how it was developed, and common myths about the safety of cyberspace. In addition, common crimes and illegal activities involving electronic devices and the World Wide Web, as well as methods to protect and reduce the amount of incidents caused by criminals will be covered. Also, the reader will be introduced to the importance of policies and procedures for organizations to protect against and prevent cybercrimes, investigative efforts to assist with the fight against cyber perpetrators, the very real threat of a terrorist acts via the World Wide Web, and the private and public efforts to reduce the number of victims from these cyber criminal actions.

Network Operations Center © agnormark via fotolia.com

What Is the Internet and Where Did It Come From?

The concept of the Internet, computer communication technology, and the World Wide Web did not simply occur overnight. In fact, a series of engineering and scientific events which spanned the course of 50 years led to the system that society now relies on for so many tasks.

The rationale for the invention of what is now the Internet occurred during the Cold War era between the United States and the former Soviet Union. During the early years of the Cold War, a race for scientific achievement occurred between the two countries. This push for scientific achievement as well as developing a method to securely communicate led scientists and engineers to develop the infrastructure and methodology that became today's Internet.

During the Cold War, continuous efforts took place to intercept and spy on the activities within both the United States and the former Soviet Union. The original intent of this secure information network, developed by the Americans, was to allow for communications that could not be intercepted and decoded by the Soviet Union. This motivation for secure communications developed what was first called "The Arpanet." This system allowed American military and governmental personnel the opportunity to communicate without using the telephone systems or antiquated methods such as Morse code (History, n.d.). The Arpanet allowed the computers used by governmental, military, and university entities the ability to transmit messages within a secure infrastructure (ciec.org, n.d.).

This initial platform for secure communication was far from being complete or finalized. During the 1970s, scientists developed the method of information disbursement and transmission of data. Through the use of what is commonly called "**packets**" or "packet switching," data leaves the originating source, breaks into predetermined "packets" and then reconfigures at its final destination (History, n.d.). The information within each packet contains a **binary code** which allows numbers to represent letters and characters then be reconstructed and interpreted by the end user. These systems were very localized and limited access to the few individuals on each network.

As time progressed and the need arose to have multiple individuals, computers, and networks able to send, receive, and interpret data, a formal program for encrypting and interpreting the information was created. This program, known as **Transcription Control Protocol** (TCP) allowed global computer networks the opportunity to send, receive, and read data. In addition, with the continued development of a global Internet system, an additional protocol, known as **Internet Protocol** (IP) afforded the transmission of information and data onto the developing system called the World Wide Web (History, n.d.). This TCP/IP technology is the common protocol used today to transmit information on the World Wide Web and will be covered in greater detail later in the chapter.

In the early 1990s, the United States Congress authorized public and commercial access to a portion of the Internet system. Originally, the concept of the public and commercial Internet was to provide a communal avenue to share information, ideas, and data. As we now know, this public and commercial system was transformed into a commonly used medium for data, information, and commerce. The initial concept of the Internet and the use of electronic devices to access the World Wide Web is now an ever-evolving system which is used for both positive and negative reasons. According to the Global Internet Report published in 2014, the number of users on the public and global Internet will triple from 1 billion in 2014 to approximately 3 billion users (Internet Society, n.d.). As our global society gains access to computers, phones, and other electronic devices that allow access onto the World Wide Web, the continued growth of threats, deviance, and criminal acts will also increase exponentially.

Internet Myths

The unfortunate reality is that the Internet is not a safe place. Users of this technology blindly and haphazardly enter into the World Wide Web oblivious to the risks and perils that lie one click away. The following is an abbreviated but common list of Internet myths facing all those using this technology.

The first myth relates to the total lack of anonymity users have while being logged into the Internet. Many Internet users fall into a false sense of security when logged in because they may be safely in the confines of their homes or using their personal electronic devices to gain access to the World Wide Web. The reality is that all Internet activities are being recorded, monitored, and stored. All actions on the Internet can be traced and recorded through the use of TCP/IP technology. A digital trail (or digital fingerprint) is generated every time someone goes onto the Internet and can be literally monitored from the originating website to the end user by design. One must remember that the systems developed by scientists and engineers for the military are equipped to store and track information from the source to the end user. The belief that a person is anonymous while on the Internet is a total misconception. This does work as an advantage for security or law enforcement in the investigations of crimes or deviant acts. This will be explained in greater detail later in the chapter.

The second common Internet myth relates to the storage and tracking of information.

Simply stated: images, files, and downloads imported onto personal computing devices can still be stored on the hard drive and exist long after the user attempts to delete the information. The image, file, or download can be imbedded into the hard drive of a computer and potentially remain for the life of the device. Also, file sharing and storage programs and sites will record and maintain all information as long as the system's management deems it necessary. This data storage can be of great assistance to security and law enforcement organizations. The information can be extracted from the device even if the user thought the data was permanently deleted. It can also be of great assistance to those who access personal data illegally.

To complicate matters, web organizations may install tracking devices onto electronic devices to monitor user activity for both positive and negative reasons. Retail outlets and advertising organizations may install these tracking devices (commonly referred to as "cookies") to monitor the sites the user visits and make recommendations to visit other websites based on previous activity. Conversely, these programs can be unknowingly installed to access data for illegal or unauthorized use. Users of the Internet must understand that any and all information can be tracked down to the end user and then, in most cases, extracted from the user's device.

Another common myth is that the World Wide Web is a safe place. Internet users can develop a false sense of security based in part on where they are accessing the system, the sites visited, or the activities they partake in. The reality is that crime runs rampant on the Internet. It has no boundaries and does not discriminate between users. When public access was granted to the Internet and with its continual global expansion, additional deviants and criminals have entered into the electronic realm in search of their next victim. Many of these deviants and criminals are perpetrating common criminal acts, only using the new medium as a platform for their crimes. As previously stated, even though the initial intent for the public Internet was based on a positive and communal rationale, the truth is that anyone in the World Wide Web can commit a criminal or deviant act against an unsuspecting or unprotected user. For many of us, we try to avoid situations on the street where we can come into harm. We take time to physically protect ourselves or become attuned to observe potentially harmful situations. Internet users must adopt the same mentality online as they do to avoid altercations on the street. This false sense of security when logging onto the World Wide Web, combined with the criminals and deviants trolling in search of their next victim, combine for a criminal or deviant act just waiting to happen. Today's Internet can be compared to the American Wild West, where crime was rampant and protection or enforcement could not keep up with the unwanted acts.

The final myth to be presented is that proactive security methods will stop crimes or unwanted acts from occurring on the Internet. Again, this is not the case. Even with the best attempts by reputable organizations that work to secure the Internet, crime and unwanted acts continue to evolve. When new programs to commit criminal or deviant acts are created, web security experts must react to the situation. This is in direct contradiction to the proactive mentality of the security industry. Unfortunately, when new digital programs are developed for illegal or unwanted use, the cybersecurity experts must find the program, dissect and analyze it, and then create a solution to the problem. This leaves a period of time when the new program or act is running rampant and gaining victims while the security experts work to stop it. This reactive style to addressing Internet crimes and unwanted programs will continue to plague the system. When an illegal or unwanted computer program is stopped, then another can and will be produced. When one individual is stopped from committing unwanted acts on the Internet, another individual arises and takes his or her place. When it comes to crimes on the World Wide Web, the concept of being proactive to stop attacks or unwanted acts may never be enough, placing additional emphasis on the user to be as smart as possible to avoid victimization.

Every time a person enters into the World Wide Web, they open a portal that allows information both in and out. This information can be of great benefit or it can produce horrific consequences. The digital realm is ripe with criminal activity where everyone and everything can be traced. Proceeding with caution every time someone logs onto the Internet needs to be the primary mind-set to avoid becoming the next victim.

Basic Components

Often ignored or taken for granted, the basic components of a computer system, what binary code and TCP/IP technologies are, and how servers and firewalls work are essential areas of knowledge when attempting to protect against crimes and unwanted acts on the Internet. Every crime or unwanted act uses or transmits through these devices or systems. The following are "the basic building blocks" for cybersecurity.

The first area of computer technology is the basic components of a computer system. Each computer system is comprised of some form of a **central processing unit** (CPU) that stores the main processor, the system's memory, and if applicable, the secondary memory. The CPU is the brains of the system that works to bring in data, store the data, and send out the information. Next are the **input devices** that include items such as keyboards, scanners, or recording devices. The sole intent of these devices is to enter the information into the CPU. The final component is the **monitoring unit** or output devices. These are used to view or listen to the data that is in the CPU or passing through the CPU (ccsu.edu, n.d.).

Computer systems run off of hardware and software. The computer hardware is the various components inside the central processing unit (CPU). The software is comprised of the computer programs and data downloaded onto the hardware (ccsu.edu, n.d.). These specific components allow the computer system to function and run the specific programs downloaded into it.

Binary Code and TCP/IP Technology

Binary code and TCP/IP technology are two of the basic elements that power the Internet. From the creation of this communication medium after the Second World War, scientists and engineers devised these systems, components, and methodologies to ensure a safe way to communicate without interception by adversarial countries. Binary code uses a series of numeric algorithms to create encrypted messages and have the ability to cipher (decrypt) the message at its destination. By creating a mathematical and algebraic system in which to communicate, in addition to the technology used for encryption, this computational platform takes the basic elements of encoding information into an electronic state (Encyclopedia Britannica, N.D).

Transmission control protocol (TCP) and Internet protocol (IP) are the electronic foundations developed to create the delivery system of the messages written in binary code. TCP/IP technology uses a packet address system to deliver the electronic messages from the sender to the user. When a message is created using the binary code system, it is addressed from the sender to the end recipient. The message then breaks up into multiple subsets (or packets) to allow for an uninterrupted and secure delivery. Each packet has a numerical code assigned to it that allows the transmission to the final destination and then reassembles in its original form. Every time information is sent via the Internet, the message breaks into the numerically identifiable packets of information to allow for possible tracking as well as sending and receiving. These same platforms and protocols developed by scientists and computer engineers for military use are still used today for the public Internet.

Servers and Firewalls

In chapter four, the reader was introduced to the concept of protection through physical barriers that includes walls for protection against outside intrusion or attack. This basic concept of using a wall to protect the inside from threats outside expresses the same primary function of servers and firewalls.

A **server** is a computer that distributes connectivity and data to a network. The server connects individual computers via hardwire, creating either a **local area network** (LAN) or through a wireless connection, creating a **wide area network** (WAN). The server (or servers) allows the networks to intercommunicate and provides an external Internet connection. It is extremely important to ensure that servers are afforded with all the necessary computer software to protect against unwanted intrusion or programs that could be detrimental to the computers connected to the network (Techterms.com, n.d.).

The **firewall** is a computer network device that has been devised on the concept of a wall within a building that is intended to withstand an actual fire from spreading. The traditional firewall constructed in a building is composed of material that will not allow a fire to spread. Unlike an actual firewall, the computer firewall is an additional device (normally the size of a server or a modem) that filters unwanted Internet content or programs from entering into the LAN or WAN. Firewalls can be programmed to block certain types of content deemed inappropriate for the network users and act as protection against potential cyber criminals (Techterms.com, n.d.). With the constant evolution of harmful web content as well as the threat of cyberattacks, the hardware and/or software within the firewall must be continuously monitored and updated to ensure the best protection possible. These additional devices that can create and protect computer networks are now essential in the continuous fight against cybercrime.

Crimes on the Internet

Whether an individual calls the Internet "the black hole" or the "electronic Wild West," it is clear that the World Wide Web runs rampant with crime, deviance, and corruption. These illegal and illicit activities take place in many forms and activities. For some of these offenses, they are old crimes in a new venue, while others are new to the field of criminal justice. The following is a short list of common crimes, acts of deviance, and corruption that can be found just one click away on the World Wide Web.

Spam is a common and everyday occurrence on the Internet. Spam is defined as unwanted and unsolicited emails and correspondences sent to Internet mail (email) users. Spam can be sent to advertise legitimate products, illegal or unethical services, or contain viruses or programs to infect computers or computer networks. The act of "spamming" unwanted or unsolicited email messages is a crime but the Internet is plagued with millions of these messages on a regular basis. Spam messages are difficult to stop and the senders may face only minor penalties if they are convicted at all. Efforts in the United States and allied countries have assisted to reduce the amount of spam on the Internet but the practice of sending unwanted or unsolicited messages remains a problem for those connected to the World Wide Web.

Hacking and **cracking** are terms connected with unauthorized or illegal intrusion into websites, computer networks, or individual computing or communication devices. Both terms share a common practice of illegal intrusion but they have distinctly different motivations. Technically, a person who "hacks" into a computer system illegally enters but only ventures to look into the network. With hacking, there is no damage to the hacked system nor is anything taken or compromised. Cracking is also an illegal entry into a computer system but the person who "cracks" into the site commits the offense to steal information, damage the site or system, or deface the content of the organization. Today's news media calls both offenses by the same name—hacking. This has created an inaccurate description of these two different actions by Internet perpetrators.

A **denial of service attack** (DoS) is a program intended to slow or stop content from traveling on the Internet. Contrary to popular belief, the Internet is not infinite or limitless in the amount of data and information it can hold. The denial of service attack works on this premise to slow or stop the data traveling to a specific end point. The DoS is a program that, in common terms, clogs the Internet portal with useless data to the point that information is either slowed or unable to travel to or from a network or user. This data and information stoppage can be highly detrimental or costly to the victim until the program is discovered, identified, and removed from the network.

Worms are malicious programs created to corrupt a computer and deter partial operations from taking place. Worms can infiltrate a computer through email or message. They then enter into the computer and traditionally slow or stop one or more computer activities from taking place. Known primarily as a nuisance program, they can attack specific computer functions such as turning on or off the system, corrupt a monitor from working, create unwanted messages viewed by the user, or direct all Internet connections to a specific (and often illegal or illicit) website. Traditionally, worms do not physically damage the computer hardware, instead they focus on disrupting the software or the functions of the actual computer.

A **Trojan horse** is a malicious computer program (also known as malware) intended to steal information or damage a computer network. The operation of this attack is based on the story of the invasion of the ancient city of Troy. In this historical invasion, the Greeks built a large wooden horse and hid soldiers inside. The rulers of Troy were informed that the giant horse was a symbolic and respectful offering to their people. The Trojans accepted the offer and rolled the giant horse into their fortified city. At night, the Greek soldiers emerged from the horse and invaded the city of Troy. This is conceptually the same premise for this computer attack. A malicious program is unknowingly sent to a computer network or system. The program is undetected and remains dormant in the system until the pre-programmed launch date. On the programed date of attack, the malicious program activates and releases the destruction intended for the system. If the program is not detected, severe damage can take place.

Spyware is another form of malicious software intended to record information from computer networks without their owners knowing. This recording program is sent to the user via an attachment or message. The program activates and begins to send the sought-after information back to the originating source. Spyware can be programed to record specific activities such as websites visited or to steal the documents and information on the computer or the system's files. The originating source can then record and sell the data obtained or use it to harm the end user.

The crime of **identity theft** is not a new act of deviance. For decades, criminals have worked to obtain the personal or financial information of unsuspecting victims and then exploit the findings for illegal monetary gain. The virtual crime of identity theft follows the same ideological format. The traditional method of identity theft involves gaining physical documents belonging to the potential victim that may include bank account information, credit card numbers, driver's license numbers, or Social Security numbers. The perpetrator then takes the information and fraudulently assumes the victim's identity, opening false or bogus accounts, buying items, or withdrawing the money out of the victim's financial accounts. Identity theft scams run rampant on the World Wide Web. Fraudulent emails, messages, and websites attempt to draw the victim in by false means. The perpetrator may pose as a government agency, bank, retailer, religious organization, or a family member. When the unsuspecting reader views the information, they believe the source to be legitimate and the false claim as true. The recipient then gives their personal information and the criminal has the data needed to assume the person's identity. A concern with this process is that the criminal may not use the absconded data immediately. They may sell the information to a person or criminal organization that may use the stolen data at a later date. In this case, not only is the victim unaware him or her information has been compromised, the victim may not be affected by the theft for weeks, months, or years. Conversely, the criminal could use the data right away before the victim realizes he or she has been compromised and violated. With either the short-term or long-term use of the stolen data, it is vital for all those giving out personal information on the World Wide Web to review bills and bank accounts for any unauthorized activities. When these activities are discovered, they need to contact the lending company, bank, or credit bureau immediately.

Cyberstalking is an electronic crime that began as a person-to-person offense. Cyberstalking is formally defined as: "The use of the Internet, email, or other electronic communications to stalk, and generally refers to a pattern of threatening or malicious behaviors," (National Conference of State Legislators, n.d.). Through the use of electronic mediums, the victim is harassed, bullied, and threatened by the perpetrator. With the popularity of social media websites, electronic mail, message texting, video communication, and other message portals such as blogs or community information boards, the victim is continuously followed and harassed. The unfortunate reality is that the person can be victimized without knowledge of the cyber stalker. This is a serious criminal offense that can lead into unwanted or harmful personal interaction or violent acts by the perpetrator or others participating in the various social mediums.

With the introduction of the public Internet, the crime of **pedophilia** found a new venue to reemerge and flourish. The crime of pedophilia entails the gathering, harboring, and distribution of sexual images of children. These images can come in the form of photos, audio recordings, or video recordings. Pedophiles that participate in this heinous offense use the World Wide Web to distribute or gather these images. They can use means such as electronic mail, private chat rooms, or clandestine media sites for their illicit means. Unlike some Internet and electronic crimes that are hard to prosecute due to a lack of enforcement cooperation, many countries will work to apprehend and prosecute these sexual deviants. Through the leadership and guidance internationally of the United Nations and the International Criminal Police Organization (INTERPOL), as well as domestic efforts through the Federal Bureau of Investigation (FBI), unified efforts can be rapidly coordinated to find, identify, and punish these offenders.

The theft or illegal distribution of **intellectual property** is also a continuous battle that has been greatly amplified through the use of electronic devices and the Internet to gather, store, and illegally distribute information. Formally defined as "Any product of the human intellect that the law protects from unauthorized use by others," intellectual property can be in the form of electronic music, movies, books, and documents as well as corporate or governmental information (Cornell University Law School, n.d.). The public access of the Internet has driven companies, organizations, and governmental entities to use this communication medium for their business practices. It also allows deviant individuals the opportunity to exploit or attempt to steal this information. The fight against intellectual property losses is a continuous effort that can be confronted by a corporation, governmental agency, or a unified effort within a specific communication industry. Without the enforcement of intellectual property laws, the global economy could be in danger of huge financial losses and governmental agencies could become compromised and rendered ineffective or useless.

The World Wide Web is inundated with crimes, predators, and malcontents. The threats to users is very real and ever changing, or it can be described as "consistently inconsistent." Even though a small portion of the potential crimes and perils found on the Internet were listed above, it is important to know that self-protection and awareness is vital to avoid being a victim of a cybercrime or cyber threat. The remainder of the chapter will offer concepts and methods for Internet protection, the importance of agencies and organizations implementing strong employee policies and guidelines for electronic use while at work, terrorism on the World Wide Web, and agencies that work to combat the criminal elements that prey on the innocent or unsuspecting user.

Protecting the System

Ultimately, the individual Internet user is responsible for protection against the predators lurking online. For some, the concept of accepting personal responsibility for their own actions can be a difficult task. In a world filled with lawsuits and litigation, our society tends to blame others instead of accepting fault. This is an important factor for Internet use because if those online do not understand that threats are one click away or that they can personally work to prevent being victimized, then the amount of unfortunate and avoidable crimes will continue to rise.

Users should accept a mentality of a "healthy paranoia" pertaining to Internet use. The term "healthy paranoia" simply means that individuals need to be cautious and protective of their best interests. What does not mean is to be scared or avoid the situation, rather to keep their eyes and mind open and adopting a protective mentality. This mind-set of being cautious and never assuming that whomever or whatever you are interacting with has your best interest in mind needs to be continuously maintained by the user. If individuals "let his or her guard down," while online, they can open themselves up to the crime and corruption that plagues the Internet.

The practice of consciously checking the validity of your Internet sources can also prove beneficial to avoid becoming a victim. The Internet user needs to keep in mind that criminals and deviants will adapt to their environment to lure in an unsuspecting victim. Giving false information or attempting to portray an honest person or business, as well as not providing the information a legitimate organization would offer are areas of concern for Internet users. Users must always "check their source" for legitimacy. This may be verifying where the person or company is located (especially for independent businesses), if there are any comments about the services, and how long they have been in business. Many formal and well-established Internet sites and services are safe and legitimate but when people start to search out other options and not verify their legitimacy this could lead to avoidable and unneeded loss and peril.

A good rule to follow when interacting online is the axiom that "if it is too good to be true, then it probably is." Applying this axiom to Internet activity and self-protection means that too many semi-anonymous predators hope that the user will fall for their false information, offers, and promises without giving a second thought to their trustworthiness. The Internet user needs to accept some responsibility to question the source and verify claims or promises. This "healthy paranoia" will be helpful to protect against becoming the next victim on the World Wide Web.

Policies and Procedures

With the tremendous amount of business conducted with electronic devices and on the World Wide Web, it is vital for companies, organizations, and corporations to develop policies and procedures for employees' use of these company provided devices and Internet access. The rationale for the development of policies and procedures is rather straightforward. These rules and regulations can help improve employee productivity, protect company equipment, avoid unwanted loss of information to competitors, and attempt to limit computer system data breaches. Depending on the type of business conducted by the organization and the concern for loss or damage through their equipment, time and attention must be taken to develop viable policies for usage that address the importance of these actions, as well as define consequences for misuse.

Some organizations or employees have a difficult time accepting the development of or adherence to these guidelines. For some, since the Internet is a public medium, it is difficult to understand how or why companies should regulate employee usage or access. It is imperative for the organization to clearly define that Internet use should be for company use only, what appropriate activity for the company is while online, and why the oversight is necessary. Thought must also be given to incorporate language for the use of company electronic equipment following the same ideology as online access. Also, organizations must consider procedures for tracking employee use of electronic equipment as well as what Internet content they are accessing while working. Although this may not be popular with the "rank and file" employees, the policy makers must keep the best interests of the company in mind while developing a productive work environment. The unfortunate reality is that without policies and procedures in place, productivity may decline, the electronics and computer infrastructure could be compromised, and the company could sustain losses of important information and finances. Electronics and the Internet have redefined how business is conducted in today's global market. Without policies and procedures guiding the employee as to what are appropriate and necessary uses of this technology, the company, organization, or corporation can become less productive and open to huge losses of information and financial capital.

Investigating Cyber Crimes

The investigation and subsequent prosecution of cyber criminals is a very difficult process. Great detail and care must be taken to determine the location of the evidence, gain approval to gather the appropriate evidence (through governmental search warrants), maintain a proper "chain of custody" to preserve the data or information, and determine how to present the details for prosecution. Public law enforcement agencies continue to improve methodologies to investigate, apprehend, and prosecute cyber criminals. Through the use of court orders requesting electronic records from Internet service providers (ISPs) and the development and use of data extraction devices to extract files, documents, and pictures off hard drives, law enforcement continues to improve the efficiency of the process.

For the positive attributes and improvements of fighting cybercrimes, some glaring deficiencies still remain. The first is a lack of law enforcement personnel to handle the huge number of reported cybercrimes. Many law enforcement agencies have limited resources or allotted time to fight cybercrimes. These agencies must still work to combat street crimes and simply do not always have the necessary personnel, time, or resources for cybercrimes. A police department may be able to take a report to track cybercrime patterns or in the case of large departments, have a cyber division or task force dedicated to combating these crimes. Even with these positive examples, there are simply not enough personnel dedicated to help investigate all the cybercrimes occurring. Law enforcement agencies are also unable to recruit and pay the top cybersecurity specialists to work for their departments. These talented individuals can command large salaries and benefit packages offered and afforded through private sector businesses. This lack of financial resources greatly hampers the ability of governmental agencies to recruit the top cyber experts to work in the public sector.

Second are issues with jurisdictional support for the investigation and prosecution of cybercrimes. For major cybercrimes committed on American soil, there is a positive sense of cooperation between law enforcement agencies, prosecutors, and the court systems. The same cooperation can hold true between the United States and their allies around the world. Countries that have solid relations tend to work together and assist each other when trying to investigate and prosecute cybercrimes. An excellent example is the efforts of Interpol, an international policing organization with approximately 190 member countries. These member countries share law enforcement information through this agency, allowing the member countries access to vast databases on crimes and criminals. Interpol may work to coordinate or assist in the investigation of cybercrimes and provide data necessary for the apprehension and prosecution of global cyber criminals (Interpol, n.d.). Conversely, if professional or friendly relationships do not exist between countries, little can be done to investigate cybercrimes or extradite the accused individuals for prosecution. This creates a major problem when countries ignore criminal activities or more horrifically, support the criminals and their actions. Because many of these cybercrimes may originate on unfriendly foreign soil, without cooperation between the governmental leaders the crimes go unpunished.

The third example is the general mind-set by the public that nothing can be done if they are victimized by cybercrimes. This is an understandable emotion but one that could be unnecessary. It is true that the fight against cybercrime can be a confusing and frustrating series of events, but without public reporting of these incidents, no investigation or prosecution can happen. Minor cyber offenses such as spam or viruses may be best prevented or eliminated by a qualified cyber technician, but major crimes such as identity theft, cyber bullying, or stalking, or being the victim of a financial crime needs to be reported to the proper authority for recording, investigating, and prosecution. Without the knowledge and information of what crimes are taking place and how people are being victimized, then positive steps cannot be taken to punish the offenders and deter future unwanted and illegal acts.

The Threat of Terrorism

The threat and concern of a terrorist act taking place via the World Wide Web is a legitimate concern for governments and their protective agencies. Grave concerns exist among governmental leaders (both foreign and domestic) that a terrorist act perpetrated though the Internet could happen at any moment. These potential crimes and acts could include penetrating and compromising governmental computer networks and accessing classified information, infiltration of the computer systems of the financial markets or banking corporations and sending the monetary markets into chaos, or illegally accessing the computer systems of critical infrastructures (such as the power grid, water systems, or nuclear reactors) and rendering them inoperable. It is a well-known fact that many of our governmental organizations are continuously under attack by would-be cyber criminals. These attacks must be met with a proactive mind-set of deterrence. In the event the cybercrime is able to compromise one of these computer networks, catastrophic results could occur. The identification of would-be cyber terrorist attacks and the perpetrators developing these threats is a top priority of governments worldwide. In an instant, unfathomable devastation could occur, ending lives and creating upheaval in our global community—all created by a terrorist attack on the World Wide Web.

Law Enforcement and Private Sector Partnership

When it comes to the protection of individuals, businesses, and organizations from cybercrime, one word can properly describe a solution. The word is collaboration. In order to truly reduce or eliminate the threat of cybercrime, the private and public sectors must continue to combine resources to fight this global threat. The private sector has the talent and personnel needed to create programs and infrastructures to dissect, deter, and detect cybercrimes. The public sector has the resources to prosecute and convict cyber criminals and terrorists. Through the collaboration of the private and public sector sharing information, data, and methodologies, cybercrimes can be reduced and greatly improve the safety of those who utilize the World Wide Web. Examples of these efforts include The Internet Crime Control Center (**IC3**), a public/private initiative though the United States Federal Bureau of Investigation (FBI, n.d.), the Critical Infrastructure Cyber Community (**C3**) through the Department of Homeland Security (DHS, n.d.), as well as international efforts such as the European Public Private Partnership for Resilience (**EP3R**) (ENISA, n.d.). These examples can be replicated at the state and local levels to fight the threat of cybercrime in all jurisdictions. These focused and consolidated efforts are becoming the new standard for combating the global plague of cybercrime.

Conclusion

The public access to the Internet has exceeded all thoughts and expectations pertaining to personal, business, and governmental usage. Our new reliance on this communication infrastructure has opened a "Pandora's Box" of criminal activities. This continuously evolving and loosely regulated threat of cybercrime will continue to plague all those who enter the World Wide Web. Only through communal responsibility and efforts to eradicate these criminal entities will the Internet become a safe place to enter. Without an all-inclusive commitment to police this medium, the reality of becoming a victim of a cybercrime or attack will continue to be only one click away.

Case Study—Former Detroit Mayor Kwame Kilpatrick

In 2008, the former and embattled mayor of Detroit was on trial facing charges in a whistle-blower suit. During the testimony, it was alleged that Kwame Kilpatrick was having a romantic affair with his former chief of staff, Christine Beatty. While under oath, Kilpatrick denied the allegations of the romantic affair. It was later uncovered through the search of the phone and text message records that evidence did exist proving the sexual affair between Kilpatrick and Beatty. Because of the discovery, Kilpatrick was also charged with perjury, the crime of lying while under oath in court (Detroit Free Press, 2008).

This case of a high-powered public official and his employee showed the general public that records of text messages can be uncovered even if the user deletes the information from his or her phone or mobile device. With each passing year, more civil and criminal cases have incorporated information from mobile phones or devices that were sent from one party to another. With this concept in mind, answer the following questions:

1. Why do you believe people think that if they delete information off their phone, mobile device, or computer that the information is no longer available for viewing?
2. Do you believe it is appropriate and ethical for Internet service providers (ISPs) to supply this information when properly subpoenaed by a court?
3. What are the positive and negative attributes of all former communications being recorded and saved by the Internet service providers?

Discussion Topic—"Putting All Your Eggs in One Basket!"

As discussed in this chapter, the public access to the Internet created a phenomenon and a new medium to communicate and conduct business. Combined with computer networks and mobile devices, many individuals now rely on the World Wide Web for communication, entertainment, shopping, banking, and business and work transactions. Our society is becoming totally immersed in the Internet for personal and professional activities. With this in mind, contemplate and answer the following questions:

1. Because of our new reliance on the Internet, has this medium created too many unnecessary opportunities for cyber criminals?
2. What do you think would happen to our business and global economies if all or part of the Internet were shut down due to a cyberattack?
3. If a paralyzing cyberattack did occur, how would you personally attempt to communicate, shop, work, and participate in school activities without access to the World Wide Web?

Research Focus—DEF CON

Since 1993, a gathering takes place every year, known as DEF CON. This event is intended for cyber hackers and for discussion about the practice of cyber hacking (DEFCON, n.d.). Search the name "DEF CON" on the Internet, read about the event, and answer the following questions:

1. Why does an event like this take place?
2. Are there any positive elements, attributes, or results that could come from the event?
3. How could the cybersecurity and law enforcement communities benefit from attending this event annually?

Key Terms

Packets	Transcription control protocol (TCP)	Internet protocol (IP)
Central Processing Unit (CPU)	Input devices	Monitoring unit
Binary Code	Server	Firewall
Local area network (LAN)	Wide area network (WAN)	Spam
Hacking	Cracking	Denial of service attack
Worms	Trojan horse	Spyware
Identity theft	Cyber stalking	Pedophilia
Intellectual property	IC3	C3
EP3R		

Sources

Central Connecticut State University. (n.d.). *Components of a computer system.* Retrieved from http://chortle.ccsu.edu/java5/Notes/chap01/ch01_3.html

Ciec.org. (n.d). *Creation of the Internet and the development of cyberspace.* Retrieved from http://www.ciec.org/trial/complaint/facts1.html

Cornell University Law School: Legal Information Institute. (n.d.). *Intellectual property.* Retrieved from http://www.law.cornell.edu/wex/intellectual_property

DEF CON. (n.d.). *About.* Retrieved from https://www.defcon.org/html/links/dc-about.html

Detroit Free Press. (2008, January 24). "Kilpatrick, chief of staff lied under oath, text messages show." Retrieved from http://archive.freep.com/article/20080124/NEWS05/801240414/Kilpatrick-chief-staff-lied-under-oath-text-messages-show

Encyclopedia Britannica. (n.d.). *Binary code.* Retrieved from http://www.britannica.com/EBchecked/topic/681536/binary-code

European Union Agency for Network and Information Security. (n.d.). *Public private partnerships (PPPs).* Retrieved from https://www.enisa.europa.eu/activities/Resilience-and-CIIP/public-private-partnership

History Channel. (n.d.). *The invention of the Internet.* Retrieved from http://www.history.com/topics/inventions/invention-of-the-internet

Internet Crime Complaint Center. (n.d.). *About us.* Retrieved from http://www.ic3.gov/about/default.aspx

Interpol. (n.d.). *Overview.* Retrieved from http://www.interpol.int/About-INTERPOL/Overview

National Conference of State Legislators. (n.d.). *State cyberstalking and cyberharassment laws.* Retrieved from http://www.ncsl.org/research/telecommunications-and-information-technology/cyberstalking-and-cyberharassment-laws.aspx

Techterms.com. (n.d.). *Firewall.* Retrieved from http://www.techterms.com/definition/firewall

Techterms.com. (n.d.). *Server.* Retrieved from http://www.techterms.com/definition/server

The Internet Society. (n.d.). *Global internet report, 2014.* Retrieved from http://www.internetsociety.org/sites/default/files/IS_ExSummary_30may.pdf

United States Department of Homeland Security. (n.d.). *About the critical infrastructure cyber community C3 voluntary program.* Retrieved from http://www.dhs.gov/about-critical-infrastructure-cyber-community-c%C2%B3-voluntary-program

Chapter Seven

Nobody Sees, Nobody Knows: The Field of Private Investigations

Introduction

In the United States, the business of private investigations formally began with William Burns during the 1860s (Jones, 2005). Bureaucratic or governmental investigations can be traced back to the 1700s, when Benjamin Franklin created formal investigative positions for the United States Postal Service (U.S. Postal Inspection Service, n.d.). Today, popular media portrayals of private investigators leave a lot to be desired. The fictional characters have state-of-the-art equipment, work in primarily safe conditions, drive expensive cars, wear stylish clothing, and solve cases by the end of the program. In real life, this fictional portrayal could not be further from the truth. The field of private investigations can be dangerous, tedious, and totally unglamorous. Private investigators need comprehensive training and education, outstanding concentration skills, the ability to blend into an area without detection, and patience. Without these attributes, the investigator can be ineffective, and most importantly, sustain unwanted injury. The private investigator takes on many different roles in our society to gather information for their employer or client.

Learning Objectives

In this chapter the reader will be presented with a broad overview of the different facets of private investigations, skills needed to conduct a successful assignment, the different styles of investigation techniques, the importance of documentation, and legal considerations that need to be considered for this career. By the end of the chapter, the reader should have an accurate and broad

Person in Car Taking a Picture © mokee81 via fotolia.com

overview of the importance of investigators, the challenges they regularly face, and the positive and negative attributes of the job.

What Is an Investigator?

The private investigator can come from a variety of different places, jobs, or employment backgrounds. There is no one-size-fits-all prototype for a private investigator. Some investigators come from law enforcement backgrounds. These individuals have policing and detective experience and then begin a second career in the private sector. Other investigators have formal college degrees and received investigative training from a contract investigative agency, a proprietary organizational department, or a business. Other investigators have formal legal, accounting, or scientific training and then apply their backgrounds for investigative purposes. People do not suddenly make a decision to "become an investigator" without relevant training and experience. The following is a list of the various types of investigators who work to gather information, protect lives, and defend businesses.

Corporate investigators (also known as proprietary investigators) work directly for a company or organization. They are assigned to investigate occurrences or events within their respective company. For larger corporations, the investigator may have a home office at the corporate headquarters and then travel to the various locations where the investigation needs to take place. Often these individuals are known to employees and do not have the luxury of anonymity. This lack of anonymity can cause other employees not to share information for fear of punishment by the company. Conversely, these investigators typically have excellent knowledge of the company or organization and can access details that may not be available to an outsider. Corporate investigators may be involved in pre-employment background checks, workmen's compensation claims, violations of company policy, and executive protection of senior management officials.

Private investigators (also known as contract investigators) work either as independent contractors or as part of an investigatory firm. Private investigators can work a wide range of cases depending on the expertise of the individual investigator. These individuals can investigate domestic and corporate cases, insurance fraud cases, workmen's compensation cases, or pre-employment checks, as well as track missing persons or accept executive protection assignments. The most advantageous role that a contract investigator can take on is an undercover assignment. Because of the relative anonymity of the investigator, he or she can work to blend into a particular environment to gain information for their client. Undercover investigative work takes great practice, skill, and a keen sense of awareness of what is going on around them. This is also a very dangerous practice due to the fact that people are very unpredictable and may react violently to the investigator if their anonymity is compromised (or in slang terms, they are "made" or their identity is "blown"). Undercover investigators can assume numerous social roles in order to obtain information for their client. They may assume a false identity and work alongside the subject of the investigation, follow the individual into any type of social or public setting, or assume a stationary surveillance position to monitor the activities of their target. Undercover investigators must be able to make quick decisions to protect themselves from harm and not to compromise the investigation.

Internal control employees are a form of investigator that work directly for a company or organization. Their role is to investigate possible breaches of company policy and maintain the continuity and adherence to organizations' rules and regulations. Internal control investigators may also scrutinize and examine company relationships with vendor clients and outside sources that may be a threat to organizational well-being. In the public law enforcement sector, those working for "internal control" departments are often unfortunately viewed with distain and disrespect. In the private sector, these individuals can be viewed as positive contributors to their organization, keeping employees safe and the company productive, and detering outside loss.

Risk managers assume a role of protecting an organization's best interests against loss, lawsuits, or harmful work situations. Frequently, risk managers assume a role of a "legal guardian" through the review of company agreements, insurance claims, and prospective contracts the organization may enter into, or review of the business credentials or practices of potential vendors and contractors. Frequently risk managers have a formal law degree (Juris Doctor) due to the amount of legal work required for the position. Risk managers may also oversee or conduct risk assessments of the organization (seeking vulnerable areas of policies, procedures, and practices) and conduct internal investigations on sensitive corporate matters. In some cases, risk managers may also represent the organization in court as one of the company's attorneys. Risk management is a growing field of expertise and is viewed as a necessary entity for corporations to protect the organization's best interest from harm.

Two emerging fields of investigations involve highly specialized professional practices. The first is known as **forensic accounting**. These individuals are trained in business and accounting practices and the appropriate legal knowledge. A forensic accountant's role is to review financial records for errors and improprieties, as well as unlawful or immoral practices. This investigator must not only have extensive training in accounting and financial matters but also have a solid grasp of all the laws, rules, and regulations that govern economic regulatory practices. These individuals are hired by an organization to completely immerse themselves into the financial practices and records of an organization.

The second type of emerging and highly specialized professional is that of a **forensic investigator**. With the development of DNA investigatory practices for public law enforcement cases, there is now a lack of qualified, publically employed forensic investigators to gather this evidence, analyze samples, and report findings. Because of this lack of public personnel, private organizations have been created to outsource forensic investigation practices. These private labs are contracted by public agencies to provide the same services as their publically employed counterparts. Because of the high number of cases needing laboratory testing, analysis, or verification, the private labs are growing in number. Forensic investigators typically have higher education degrees in biology or chemistry as well as basic investigatory procedures. Both of these hybrid investigators now serve a growing need in their respective fields.

Finally, there are workplace situations where individual employees can act as investigators, offering tips on possible violations of company policy or wellbeing. In the 1970s and 1980s, "silent witness" programs were developed to give employees an anonymous way to inform the organization of wrongdoings or improprieties. These silent witness programs can be managed internally within an organization or contracted externally through a contract security or investigative company. The employee is afforded the opportunity to submit an anonymous tip explaining the impropriety or problem. The report is then investigated through the assigned individual or department. This form of reporting can have a profoundly positive impact on an organization, providing it is operated with professionalism and integrity.

The need for investigative services continues not only to increase but also become a specialized field. Highly qualified and well-trained professionals can produce significant results through investigating incidents and cases. Like their colleagues in the private security industry, private investigators and investigatory services will continue to grow in number as well as improve in professional practice. These individuals serve a wide variety of services in the ever-growing investigatory field.

Types of Investigations

Generally speaking, investigations may be broken down into two broad categories: domestic/personal and corporate/business. The basic qualities of conducting these investigations are consistent but the circumstances, preparation, and dangers are uniquely different.

Domestic or personal investigations can be extremely dangerous and unpredictable due to the instability of the subject being followed and the possibly emotional circumstances. Even after the information is gathered for the client, their personal emotions must also be guarded against for a sudden outburst, despair, or even rage. The investigator may become the unintended victim of the client's extreme emotions.

Infidelity or possible infidelity can be a reason for a domestic investigation. The client may hire the investigator to confirm or deny that their spouse or partner is involved in an affair with another person. Infidelity investigations can be extremely emotionally charged for the client as well as their partner and potentially dangerous for the investigator. To complicate matters, if the couple also has children the investigator's findings could have an impact on child custody and the payment of child support. The investigator must take great care not to be identified by the subject being followed. Keeping a safe distance and working to blend into the surroundings is extremely important to avoid an unwanted confrontation with the subject. Instances have occurred when the subject notices the investigator and reacts in an explosive and violent manner. The investigator may need to follow the subject at all times during the day and night and in different types of environments. Typically, the request for domestic investigations may increase during the December holidays and around

St. Valentine's Day. During these specific times of the year, a cheating spouse or partner may want to meet up with the person they are having the affair with. As the amount of infidelity and divorce rates rise, more requests for investigatory services have taken place to verify or deny an affair. If the investigator accepts this type of case, his or her personal safety must always be the first priority during the process.

The horrific crime of domestic abuse may also warrant an investigator's services. As in the case of infidelity investigations, domestic abuse cases are potentially highly volatile not only for the investigator but also the alleged victim. With cases of domestic violence, the investigator may need to prove not only physical abuse but also emotional or psychological manipulation or exploitation. In these cases, the investigator may be hired by an immediate family member or a close friend to the alleged victim. As with too many domestic abuse cases, the victim will not seek assistance or file criminal or civil charges against the perpetrator, instead tolerating the abuse out of fear or a false sense of security, acceptance, or fear of additional harm. With domestic violence cases, the investigator may need to obtain any existing police records and interview family members, friends, or acquaintances as well as attempt to gather documents to prove the abuse. Investigators must always work to ensure their personal safety from a potential violent attack as well as maintain emotional distance from the case. Domestic abuse cases can be disturbing for the parties involved as well as the investigator.

Missing children cases are another domestic case where a private investigator may be required. In some cases, the parents or guardians of the missing child may request assistance from an investigator to work in conjunction with law enforcement authorities. In other cases, the investigator may be asked to continue the search for the missing child after the police are forced to stop their efforts or pull their resources. Investigators may attempt to gather similar information as the police detectives working the case. The investigator may interview possible witnesses, family members, or friends as well as work with cellular phone or credit card companies to attempt to trace the possible travel patterns of the missing child. Specialized investigators may also be called to use tracking dogs or conduct physical searches in areas where the child may have been last seen. The private investigator may also need to cross jurisdictional boundaries into other states or countries to follow up on possible leads and work with local authorities to gather information. Frequently, children may be apprehended by a non-custodial parent or sympathetic family member who believes the court assigned custody is unfairly disproportionate toward the other parent or guardian. Also, children may be abducted by mentally imbalanced or deviant individuals and in some cases, kidnapped for possible ransom. The investigator must be prepared to work in a multitude of environments to track down any leads or traces of the mission child.

The final domestic investigation that will be addressed are verifications of police investigations. With these cases, an investigator is hired to verify or disprove the information and claims made during a formal police investigation. Family members, attorneys, insurance companies, or advocacy groups may hire an investigator to verify the accuracy of evidence, recreate accident or crime scenes, or completely reinvestigate the crime, seeking to uncover evidence that was inadvertently or intentionally overlooked. This type of an investigation takes great diplomacy and political savvy. Depending on the case, when the investigatory file is closed by the police, the investigator may be met with resistance or animosity from the department. Yet, in other cases, the police may be either non-committal or even supportive of the effort. Investigators must be continuously aware of the rationale for the investigation for their client. The client's needs must remain the motivating factor for the investigatory process.

Corporate or business investigations may present a different type of work environment for an investigator as compared to domestic cases. In many situations, corporate investigations may become procedural and less emotional, depending on interaction with the subject. Corporate investigators may be needed by the organization the subject of the investigation works for, insurance companies, or licensing or bureaucratic organizations. The following is a partial list of investigations conducted for the corporate or business sector.

Time theft is a reoccurring problem for many companies. With this violation of company policy, employees intentionally avoid working while on the job or falsify time records to show they were on the job when they were not. Time theft not only depletes productivity but also creates staggering losses. Investigators may need to review pay records or work undercover to find employees attempting to cheat the system. In addition, the investigator may set up surveillance at local bars or restaurants frequented by employees or watch the employee's residence to see if they return home while they claim to be on the job. When the information is gathered by the investigator the organization could discipline, suspend, or terminate the employee for his or her actions.

Another systemic problem in the workplace is internal theft. Many employees steal company property for personal use or profit. In some cases, employees will steal from employers because they believe that they are either underappreciated or undercompensated for their duties and responsibilities. The theft of company property can range from small items (such as office supplies), to large items (such as manufacturing parts or electronics), or even to company information. The investigator can use a variety of methods to uncover internal theft, from a review of company purchasing records to an undercover operation. The company employing the investigator will set the parameters of the investigation based on the losses incurred and the budget for the operation.

Drugs in the workplace are another problem for employers. Illegal drugs could be taken by employees at work or sold during work hours. As previously discussed in the text, drugs in the workplace can deplete productivity, cause workplace accidents, and create an unsafe work environment with the visitation of drug dealers. Investigators can be used in an undercover effort to observe employees buying, selling, or using drugs in the workplace. Surveillance equipment could also be used instead of an actual investigator to uncover the drug interactions as long as the potential area for the activities is known and the equipment does not violate company policy or labor agreements. If an undercover investigator is used, he or she must be very careful not to partake in the drug activity or become suspected of working on behalf of company management. If the undercover effort is discovered, the investigator could be in grave danger of retaliation by the drug abusing employees and should abandon the operation immediately. If the undercover operation is successful, company management could discipline or terminate the employee(s) involved or possibly seek criminal charges.

The misuse of company equipment is also a concern in the workplace. In this situation, the employee uses company equipment, without authorization, for personal gains. This misuse commonly happens on company property with items such as machinery but could also include desktop or laptop computers or cellular equipment. This misuse of equipment could reduce productivity but also becomes a liability issue if the employee is hurt using the equipment or is found using company property for illegal or illicit gains. Investigators can use surveillance equipment with the permission of management to view activities or gain access to electronic use records to determine if the devices were used for non-authorized activities.

In the case of medical personnel, healthcare, insurance, or regulatory organizations may require investigatory assistance to prove possible medical malpractice. Cases occur where doctors prescribe unnecessary prescriptions, order unwarranted surgical procedures, or authorize medical leave for employees who are not hurt or sick. These problems create an economic strain on healthcare systems but also can result in higher insurance premiums for unpaid bills. Investigating medical malpractice or fraud requires cooperation between the investigator and the healthcare organization. Great caution must be taken not to violate patients' medical rights under HIPAA while uncovering the necessary information to identify unethical or illegal medical practices. Investigators may have a need to review patient or physical records as well as interview patients or medical employees to determine violations are present. These investigations may be requested by the individual healthcare organization, insurance companies, or in some cases, the patient. If medical malpractice is discovered, the doctor could lose their right to practice medicine, face disciplinary charges including termination, or have charges rendered in a civil or criminal court.

Embezzlement is another issue in the workplace which may require an investigation. When individuals in trusted positions use their employment status to steal money from their employer, an investigator may be needed to uncover the fraudulent or illegal activities. Money, stocks, or company financial assets can be illegally appropriated by an employee for personal use. Investigators must be afforded access to company financial records and be trained or highly qualified to search for monetary discrepancies. Depending on the specific type of embezzlement taking place or the discovery of employees appropriating company money or financial assets, the organization may discipline or terminate the employee, seek civil restitution or recovery, press criminal charges, or report the employee to the appropriate regulatory body for punishment. Embezzlement can happen in any type of public or private company, governmental organization, school district, or even in a church or religious community. The losses could be minor or astronomical and could occur one time or over a period of years. Depending on the depth and length of the misappropriation of funds, investigators may need to immerse themselves in numerous financial records to find the losses and connect them to the employee or employees.

The final corporate or business investigation that will be addressed is insurance fraud. In this case, an employee fraudulently claims an injury taking place while at work with the hope to be given paid time off through workmen's compensation benefits. Businesses and organization will carry workmen's compensation insurance for occurrences where employees legitimately are injured while performing the duties and responsibilities at work. When this occurs, the insurance claim will pay all or part of the employees' wages for a predetermined time while they are recovering. Often, immoral employees will submit bogus injury claims and lie to an examining physician to attempt to get paid time off from work. Investigators may be hired by either the company or the organization to observe the individual. If the employee is discovered by the investigator to be at home or in public without showing signs of the alleged injury, the insurance company may reject the claim and seek restitution for the monies paid, and the company may discipline or terminate the individual. Insurance fraud can also take place when property owners make false claims that property has been stolen or damaged with the hope of filing the item as lost or damaged. At that point the insurance company will pay a claim and the company owner or manager will illicitly earn money for the item's replacement. In these scenarios, investigators may be used to locate the property and gather evidence that the "missing" item is still intact, being used, and not damaged. The investigation may uncover that the item was personally damaged by the owner, the loss was part of a larger conspiracy involving acquaintances of the owner, or that the item was sold to a third party and reported as stolen. When this occurs, the insurance company may cancel the insurance policy as well as file criminal charges against the policy owner, and file civil charges to recover lost money and financial damages as the result of the false claim.

Deviant, immoral, and illegal acts by individuals can result in a great need for investigatory services. Acts of infidelity or immorality, civil violations, or criminal acts may require the use of a private investigator due to a lack of law enforcement personnel or actions that may violate organizational policies and procedures. Because of ever present-illegal or immoral actions by people, private investigators or investigation firms will continue to be needed to protect the well-being of individuals and organizations.

Investigative Operations

Conducting any investigation takes an immense amount of time and attention to detail. One does not simply begin to "follow someone" without adequate research and preparation. In most cases, the more time an investigator spends researching and preparing for a case, potentially the smoother the operations may go. This does not mean that the operational landscape during an investigation may not shift or change. What it does mean is that preparation is key to a potentially successful operation. The following are some basic practices that can help an investigation be successful and decrease the amount of problems or issues while on a case.

It is vitally important for an investigator to "blend in" to his or her surroundings. In order to accomplish this, investigators must gather as much information as possible on the geographic areas where they may be working; physically visit the areas prior to the operation; and observe the people, the activities taking place, and the physical surroundings. Investigators will then need to adapt their appearance to "fit in" to the area. The ultimate goal for the investigator is to go into the geographic area, gather the information needed for the assignment, and then leave without drawing attention. This can be a challenge for the investigator depending on the area where the work will be conducted. Larger investigative firms have a potential advantage with this because they can select an investigator who can fit the demographics of the area. For those working with smaller firms or independently, they will need to do the best job possible to blend in and gather the appropriate information.

The next area of importance when preparing for an investigation is to know the subject they are observing. The investigator must take time to gather as much detail as possible about the subject. This includes a physical description, the type of vehicle they may drive, their travel pattern, their work location, and social areas they frequent, as well as any other pertinent information on their description and travel patterns. These important details will assist the investigator to recognize the subject and allow them to gather the information without detection.

Another vitally important area of pre-investigatory research is to understand the traffic or pedestrian patterns where the surveillance will take place. The investigator will need to physically visit the locations and study both pedestrian and vehicular traffic patterns, surrounding buildings, and any potential physical or geographic obstacles they may encounter while conducting the surveillance. It is essential that the investigator personally review the geographic area for traffic and pedestrian patterns and not rely on geographic positioning system (GPS) devices, Internet map programs, or information given from the client or a colleague. The investigator must understand that these resources could be of help but without physically viewing the area in question, they may not fully understand the activities in the area or be able to plan a feasible escape route in the event the investigation is compromised.

The final general area of pre-investigative importance is to know how to operate any recording equipment and ensure that all the devices are in proper working order. The investigator must avoid not knowing how to work the hardware needed for recording, determining that the device may be inoperable, or that he or she does not have sufficient back up power to operate the equipment while conducting the operation. Investigations can take prolonged periods of time, so it is vital for the investigator to properly prepare the equipment for elongated use. This preparation includes the use of any surveillance equipment, computers, or vehicles. Another frequently overlooked area of preparation is the planning for the physical well-being of the investigator while on the case. Food, water, heat, cooling, communication devices, lighting, or methods for bodily relief must be considered prior to embarking on an assignment. As previously stated, surveillance work can be long as well as very tedious. The investigator must spend a significant amount of time preparing for the assignment to ensure a successful surveillance and investigatory process.

Types of Investigations

Gathering the information during an investigation is critical for the success of the operation. The investigator must take into account all the different nuances and factors for conducting a successful operation as described above. To further complicate matters the investigator must decide what type of investigation is needed to gather the information. Many surveillance operations may fall into the "99%-1% rule." This means that 99% of the time absolutely nothing occurs until the event takes place (the 1%). The investigator must be able to maintain his or her focus on the case and not become distracted in any way, shape, or form. Surveillance methods for investigations may be categorized into two types: stationary and moving.

A **stationary surveillance** at first may appear to be relatively easy, but the investigator must hone their craft and abilities to avoid being noticed and still record the information needed. Prior to beginning any surveillance, investigators should contact the local police authority and notify them of the activity, develop a solid cover story in case someone inquires or challenges their activities, develop an alternate plan for gathering the information in case their cover is compromised, and know the fastest way to abandon the surveillance to avoid the threat of harm. These four steps are necessary and essential for all investigations, both stationary and moving.

For a stationary surveillance, the investigator can take up a position in a concealed area where he or she may not be noticed, sit in a vehicle to obtain the information, sit in an open or public area, or stand in an open or public area to gather the information. Sitting in a concealed area offers the easiest way to gather the information. This gives the investigator the flexibility to use any necessary equipment to gather the information as well as the best way to avoid unwanted contact with the subject or another inquisitive citizen. A concealed investigation could be in an adjoining building or house, a cabin or hunting blind, or in extreme cases, camouflage netting. The goal for this type of information gathering is not to be noticed and still be able to use the equipment necessary to record the events and take field notes.

Conducting an investigation in a stationary vehicle can be a difficult task. First, the vehicle itself must not attract any unnecessary attention and "fit in" to the environment. Panel vans used by service or repair personnel can be a solid base of operations. In the event the investigator must remain in the vehicle for a prolonged period of time, he or she must be sure to stay quiet, not move around to shake the vehicle, and have the proper provisions needed for a prolonged stay. The goal is to be able to gather the information but have the public ignore the vehicle. If a domestic vehicle is used, the investigator must take great care not to remain there too long, especially if the vehicle is parked in busy or populated areas. Passersby, residents, or those who work in the area can approach the vehicle and question the investigator. The same dilemmas can occur if the investigator is conducting surveillance in an open area, either sitting or standing. In these cases, it is imperative that the investigator "fits in" the area. Whenever sitting in a coffee shop or restaurant, on a city bench or standing in a mall or airport the investigator must look like he or she belongs or has business in the area. To complicate matters, the investigator must be able to have a clear view of the subject and be able to properly conceal any recording equipment deemed necessary.

Moving surveillances are extremely complicated operations. Investigators must ensure their vehicle has no identifying marks or paint colors that would bring attention to their surveillance. Even simple items such as decals, stickers, vanity license plates, or items hanging from a rearview mirror can be a way for the subject to identify the investigator. Standard or factory paint and wheels on the vehicle are preferred. Any enhancements to the appearance of the vehicle can bring about unnecessary attention. The investigator must also stay a safe distance away from the subject and not follow too closely or directly from one lane to another if possible. This can be complicated in the event the subject makes sudden lane changes or abruptly exits a highway. The best case scenario is for a team of investigators to work together trailing the subject. The investigators can take turns following closely and then switch positions. This can help not to raise the suspicions of the subject that he or she is being followed. Also, in the event of an abrupt exit by the subject on the highway, the trailing investigator can make the exit and keep the surveillance intact.

Surveillance work takes time and practice to develop the necessary skills in order to be successful. These operations take great preplanning and thought to understand the possible movements of the subject, any risks that may occur during the operation, and the ability to record the activities. Stationary or moving surveillances can quickly become dangerous and the investigator's well-being can be in jeopardy instantly. It is essential for investigators to practice these surveillance methods before attempting to follow a subject. An investigator who is not properly trained or briefed can quickly be identified and the operation as well as the investigator's life may be in peril.

Documentation

The ability to document findings and activities during an investigation is crucial for this occupation. If an individual cannot properly compose notes or a report and cannot utilize the necessary recording devices, any and all efforts will be futile, at best. Documenting and recording events are the cornerstone for any investigation. Without proper documentation, the investigator's account will lack credibility and value.

Taking proper field notes during an investigation is vitally important for all reports. The investigator must begin by listing the time, date, and location as well as what is going on around him or her. Throughout the investigation and surveillance, the notes taken can be invaluable for denoting information that a recording device cannot detect, act as a journal for the investigator to refer to, be used to list important information to be remembered, and act as a backup to recorded documentation in the event a recording fails. The investigator should rely on the old fashioned method of paper and pen/pencil for note taking and avoid the temptation of using electronic devices. Writing out the information longhand will assist the investigator to remember the information accurately and reinforce recall of the events. Being able to take written notes and then to be able to translate them later will be a great assistance to the investigator when it becomes time to compose the report.

Still pictures (photographs) were once a common way to record events during an investigation. With the development and advancement of electronic recording devices, many have fallen away from using photography to obtain additional data from investigations. Still photographs remain a reliable way to gather and record data. Digital cameras that allow interchangeable lenses can deliver a clear and up-close picture of events taking place. Professional-grade cameras can allow pictures to be taken in rapid succession, allowing for a photo journal of the event. Long-range lenses combined with a digital camera cannot only provide important images, they can also record the time and date of the photo, which can be invaluable for the case. Best of all, a reliable long-range camera can also keep the investigators a safe distance from the event taking place.

Video images are a very popular way to record events during an investigation. Video images may be used with or without sound to record a subject's activities. Investigators should only use commercial-grade video equipment and avoid using low-cost devices or recorders on handheld phones. Commercial-grade equipment will provide a superior image with better clarity and provide a "time stamp," showing the date and time of the recording. The investigator must also avoid being detected using a video device by an inquisitive citizen, avoid being noticed by the subject, and avoid being harassed by a passer-by. Attempting to conceal the video recorder can allow the investigator to safely document the event while taking field notes.

Listening devices can be an acceptable alternative to gathering information when video devices or cameras are not feasible. Video recording devices can be very complicated to install and monitor, and it may be difficult to retrieve information. They must be of commercial and professional quality to ensure a clear recording. They also can pick up secondary conversations or noises that can disrupt the conservation with the intended subjects. Audio recording devices can be used for gathering information but are not used as frequently due to reliability and installation concerns.

Video and audio devices can come in many different forms. Traditional video cameras and audio microphones still exist but advancements in technology have also created recording devices in different sizes and forms. Aside from recording devices on smart phones, the ability to record images or sound can come in a myriad of different shapes. The creation of pinhole lenses can now result in the recording of quality video with a very small lens. Video cameras can be implanted into baseball caps, clocks, children's toys, burglar alarm equipment, pens, watches, or key fobs. It is essential that the investigator understands how the devices work, how long they can record, if they need a wireless recorder for the images, and what the recorded image will look like. The price of the video recorder will frequently determine the quality of the picture and the operational reliability of the device. Time and research must take place prior to selecting a video device.

Like the different shapes and forms of video devices, the same is true with audio devices. Wireless voice recorders come in various shapes, forms, and sizes. They may be incorporated into pens, key fobs, or computer flash drives. Audio recorders can also be handheld, battery operated, and provide digital recordings. These recorders are not covert, so care must take place to determine the location and use of these devices. Background or ambient noises can detract from the quality of the audio recording. Without state-of-the-art audio engineering equipment to filter out unwanted noises, audio recording can be less reliable than video devices. It is again essential for the investigator to research and understand the parameters of the audio recording device to ensure proper use and the ability to integrate it into the investigatory process.

The end result of note taking and video or audio recording is the compilation of the final written report. These reports must be accurate, detailed, and composed in a professional manner free of compositional errors, slang language, or unsupported information. All reports need to be complete and properly reviewed and edited prior to submission to the client. All investigative cases must contain a professional and detailed written report. These reports along with any supporting pictures and video or audio recordings can be admitted into a civil or criminal court case with or without the investigator being present. In fact, the report should always be prepared as if it will be admitted in a court case. A complete and professional report will assist the client with personal or professional matters and may help the investigator avoid confusion as to what occurred while on the case. This report is the final phase of all investigations and needs to be consistently composed with a professional level of accuracy.

Legal Considerations and Concerns

In this chapter, various investigatory techniques, methods, and devices have been introduced to the reader. The occupation of private investigations must be treated not only with professionalism but with the complete understanding of any local, state, or federal legal considerations or laws. For example, some states will require independent private investigators to apply for licensing, maintain insurance and/or operational bonding, and pass a background check or test prior to starting business. The independent investigator must also abide by all laws and regulations pertaining to taxes, insurances, and business requirements and regulations. In addition, laws may exist pertaining to the use of video images or audio recordings. The private investigator does not have to abide by all the legal requirements of the public police or law enforcement, but legal issues can exist regarding invasion of privacy, trespassing, or the following of a subject.

It is the full responsibility of both private and corporate investigators to know all laws, regulations, or policies that may affect their job. The phrase "ignorance is not a defense," strongly applies to this scenario. No investigator who violates the law will be granted immunity for not knowing the rules or statutes that apply to their industry. The investigator, organization, or department must research all potential local, state, or federal regulations, abide by all the requirements, and provide any and all proper reporting documentation to bureaucratic agencies to ensure legal and ethical operations.

Conclusion

The role of an investigator is an important one in today's society. They can serve both corporations and the general public in a variety of ways. It is essential that an investigator is properly trained and maintains ethical and professional business practices. Serving in an investigative role requires detailed training, understanding of the law, and knowing their subject and the environment they will be working within. This profession can be extremely rewarding yet also very dangerous. The investigator must also be highly observant and have the ability to make accurate and intelligent decisions at a moment's notice. Only trained professionals should work in an investigatory role by gathering information and helping their employer or client protect their best interests. As the need for information in bureaucratic, corporate, and domestic arenas continues to grow, the need for quality private or corporate investigators will increase accordingly.

Case Study — The Heartbroken Mother

A concerned mother, living on the Eastern Seaboard of the United States, contacted an investigator to look into concerns that her daughter was involved in an abusive relationship at college. When the mother had conversations with the daughter on the subject, the daughter would at first avoid the subject and then chose not to speak to her mother for any reason. Over the course of two weeks, the investigator gathered the demographic information of the daughter, confirmed her location at a college in the midwestern United States, and located the residence of the alleged abuser. The investigator then conducted interviews with neighbors and worked with the campus police to view multiple reports of verbal abuse by the boyfriend. In addition, reports were filed of possible physical abuse by the boyfriend but the daughter never pressed charges. She claimed for the reports that the boyfriend loved her and was having a bad day. During the course of the investigation, it was found that the boyfriend was a religious studies major, working toward a career as a church pastor. The information was compiled into a written report and sent to the victim's mother. The investigator followed up with the mother via telephone to see if she had any questions about the report or desired any additional information. The heartbroken mother continuously cried on the telephone while thanking the investigator, but her worst fears were confirmed. The case was extremely emotional and the investigator was dismayed at the pain and suffering caused by the boyfriend studying for a career in religious life. In the post-case briefing with the investigative manager, the investigator was commended for his work but strongly advised to distance himself from the case. The investigator was told that the agency's work was complete and he should prepare for the next case. After reading the case study, answer the following questions.

1. Was the investigator wrong to have personal emotions at the end of the case?
2. How can personal emotions benefit or hurt an investigator when working on a case?
3. What could the investigator have done to separate his personal emotions from the case?

Discussion Topic—Privatizing Forensic Science

As stated in the chapter, due to the high demand for DNA evidence in criminal prosecution cases, publically funded forensic labs are unable to keep up with the demand for the scientific verification of criminal activity. This ever-increasing demand for scientific evidence has created a new business and for-profit opportunity for private forensic laboratories services. After contemplating this new business venture, answer the following questions.

1. Do you believe that private forensic laboratories will produce reliable investigations?
2. Do you favor public organizations using taxpayer funds to pay these new laboratories?
3. What type of regulatory oversight do you believe these for-profit labs should have to ensure quality and accuracy?

Research Topic—"Spy Stuff"

Go onto the Internet and search the phrases "spy equipment" and "spy devices." Visit at least three to four different sites that sell equipment that can spy on individuals. After visiting the sites, answer the following questions.

1. Who can purchase these items?
2. Are there any noted regulatory or legal concerns listed on the sites to warn the buyer?
3. Do you believe that these products could be used to violate personal rights and freedoms?
4. Should the government do anything to possibly regulate this industry?

Key Terms

Corporate investigator	Private investigators	Internal control
Risk managers	Forensic accounting	Forensic investigator
Domestic investigations	Corporate investigations	Stationary surveillance
Moving surveillance		

Sources

Jones, G. M. (2005). *Criminal justice pioneers in U.S. history*. Boston, MA: Pearson Education.

United States Postal Inspection Service (n.d.). *A chronology of the United States Postal Inspection Service*. Retrieved from https://postalinspectors.uspis.gov/aboutus/History.aspx

Chapter Eight

Shrinking the Shoplifting: Retail and Shopping Center Security

Introduction

The pattern of activity happens every day. Shipments arrive; they are sorted, marked and priced, and then placed on shelves for the customer to purchase. This pattern occurs in thousands of retail stores and outlets around the country in order to serve millions of potential customers. According to the Internet site eMarketer.com, total retail sales in the United States for 2013 exceeded 4.5 trillion dollars (2015). The retail sales total for 2014 is estimated to exceed the 2013 total by approximately 4 percent (census.gov, 2015).

The world of retail sales is complicated and difficult. To the outsider, the process appears simple, but for retailers, they must be continuously vigilant to efficiently and effectively operate their stores to ensure success and profitability. The threats of shoplifting, retail fraud, and employee theft are a constant peril to retail establishments. In some cases, these illegal acts can cause retailers to lose money and eventually be forced to close their businesses. Criminal and unwanted activities in shopping centers can also deter patrons from visiting and purchasing products from the individual stores. The threat of loss and illegal activities in stores and shopping centers is a continuous battle for loss prevention and security professionals today. Customers, employees, products, and facilities must be made safe and free of crime. Because of these threats, these loss prevention and security professionals must be able to identify the potential causes of loss and institute numerous proactive measures to maintain a safe and profitable shopping environment.

Person Shoplifting © Steve Lovegrove via fotolia.com

Learning Objectives

In this chapter the reader will be introduced to basic concepts of retail and shopping center security. Common terms pertaining to the protection of these stores and centers will be presented and explained. In addition, a vast array of threats to retail stores and shopping centers will be explained as will various methods to prevent loss and maintain safety and order. Finally, the importance of a public and private partnership pertaining to loss prevention and security will be presented. By the end of the chapter, the reader will have a sound, basic understanding of the immense number of threats and preventative methods used to thwart these unwanted and illegal activities.

Controlling Shrink

When the average shopper looks at a retail store or shopping center, he or she may never understand that a majority of these owners or companies only make a small profit on each sale. As an average estimate, retail establishments earn a profit of one to two percent (1%–2%) on every sale. This can leave buyers wondering, "Where does the rest of the money go?" The "cost of doing business" for store owners is a complex issue. They must buy the product from the supplier or buy the items to make the product, invest in various methods of advertising to attract customers, and pay for their store (including physical supplies, rent, taxes, insurance, and applicable licenses), in addition to hiring, training, and compensating employees (which also includes licensing and taxes). By the time all the bills are paid (known commonly as "overhead"), the retail owner is left with a gross or total profit of one to two percent.

When an item is stolen or destroyed, the retail owner is still responsible for paying for the overhead associated with the item. As an example, if a ten-dollar item is stolen from the store, the owner may have paid five dollars for that item. If the profit from that item would have been a mere twenty cents, the store owner must sell additional items to make up for that loss. It takes a lot of items at a profit margin of "pennies on the dollar" to make up for that original loss. This is why it is vitally important for retail owners to protect their investments and avoid loss or damage to their products.

The term "**shrink**" is used to calculate and describe losses suffered by retail stores. As retailers continually count and track their inventory, they can compare the amount of items sold versus the amount of items no longer in the store or available for sale. This difference between actual sales versus the total number of items no longer available to the customer is what creates "shrink." Shrink is normally described in a numeric manner (the cost of the losses) but could also be described by the number of items lost in the store. Controlling the loss of items for sale to the customer is a regular and viable threat to retail establishments and must be controlled for the business to remain profitable and viable.

Internal Threats

Threats to retail establishments arise from the inside and outside. Internal threats are just as important to protect against as external threats. For some employees within the retail sector, they may have a difficult time comprehending the fact that their coworkers, employees, or vendors may be stealing from them.

Pilferage is the act of employees stealing from their employers. These thefts unfortunately occur on a regular basis. For employees, they may justify their actions based on the lack of compensation they receive, a false feeling of entitlement because "they earned it," or the justification of the theft because the organization "will never miss it." In the retail sector, this threat is real and can cause great harm in the store's financial viability. Part-time or seasonal employees who have no incentive or obvious opportunity for advancement may use this factor to justify stealing from their store. Items may be taken for personal use, sold, given to friends or family, or taken to illegal or illicit sources for money. Any and all employees are capable of stealing from their employer. This reality must be considered to keep a vigilant and watchful eye over the employee base to detect and thwart the employee from pilfering from the employer.

Suppliers or vendors may also be a threat to the financial well-being of the store. Retail outlets purchase a substantial amount of goods from various suppliers. The retail establishment must thoroughly vet (investigate or check-out) the possible suppliers prior to purchasing goods from them. If the supplier is found with a history of complaints or a high turnover in their customer base, the store should view these issues as a potential threat. Multiple potential vendors or suppliers for a product should be properly investigated prior to entering into a business agreement. After an agreement is made, the retail organization must continuously inspect products purchased to avoid buying damaged or defective items. Also, shipments must be inspected before accepting delivery to ensure accuracy in the order. Many people blindly accept orders from suppliers without inspecting the shipment and receive incorrect or damaged goods. These discrepancies may be caused by human error (not paying attention) or may be intentional with the hope that the retailer is now "stuck" with the damaged goods or inaccurate shipment. As a general rule, all shipments should be inspected for accuracy and potential damage prior to accepting and signing for the items.

The transportation of goods can also be a cause for concern. Suppliers who produce the items may use various methods to transport the items from the factory, to a warehouse, and finally to the retail outlet. Depending on the shipping process, numerous shipping agencies and employees may come into contact with the products. Traditionally, it can be the supplier's responsibility for the items to be delivered to their final destination. But some suppliers subcontract the transportation of their goods and depend on the shipping organization for delivery. During the shipping process the goods can be damaged, lost, stolen, or delayed. When these circumstances occur, they can have a negative impact on the retail outlet. When ordered items fail to arrive or arrive damaged, the store is unable to sell the goods and misses an opportunity to earn money. Larger retail corporations rely on their own internal shipping and transportation services while smaller retail establishments use a myriad of suppliers and shipping options to receive their ordered goods. In any case, the final destination of the goods must have provisions in place for missing, late, or damaged shipments. Tracking of the shipments and having a solid working relationship with the supplier or the company transportation employees can be critical to ensuring the successful delivery of the goods as well as tracking lost or delayed items or the replacement of missing or damaged deliveries.

All of these internal threats to the store, retail outlet, or the retail chain can have a tremendous impact on the success of their business. A store cannot sell items it does not have. Continuous and diligent oversight of employees, suppliers, and transportation services can help to reduce or minimize the loss of items intended for the customer.

External Threats

The external threat of loss for retail establishments can be broad and continuous. The threat may range from a child looking for a cheap thrill to organized crime rings pilfering thousands of dollars of merchandise. Because of the wide range of potential perpetrators seeking an even wider range of goods to steal, retail stores and their loss prevention efforts must be ever vigilant and watchful.

Shoplifting

The crime of shoplifting can be categorized in numerous ways. Terms to describe these crimes include not only shoplifting but retail fraud, pilferage, larceny, and petty theft. In any case, this crime can have an astronomical impact on stores, their profitability, and overall business existence. Left unchecked or unaddressed, shoplifting can result in higher prices for consumers, continuous losses for retail establishments, an overall burden on the criminal justice system, and impacts on the overall national economy. According to the National Association for Shoplifting Prevention (NASP), it is estimated that there are 27 million shoplifters in the United States. Of these millions of criminals 25% are children and 75% are adults, with 55% of the adult offenders claiming to have begun their shoplifting activities as a child. The NASP also speculates that shoplifting is a crime of spontaneity (impulse or opportunity) with 73% of adults and 72% of juvenile offenders claiming they do not plan their thefts in advance. They also claim that they are caught only once in every 48 times they steal an item (2015).

The rationale for committing the offense varies with each individual. Shoplifters can be categorized into various groups, depending on need, skill level, and methodology used. Some shoplifters are known as "thrill seekers." These individuals have money to pay for the stolen items but commit the crime for the adrenaline rush. When these criminals are apprehended, they frequently have adequate money or funds with them to pay for the item but are looking for a physiological thrill. Mentally ill individuals or those under the influence of drugs and alcohol are also known to steal items. For these people, their mental condition or impairment may cause them not to realize what they are doing as a wrongful act. Other mentally ill individuals can have episodes that force them to believe that the item actually belongs to them and they found it after misplacing it. Also, the poor and elderly may turn to shoplifting as a way to survive. Because they do not have money and do have a need for the item, these people may steal to maintain a basic lifestyle or to provide the for the basic needs of their families. The rationale for the theft can vary with every perpetrator. It is important for retail management and loss prevention agents to keep a watchful eye on those potentially acting suspicious.

The methods used for shoplifting can be basic or well thought out. Some of the basic techniques of retail theft include placing the item in a pocket, hiding the item in a purse or bag, wearing an item out of the store, or even hiding the item in a baby stroller. Advanced or blatant methods to commit retail crimes are distracting a store clerk while a partner takes an item, forcefully breaking a display case to grab an item and run out of the store, or constructing an apparatus such as a "booster box" with a false bottom allowing the shoplifter to place the box over the item and carry it away in the device without suspicion. These basic methodologies remain a threat today but can develop into various other forms or advancements of technique.

Organized retail crime represents a small percentage of the crimes committed but results in staggering financial losses. The NASP cites that only 3% of shoplifters are professionals. These individuals steal as their profession or work with gangs to supplement the organization's income (2015). For these criminals, time and effort is taken to investigate a potential target. They will seek out the location of the high-end items to take, the location of the items in the store, the general layout of the floor plan, and what security systems or methods are in place to slow or deter the process. These retail crime rings operate on a national and international basis. They frequently strike when the retail establishments are closed or have few customers or employees in the area. Their methodologies are quick, at times silent, and attempt to be transparent. What looks to the outsider like a crime that takes a few, short minutes can actually take hours to prepare and execute.

Retail fraud continues to plague establishments today. In the past, retail fraud could include the removal of a price tag and debating with a clerk that the item costs less, placing a lower price tag on the item before purchasing or working with a store employee to enter a different price into the register and buying it for a lesser amount. With today's computer generated pricing and tracking, these methods of deceit have decreased through the years. The threat of retail fraud still exists today. Those who program the prices into the computer systems can enter an inaccurate amount for the item. Cashiers and supervisors can override a price if adamantly contested by a customer or in the event the store employees are working in conjunction with the customer to perpetrate the fraud. Although advancements in technology have worked to decrease or deter the amount of retail fraud, it still exists and can become highly detrimental to the retail establishment if left unchecked.

Retail management, their employees, and loss prevention staffs must be ever vigilant in the fight against internal and external theft. Information on individuals committing these acts as well as their methodologies should be shared with other retail stores and local law enforcement agencies. With the sharing of information and a true collaborative effort among store owners, the education process will assist to thwart or deter these crimes and to save consumers, retail establishments, and the general economy millions of dollars every year.

Prevention

A continuous fight goes on to detect, deter, and prevent losses in retail stores. The goal of security and loss prevention methods must be to work toward the complete elimination of losses due to theft, unnecessary damage to products, or record keeping errors. Although some may believe that this is an unachievable goal, this fight against loss must take place one day at a time and should never be given up. If stores were to forgo this fight, it would only be a matter of time before the losses become so great that they will be forced to discontinue business.

Company Policy

Preventative measures against loss in retail environments can take many different forms. The cornerstone of all loss prevention methods is the creation of sound policies to address this issue. Policies created to address loss prevention should identify all possible and viable aspects on the topic. These may include creating a zero-tolerance policy for employee theft, procedural methods to address and confront store loss and shoplifting, the banning or prosecuting of apprehended individuals, and employee incentives for apprehension and the reduction in store loss. The policies must be created and accepted by store management and reviewed and critiqued by a properly trained legal professional. When the policies are created, accepted, and implemented, they must be consistently followed and enforced. The failure to consistently follow and enforce the vetted procedures could result in civil suits filed on the basis of discriminatory practices. The policies and procedures for combating loss are not only the cornerstone of prevention efforts, but can act as a legal "safety net" protecting the organization against legal actions.

Customer Service

Superior customer service is another key to thwarting unwanted loss. Organizations that stress customer service and continual interaction between the employee and the patron can reduce loss simply by human interaction. Shoplifting can be and often is a crime of opportunity. If the store emphasizes tactful, polite, and continuous customer interaction, the potential shoplifter will not know when the next store associate may approach him or her. If an employee gets a detailed look at the customer's face and physical features, then the patron may decide not to steal. Because of these factors, superior customer service is a policy that may provide a welcoming shopping environment and prevent the threat of loss.

Loss Prevention

In addition to employees offering superior customer service, stores frequently employ loss prevention professionals to specifically focus on eliminating internal and external loss. These professional are formally trained to detect, prevent, and apprehend potential shoplifters and illicit employees. Loss prevention employees should be trained in observation skills, the understanding of shoplifting and theft techniques, and the proper procedures to apprehend a suspect. Many states have instituted "**shopkeeper's privilege**" laws intended to assist retail establishments in the apprehension of criminals. These laws allow store personnel the right to detain those caught shoplifting or stealing until law enforcement authorities arrive. These laws are intended to give private citizens working in retail establishments the ability to legally detain a suspect with the purpose of turning the individual over to law enforcement. For some retail establishments, employees or managers are trained and allowed to initiate the apprehension and holding of suspects. For other stores and organizations, they will rely on their loss prevention agents to apprehend and hold suspects until the police arrive.

Loss prevention agents also utilize numerous observational techniques and physical security tools to detect and apprehend potential criminals. In addition, loss prevention agents can share the information gained within their own store with other stores (both inside and outside their store chain), and with the police. Loss prevention agents and departments must be properly trained and expected to stay abreast on relevant issues as well as all laws affecting the protection of their store. The professionals must also have excellent written and oral communication skills because reports will be written for all encounters and can potentially be entered as evidence into court.

Stores and their loss prevention departments may also use a legal statue known as "**civil recovery**" as a method to regain the financial loss of a product. This practice allows stores and retail organizations the opportunity to sue for losses against a patron or employee stealing or damaging a product. Depending on the legal jurisdiction, the store may receive a multiplied compensation for their losses, as well as time and effort to apprehend this individual. For example, stores or retail organizations may receive two or three times the amount of the object lost, up to a predetermined or "capped" financial amount. This allows the retail organization the opportunity to recover the cost for the lost item as well as help pay for some of the time and effort of the retail establishment to address the issue. The field of loss prevention and the employment of loss prevention staff is a multimillion dollar investment of time, wages, training, and resources to deter, detect, and eliminate the threat of loss within the retail organization.

Store Design

The design of the facility (both internally and externally) may also have an impact on the threat of loss within a store. Store shelving, clothing racks, signs, and decorations intended to motivate sales can also offer or create the threat of items being stolen. When store employees and loss prevention agents fail to have "clear lines of sight" they are unable to easily detect and view a potential theft taking place. A large number of items for sale packed within a small or confined area allow thieves ample cover to conceal their illegal actions. This issue continues to be a point of conflict between store management and those charged with the protection and apprehension of criminals. For store management or ownership, the items need to be available for the customer to purchase and the stores need signs and decorations to inform the consumer of the sales. For those charged with the prevention of theft, these efforts create additional opportunity for people to conceal and potentially steal the item. The two internal sides must work together to create an environment that is appealing to the customer but does not encourage the theft of items.

Audits

Routine **audits** of items within the store will afford the retail establishment the data to show if loss or theft is a systemic problem for their store. Even with modern-day electronic recording systems and customized software, the auditing process takes time, attention to detail, and patience. As items enter into the store they are recorded into the store's inventory. When the item is sold, the transaction is also recorded and categorized as sold. At strategic times and intervals, the remainder of the items left in the store must be counted and recorded. In a perfect situation, the amount of items recorded upon arrival, less the items sold to customers, should equal the number of total items left in the store. The unfortunate reality is that this equation never ends up as being accurate. The unaccounted items can then be categorized as stolen, lost, or damaged. This auditing process informs the store management how much inventory is being lost and if loss prevention efforts are needed or effective. These numbers account for a sizeable segment of a store's profit and losses. They are needed for corporate reporting or for financial records and their insurance organizations. Without this routine audit process taking place, a retail establishment will never have accurate information on the inventory, sales, and losses needed to properly operate the store.

Physical Security Measures

With appropriate and well-composed policies and auditing practices in place, many retail organizations and stores invest in physical security measures to protect their items from loss or theft. These devices are intended to view potential thefts in progress, provide a physical and psychological deterrent from theft, and notify the store employees of items that are being taken from the store. The following items described to deter theft are commonly found in many retail outlets and stores but represent a sampling of the technologies used.

Devices used to watch customers and employees include digital cameras and anti-theft mirrors. Digital cameras offer store management and loss prevention staff the opportunity to watch or record the activities taking place within the entire store. These cameras can be overt (out in plain view) or covert (hidden). Digital cameras provide a clear picture of the areas surveyed as well as offer the ability to pan, tilt, or zoom from their mounted position. Cameras may be interfaced into either digital recording devices or computer programs to allow for a review of activities in either real time or at a later date. Depending on the size of the store and the number of employees charged with loss prevention working at the time, it can be difficult to view live camera images and then enter into the store's main floor for possible apprehension and recovery of an item. This is why it is critical for stores to digitally record images, providing evidence for future disciplinary measures or prosecution.

Anti-theft mirrors are devices that allow security or loss prevention personnel the opportunity to watch employees and customer around corners or down adjacent aisles. With the use of these devices, the security or loss prevention employee is actually on the store's shopping floor so he or she can use the mirrors to personally approach the alleged thief. It needs to be noted that the installation and placement of cameras and anti-theft mirrors need to be approved by store management or the store's designated legal authority. Cameras or anti-theft mirrors should never be placed in dressing room areas. Viewing customers in dressing rooms can result in legal action taken by the customer for invasion of privacy.

Devices used to physically deter the theft of items include secured display cases, as well as cables and locks to secure the items to a heavy or stationary object. High value and smaller items such as jewelry, perfume, or cologne as well as highly popular items such as electronic video games and their control unit should be continuously secured in a locked cabinet. In the event a customer wishes to look at an item, they will need a store employee to open the locked cabinet and wait with the customer until they decide to purchase the item. For other frequently stolen items, such as tobacco products, alcohol, or baby formula, the store may keep these items behind a customer service counter. These items are placed out of reach of customers and force the customer to immediately purchase the item, thus minimizing the potential theft of the items. For larger and expensive items placed on the store floor, such as leather clothing, items made of fur, or even shotguns or hunting rifles, these items can be secured with a cable and a lock. The item is secured onto a display stand or other heavy object that will deter the potential thief from simply grabbing the item and walking out. Much like the locked display cases, the customer must gain assistance from an employee to unlock the item.

The final locked device used to deter theft is an ink tag. These tags are securely attached to the protected item. When a customer purchases the item, the cashier or customer service attendant unlocks the ink tag. In the event a potential thief attempts to forcefully remove the tag, the ink vial inside the device breaks open and stains the item. This method of deterrence can be controversial because the store sacrifices the potential loss of the item to disallow the thief from illegally taking the object. These "lock and key" methods or deterrents can prove highly cost effective and provide an adequate measure of security for the item.

The final category of protective devices is designed to activate an alarm for deterring theft and the possible apprehension of the thief. These devices are known as radio frequency identification devices (**RFID**) or electronic article surveillance devices (**EAS**). With this form of protective equipment, a device is either openly attached or hidden into a product to alarm in the event the item is removed from the protected area. An example of an overtly attached item is a spider wrap. This device physically covers with a sensor and cable and activates an alarm on the object if the cable is cut or compromised. Additional attached protection includes alarm caps placed on bottles. The caps require a specific style of key to remove the protective device and will activate an alarm if taken out of the store.

Hidden or covert RFID or EAS tags can be placed, attached, or affixed into the item. When the protected item is purchased, it is scanned at the register and the device becomes deactivated. In the event a thief attempt to take the item out of the store, the item will pass through a detection scanning device (that acts as a receiver) and triggers an alarm. Many stores choose to install and utilize these electronic devices because of the long-term cost and their effectiveness. The installation of the tag deactivation scanners and the scanning devices can be an expensive initial investment but after the systems are installed, the RFID or EAS tags are relatively inexpensive and provide adequate deterrence and apprehension methods to protect the item.

All of the physical security items listed have negative attributes as well. For these items to work, employees must properly use them in accordance to the manufacturer's specifications and the written policy of the organization. If employees fail to use the protective items properly, the store or retail organization has wasted time, effort, and money to protect the item. The other concern is the de-sensitivity many people now have to alarms. If an alarm is activated, store and loss prevention personnel must immediately investigate the warning to address the situation. If the alarm device or system is failing to work properly and creating false alarms, the organization must address the deficiency immediately to ensure the device works as intended.

The use of physical security devices to protect items from theft has become commonplace in today's retail community. The common use of these devices illustrates that retail organizations and stores are willing to invest in evolving technology to deter and apprehend the criminal element.

Employee Incentive Programs

The final method to deter theft and loss, utilized by retail organizations, is **employee incentive programs**. This form of deterrence involves an employer offering some type of an incentive to employees who discover shoplifters or cases of retail fraud. The employee could be offered cash rewards, gift cards, or additional discounts on store items. In some cases, groups of employees can be rewarded for reduced losses at their store. These "contests" to slow or limit loss can reward the entire store or smaller groups. In some circumstances, the employee can be formally recognized by the company for his or her efforts. These incentive programs can be useful as long as the employees share a sense of pride for their work and understand the benefits of controlling losses. In circumstances where employee morale is low or negative, these incentive programs could help to bolster morale and productivity. It is essential for management to strongly promote these programs and give an appropriate amount of compensation for the employee to feel their effort is worth the reward.

The common denominators for these efforts to control or stop loss is that the organization or store must invest in the protection of their assets and ensure that all efforts to control loss are legally and consistently implemented. If any of these factors are not adhered to, the company may suffer a bad financial investment in loss prevention devices, demotivate employees from working to control loss, and ultimately provide an ample environment for criminals to steal. The reality of loss preventative measures is that without them, the store may lose too much money and be forced to close. Successful implementation of these measures will control loss, keep operational costs down, and promote a positive retail experience for the customer.

Shopping Center Security

Today's shopping centers come in different styles and sizes. Stores can be grouped together in fewer numbers to create a "strip mall" or placed in an open-air market style of a configuration, as well as appear as the traditional enclosed shopping center. With the rise in Internet purchasing deterring patrons from traveling to the traditional shopping malls, the owners of these properties are turning many of these structures into entertainment and retail centers. In addition to retail stores and restaurants, shopping centers are adding movie theaters, live entertainment, amusement park rides, gaming centers, art galleries, and aquariums. As these facilities work to bring in patrons for a wide range of activities, it becomes essential to have quality security at these locations. Security at shopping centers must be ready to address numerous threats while maintaining customer service as well as creating a safe and welcoming environment.

Policies and Procedures Manual

The cornerstone for success for the shopping center security department is to create, maintain, utilize a detailed policy or operations manual. This manual must contain detailed rules, regulations, and operational procedures for the security staff. Inside the policy manual, procedures for each of the various responsibilities of the staff positions must be detailed. In addition, guidelines for report writing, changing shifts, and emergency procedures need to be included. These manuals must be readily available to the security staff for review or guidance. The security managers and supervisors must continuously train and review these policies and procedures with the staff to ensure efficient performance and reduce the threat of liability.

Jurisdiction of the Security Staff

The jurisdiction of the security staff is another important and vital aspect to determine and establish. Larger retail stores in the shopping center (commonly referred to as "anchor stores") may employ their own loss prevention teams. They may not need nor want the assistance of the shopping center mall staff or only call upon them for assistance in case of an emergency. Other stores may not desire to have members of the security staff in their stores over concerns that their presence may deter patrons from coming in. In these cases, the stores may call the shopping center security in case of an emergency. Yet, some establishments in the shopping center may welcome the security presence as long as it does not become a deterrent to customers and employees. Another important aspect to the jurisdiction of the security staff is ensuring they understand how far they are to protect outside the physical shopping center structure. In most cases, the security staff's jurisdiction ends with the property line of the shopping center. Unless there is some type of contractual or mutual aid agreement with neighboring properties, the security staff should only protect the property owned by the shopping center management. If a security officer leaves the property and causes harm or damage, the shopping center, security staff, and the officer can be held liable and face a civil suit (or in rare cases, criminal charges). The security staff must understand that their authority and the protection offered by insurance (in case of harm or damage) only goes as far as the property line.

Shopping Center Threats

The threats to a shopping center and their patrons are broad and continuous. The security staff must be ready to respond and confront a myriad of situations within the shopping center property. These threats include (but are not limited to) injured patrons, thefts from stores, fights or domestic confrontations, vandalism, unruly patrons, vehicular theft or damage, vehicular accidents, patrons being assaulted or robbed, bomb threats, arson, acts of organized terrorism, or damage from natural or weather related events. With the emergence of shopping centers that include entertainment venues, large crowds may congregate and create an opportunity for loss, deviance, injury, or damage. The security staff must be properly trained on how to react to an emergency or a threat on the property.

Security and Customer Service

While the security staff is trained to respond and react to the multitude of situations that may occur on-site, implementing excellent customer service is vital. Shopping centers want to have a safe and friendly environment for their patrons. Because of this, the security staff must employ tactful enforcement of the rules and regulations. The security staff may be asked to operate customer service desks and information centers, provide valet parking, escort patrons and employees to their vehicles, locate lost family members or friends, and assist with vehicular issues. Uniformed security officers are a visual deterrent to crime and problems. These same uniforms also attract attention and can represent help and assistance. Because of these visual human perceptions, shopping center security staffs must always understand that they are "under the microscope" and are continuously being watched. A friendly and professional demeanor will help not only to deter unwanted crime and activities but promote a positive shopping and entertainment environment for all patrons.

Crowd Control

Crowd control is another key responsibility of shopping center security. Through the physical design of the center, adequate exit points, and open and unimpeded spaces, combined with a continuous security presence, crowd control can be maintained and managed. The security staff must have detailed policies and procedures in place to react and respond to a panicked or unruly crowd. Continual oversight of customer activities can detect possible negative situations that could incite violence or agitate a crowd. Confronting and controlling this situation in an expedient and professional manner can help to avoid these negative circumstances. In the event of fire or a natural disaster, security will be responsible to help guide patrons away from the threat and escort them to safety. These emergency and evacuation plans must be well written and the security staff must regularly review the procedures. The unfortunate reality is that some of these situations may occur spontaneously and without notice. Security will need to properly react to the event, notify police or fire personnel, and work to restore order.

Parking Lot Protection

Protecting parking areas can be a tiresome and potentially stressful situation. Parking lots and parking structures can be prime areas for unwanted or criminal activity. Security departments typically use electronic security measures such as closed-circuit television systems, sufficient lighting, and emergency call boxes to help deter crime. The security staff must also continuously patrol the parking areas either in a well-marked vehicle or on foot. While on patrol, the security officer must be aware of potential suspicious activities such as people loitering or sitting in vehicles for extended periods of time. Common threats to parking areas include breaking into vehicles to steal items, the theft of vehicles, customers being accosted in the parking lot and having their personal items or packages stolen while walking, or extreme cases of abduction or sexual assault. The parking areas need to be continuously patrolled and kept under surveillance to limit the number of potential crimes and unwanted activities that take place.

Police Presence

For many larger shopping centers, local police departments may have a small "mini station" within the premises. Frequently, the shopping center management or ownership will make legal and financial arrangements with the local municipality to have the police officers staffed on-site. The benefit of such an arrangement is to offer additional protection to patrons as well as an arresting authority on-site in the event a crime is committed. It is essential for the security staff and police authority to understand their differences in duties and responsibilities and to assist one another as needed. With mutual respect and understanding of responsibilities, having a full- or part-time police presence at the shopping mall or center can be a sound investment to protect the patrons, maintain order, and ensure a pleasant experience for all shoppers.

The protection of shopping malls and shopping centers takes time and constant patience, attentiveness, and professionalism. As shopping facilities continue to change into shopping and entertainment facilities, the role of security is essential to maintain a customer-friendly and welcoming environment. If patrons believe and see that the shopping center is safe, they will continue to patronize the stores, restaurants, and entertainment venues located there.

Public/Private Partnerships

Since the 1980s an increase in public and private partnerships involving law enforcement and security/loss prevention personnel has taken place. These groups, when collaborating, can share vital information and resources to make the community a safer place. Organized professional groups dedicated to slow and stop shoplifting and retail crimes exist. These organizations will meet formally on a weekly, monthly, or quarterly basis to share information and learn about emerging threats and protective methods. These smaller groups may be part of larger national or international organizations dedicated to education and the prevention of retail crime. The groups provide a vital source of information that can help both the private and public sectors deter and prevent retail crimes. More importantly, professional groups work to create trusted professional relationships among the members. These trusted professional relationships open the door for frequent communication and information sharing vital to the prevention of these crimes.

In addition to information sharing, these individuals, groups, and organizations can share physical resources in the quest to protect lives and property. In addition to mini police stations within shopping centers, the shopping center management can share access with law enforcement agencies to closed-circuit television systems via remote access. This allows the law enforcement agencies to have open access to the designated cameras on the shopping center proper to also watch pedestrian and vehicular activities. In some cases, the shopping center management will allow police or crime prevention organizations to place their own cameras on the shopping center proper to monitor public spaces. These efforts to share information and resources are sound business and enforcement practices where all parties will benefit. Any time professional biases and inaccurate negative attitudes are placed aside, everyone affiliated with these groups will benefit from the interaction, cooperation, and collaboration.

Conclusion

The continuous fight against retail theft, fraud, and shoplifting is an ongoing effort. As methods to commit these crimes shift and change, the professionals tasked to slow or stop these civil and criminal violations must remain vigilant and adapt to criminal processes. The constant investment of time, resources, and money to combat retail crimes must be continuous and never wavering. If retail organizations give up this battle or fail to slow these criminal efforts, local, state, and national economies will be negatively impacted. This negative impact can result in the closure of stores and shopping facilities, the loss of jobs, and an overall detriment to the economy. Retail management and ownership must continue to support and fund this effort to ensure a positive shopping experience for all involved.

Case Study — Excessive Force

A shopping center in a large metropolitan area was the victim of a truly unfortunate incident between a security officer and a patron. The case involved a perpetrator of a retail crime attempting to flee from the shopping center on foot. The security officer was able to run down and intercept the alleged perpetrator. The result was a physical confrontation between the two where the security officer placed the alleged perpetrator in a lethal choke hold, killing the person.

After reading the textbook, including this chapter, how do you believe the security officer should have reacted to the situation? How could the security officer have acted differently? How can the shopping center management prevent unwanted incidents such as these from happening in the future?

Discussion Question — Civil Liberties vs. Loss Prevention

Loss prevention professionals will readily admit that changing rooms are areas where many retail thefts take place. The criminals will enter into a changing room and attempt to hide an item in their purse or bag in addition to putting the item on and attempting to wear it out of the store without payment. In your opinion, what could be done to consistently monitor these areas without crossing the line and violating a shopper's right to privacy and potential civil liberties? Is there a method or process legally available to monitor activity within a changing room to prevent the ongoing threat of theft?

Research Focus — Loss Prevention Devices

Log on to the Internet and search the phrase "loss prevention devices." In a simple search and after viewing 10 to 20 listings, answer the following questions:

1. How many different devices did you encounter?
2. What is the price range of these devices?

3. Do any of the manufacturers or sellers offer "volume discounts" when ordering a large number of items?
4. What device do you believe would be the best solution to prevent shoplifting when considering quality and price?

Key Words

Shrink	Pilferage	Shoplifting
Organized retail crime	Retail fraud	Shopkeeper's Privilege
Civil recovery	Audits	RFID
EAS	Employee incentive Programs	

Sources

eMarketer.com. (n.d.). *Total US retail sales top $4.5 trillion in 2013: Outpace GDP growth*. Retrieved from http://www.emarketer.com/Article/Total-US-Retail-Sales-Top-3645-Trillion-2013-Outpace-GDP-Growth/1010756

National Association for Shoplifting Prevention (NASP). (n.d.). *Home page*. Retrieved from http://www.shopliftingprevention.org/?=PPC

United States Census Bureau. (2015, February). Advance monthly sales for retail and food services: January 2015. Retrieved from http://www.census.gov/retail/marts/www/marts_current.pdf

Chapter Nine

Keeping the Currency and Its Customers Safe: Banking and Financial Security

Introduction

Historically, banks and financial institutions have been targeted by criminals for burglary, robbery, extortion, and terrorist attacks. Early attacks on financial institutions included daring armed or unarmed robberies by a myriad of criminal rogues and burglaries during hours when the facilities were closed. The threat of attack and violent acts inside financial institutions has forced the industry to take measures to protect the lives of their employees as well as the assets they house. Because of the large number of threats to financial institutions, the United States federal government created a law mandating minimal security protection for these businesses.

Today's banking industry faces threats from individuals who work for the institution as well as outsiders. These modern-day threats involve the traditional crimes of robbery and burglary but now also include employee crimes such as pilferage and embezzlement. Complicating matters is the continuous expansion of these institutions to conduct business and offer services on the Internet. This electronic access affords breaches of financial documents and assets twenty-four hours a day, seven days a week. To combat these ever-present threats, today's financial security professional must be well versed on the latest technologies to protect lives and property as well as understand the internal, external, and cyber threats.

Learning Objectives

In this chapter, the reader will be introduced to various aspects of the banking and financial security industry. These topics will include historical crimes

Bank Vault © iuyea via fotolia.com

and legislation, specific threats to these businesses, as well as various physical security measures and employee training procedures to deter unwanted crimes.

Banks Historically as Targets

Banks have been used to retain and distribute money, provide loans to qualified customers, and hold items of value for their clients. Because of the nature of this business, they have been regular targets for crime. Even with the evolutions of protection and protective measures of these facilities, criminals work to find weaknesses and opportunities to rob and steal the bank's contents. In addition to the theft of the bank's contents, numerous robberies have resulted in the loss of human life due to the actions of these criminals.

Throughout history, the stories and reports of bank robberies became somewhat romanticized. Tales of bank robbers storming a bank on horseback or in an automobile while wildly shooting, taking money, and then living as a fugitive have been well documented in our records. These criminals became well-known public outlaws through the reporting of these events and gained popularity as their illegal activities continued. For some, the bank robbers were a symbol of a "Robin Hood" society where the poor and downtrodden rise up to steal from the rich and wealthy. No matter how these events are recorded and told, they are crimes against the financial institution and society.

The first recorded bank robbery in the United States occurred in 1789 in the city of Lewistown, Delaware (now known as Lewes). The crime resulted in the loss of over $160,000. In this case, the criminals were apprehended when banks in the region noticed large monetary deposits and were able to trace the money to the perpetrators (Avery, n.d.).

During the 1800s and into the 1900s, bank robberies and burglaries were committed either on a one-time basis, or as part of a crime spree. During the 1800s, notorious and publically known bank robbers included Frank and Jesse James as well as Ma Barker and the Barker-Karpis Gang (FBI.gov, n.d.). As the Great Depression in the early 1900s decimated the United States economy, those reading newspapers and watching the newsreels at movie theaters learned about serial bank robbers such as "Baby-Face" Nelson, Bonnie Parker, and Clyde Barrow, as well as the Federal Bureau of Investigation's public enemy number one—John Dillinger (Okomo, 2014). Americans were outraged and aghast at the violent nature of these crimes that also included shootings and murder. This heightened awareness of bank robberies by the news media not only informed the general public of these crimes but also illustrated the need for improved security at financial institutions. As bank robberies and burglaries continued to plague the United States, banks professionals and governmental leaders worked to implement new rules, regulations, and methodologies to help protect the vulnerable financial institutions.

The Bank Protection Act of 1968

Created in 1968, the Bank Protection Act established minimal security practices and procedures intended to deter crimes within savings and loan institutions. This act calls for each banking organization to appoint a "bank security officer," normally an employee in a management or executive position, to oversee the protection and compliance set forth in the legislation. Saving and loan institutions are also required to establish and maintain security procedures, regularly train employees on security methods, and develop formal opening and closing practices, as well as maintain records of all robberies, burglaries, and thefts (FDIC, n.d.).

In addition, the Act also directs these institutions to install and maintain physical security methods and develop protective procedures. This directive represents one of the only federal acts mandating physical security in private sector businesses. The minimal security protective measures include adequate lighting during nighttime hours, the use of alarm systems (hold-up or panic alarms) to notify authorities in the event of an emergency, safes and vaults to store cash and valuables, tamper resistant locks on all exterior doors, and maintaining at least one camera to record events. The regulations also call for the regular inspection and maintenance of these security items to ensure proper function and use by the employees. These federal regulations represent the minimal protection needed for banks and financial institutions (FDIC, n.d.). Many of these organizations use additional security products and developed detailed procedures to reduce the threat of internal or external loss.

Bank Security Officer

As directed by the Bank Protection Act of 1968, the bank security officer holds far greater duties and responsibilities than the image of a typical security officer. To properly visualize the responsibilities of these employees, think of the word "officer" in comparison to a military organizational structure. These banking officers hold positions of authority like those of their military counterparts. In this case, these individuals are normally mid-level to senior managers who are responsible for all security and protection responsibilities. Many of these bank security officers have a background in the banking industry and have detailed knowledge of banking policies, procedures, laws, and auditing processes. These individuals may also have risk management responsibilities in addition to their security duties. In some cases, the bank security officer may have acquired security training and education prior to their appointments.

All of the above listed educational and procedural areas of knowledge are imperative for the bank security officer. They must be very well versed in the laws that surround and encompass the banking industry, in addition to the federal mandates. The bank officers may be responsible for the development and adherence to the security policies and procedures; the design, testing, and upkeep of the physical security equipment; and the regular training of bank employees to adhere to the security policies. The bank security officer may also conduct internal investigations pertaining to security or auditing breaches and consistently work with senior bank officials to ensure the protection of their banking organization.

Another important role of the bank security officer is interfacing and communicating with law enforcement officials at the local, state, and federal levels. In the event of a criminal act or a breach of security, the bank security officer may be the primary point of contact for local or state law enforcement agencies as well as federal organizations such as the Federal Bureau of Investigation and the United States Secret Service. In addition to these agencies, the bank security officer may also stay in contact with other banking and security officials to share pertinent and necessary information to avoid and deter criminal acts.

Threats to Banks

As stated in the beginning of the chapter, threats and criminal acts directed toward the banking industry are not a new phenomenon. For decades, the criminal element has been targeting banks as a method to gain sums of currency and valuables. It is important for those charged with the protection of these financial institutions to understand the types of threats they may encounter, in order to properly protect against the unwanted acts from occurring. The following is a broad list of the potential threats against banks and the financial industry.

Robbery is a common attack against a financial institution. A robbery occurs when a person or persons use force or the threat of force to physically remove items. In the case of financial institutions, these items are most commonly money that is placed in the bank teller's cash drawer. Robberies may occur when the bank is open for business to the general public or when the facility is closed but employees are entering or departing the facility. When the financial institution is open, robbers may come in and verbally demand the items or attempt to be unassuming and pass the bank employee a note with their demand. In other cases, the robber may apprehend bank employees as they enter or depart the financial institution and force them back inside to open cash drawers, safes, or vaults. The robber may brandish a weapon or an explosive device, or imply that they are carrying such an item. Whether armed or unarmed, the robber demands cash or other items like those found in safe deposit boxes, safes, or vaults. The key with the classification of a robbery is that the perpetrator has physical contact with a bank employee, demands cash or valuables, and may threaten the employee with bodily harm if he or she does not cooperate.

Burglary is a criminal act when a person enters into a facility either illegally or without authorization to remove items or valuables. In the case of financial industries, many attempted bank burglaries are perpetrated by those with skills and tools to possibly remove safes or to force open safes and vaults. With the advancement of physical protective devices, the amount of burglaries of financial institutions has become a less frequent occurrence. Nonetheless, financial institutions can become a target of burglaries.

Employee theft is also a real and viable threat to financial institutions. Immoral employees may feel justified or have a personal and immoral excuse to steal from their employer. These thefts may include small items such as office supplies and other proprietary items or the employee may attempt to steal cash. Another major threat is the loss of internal information perpetrated by the employee. A disgruntled employee may give outsiders key information pertaining to the financial institution such as client lists, earning and loss reports, or combinations to safes and vaults, as well as access codes into the computer system. Bank protection and risk management employees must stay vigilant to review computer activities and correspondence on company owned phones and computers, as well as review activities on closed-circuit televisions and alarm systems. Continual review and audits of these mediums are essential to protect the financial institution against the threat of inside loss or theft.

Fraud can be a crime that can plague financial institutions and their customers. Fraud is a crime when someone attempts to gain access to accounts, files, or information by portraying themselves as another person. The individual committing the fraudulent act is in sense lying to the financial institution to gain access that they are not authorized to obtain. In the past, people would take bank transaction slips or monthly activity reports and then use that information by claiming they are the account holder. By receiving this unauthorized access, the perpetrator can withdraw money from accounts or open lines of credit (loans or credit cards), defrauding the bank and the customer of funds. In today's electronic society, these threats are viable and will be covered in greater detail later in this chapter. Often these crimes are discovered "after the fact" when a customer or employee notices and confirms the illicit transactions. According to consumer loan expert John A. Dasky, immoral customers are continuously attempting to cheat the loan process with fraudulent loan applications. The losses suffered by the bank or loan institution due to these bogus loans are eventually passed along to all consumers (John A. Dasky, personal interview, November 2015). Once discovered, the financial institution can conduct an internal investigation to determine the loss and possible method for the transaction. They then have the choice to deal internally with the crime or turn it over to law enforcement depending on need and legal regulations.

Counterfeit currency is another threat faced by financial institutions. Counterfeit currency can come from various sources. This illegal currency can come into the financial institution from a direct deposit from an individual or from a commercial client that accepted the bogus money as part of a sale or other business transaction.

The sources of the illegal currency can vary depending on the target they intend to defraud and the tools the criminal possesses to create the money. The individuals creating the counterfeit currency can vary from amateurs using laser printing technology and circulating the monies at fast food establishments and convenience stores to international organized crime rings mass producing currency to deflate the value of the nation's money within the global economy.

With the increase of the production of counterfeit money, countries have been forced to redesign their currency. The changes have primarily been applied to paper currency (also referred to as bills) rather than metal coins. These changes include the redesign of the appearance of the money, the use of color shifting inks, and the incorporation of plastic or foil into the bill's paper. In the United States, the creation of money is the responsibility of the Treasury Department and produced through the United States Bureau of Engraving and Printing (commonly referred to as the U.S. Mint). Even with the physical and compositional changes in the currency, older and smaller denominational currency is still in circulation and accepted by businesses and banks. These smaller and older bills can still create issues for financial institutions when discovered.

In the event that counterfeit currency is discovered, banking security officers and officials can conduct internal investigations for the delivery of the currency and work with local, state, and federal law enforcement agencies. The primary responsibility of protecting the currency in the United States rests with the U.S. Secret Service. Founded in 1865, the Secret Service Division was charged with the protection and apprehension of counterfeit currency. Today, the United States Secret Service is still charged with safeguarding U.S. currency both domestically and abroad (United States Secret Service, n.d.). All counterfeit currency legally has no value. In the event illegal money is accepted and discovered by the financial institution, they must take a financial loss on the transaction.

In recent years, the threat of **electronic crimes** against financial institutions has arisen and can become costly. Financial institutions, like many businesses, conduct regular business electronically and via wide area networks and the Internet. Because of this open access into the World Wide Web, criminals who possess the knowledge and ability can gain access into the electronic computer systems of financial institutions. When these criminals silently and illegally access the computer networks, they can electronically transfer funds and steal vital customer data. In the event customer data is stolen, fraudulent activities such as unauthorized withdrawals and creating bogus accounts and lines of credit may occur. These illegal attacks on financial institutions force the organizations and their customers to be constantly on guard to recognize and defend against such an occurrence.

Direct and virtual threats against financial institutions create a need for continual vigilance. These perils can potentially force losses to the institution and even impact the global economy. Because of this, financial institutions must use multiple preventative measures to protect the lives, currency, and property within their organizations.

Protective Measures

Because financial institutions are a continual target for criminal activities, various physical security measures are implemented. The minimum physical security protections are mandated in the Bank Protection Act of 1968, but many financial institutions incorporate additional security resources to protect lives and property. These physical security measures protect a wide range of areas within a financial institution and work best when applied redundantly. The redundancy of the security equipment provides multiple layers of protection to thwart criminal activities.

Vaults are sizeable structures that protect currency, safe deposit boxes, and valuable property. Traditional vaults are found in the lower levels of the financial institution due to their size and weight. Composed of concrete block and potentially combined with steel walls, these protective rooms offer superior protection against unwanted entry. The outer doors of the vault are solid steel with locking mechanisms which are designed to elude or deter multiple measures to break in. The inner vault door (or day door), allows easier passage into the vault during business hours but is also equipped with a locking device to allow only authorized personnel to enter (Collins, Ricks, & Van Meter, 2000). In newer financial institutions, modular vaults can be installed, affording the necessary protection against unwanted intrusion. The modular panels are composed of steel walls filled with concrete and reinforced steel bars, known commonly as rebar. The vault door also is constructed to meet industry designs and requirements for protection. These modular vaults allow financial institutions to design the size of structure needed for their currency, safe deposit boxes, and valuables. The panels (walls) can be constructed and inter-locked to provide the required protection. Both the traditional vault and the modular vault are expensive to build but afford excellent protection.

Safes are smaller and potentially portable structures to house currency and valuable property. The use of safes is common in financial institutions. For bank branch locations that do not require the protection of a large vault, safes offer reliable protection. Safes can be placed behind the bank teller lines, or in separate rooms where cash is held. Safes are constructed from laminated or solid steel and include a door with a mechanical locking device (Collins, Ricks, & Van Meter, 2000). It is imperative that financial institutions understand the composition of the safe, if the device can be secured to prevent unwanted movement, and what threats it can deter. It should be noted that professional-grade safes are far different that smaller home safes. The professional-grade safe is constructed to meet the needs of not only the financial institution but the specifications required for operation and insurance.

The protective ratings of safes and vaults allow the financial institution to understand what these devices can protect against and for what duration of time. Insurance companies may require certain protective standards for these devices prior to offering a policy. Governmental organizations could also require minimal requirements to afford protection against unwanted intrusion. Underwriter's Laboratories (UL) provides testing of safes and vaults and offers protective ratings for these devices. Founded in 1894, Underwriters Laboratories' mission is to promote safe living and working environments through the inspection and evaluation of products (Underwriters Laboratories, n.d.). These ratings provide what device the safe or vault can protect against and the duration of time the attack can be withstood. For example, safe protection can be categorized by the following:

Tested attacks against the door and front face:

- Tool-Resistant Safe — Class TL-15
- Tool-Resistant Safe — Class TL-30
- Torch- and Tool-Resistant Safe — Class TRTL-30

Tested attacks against the door and body:

- Tool-Resistant Safe — Class TL-15X6
- Tool-Resistant Safe — Class TL-30X6
- Torch- and Tool-Resistant Safe — Class TRTL-15X6
- Torch- and Tool-Resistant Safe — Class TRTL-30X6
- Torch- and Tool-Resistant Safe — Class TRTL-60X6
- Torch-, Explosive-, and Tool-Resistant Safe — Class TXTL-60X6

UL 687 — Standard for Burglary-Resistant Safes. Source: Underwriters Laboratories, (2015).

The Underwriters Laboratories standards define the type of attack, the length of time the attack can be endured, and which sides are designed to withstand the incident. For example, the TXTL-60X6 safe is able to withstand a tool, torch, and explosive attack for 60 minutes on all six sides.

Safes and vaults can also be connected to alarm systems used throughout the facility. Some alarm systems can be adapted to include protection against the unwanted opening of a door or movement of the safe. The use of alarm systems in financial institutions will be covered later in the chapter.

For banks' security executives, it is extremely important to understand the designs of the equipment, what is going to be placed inside the safe or vault, and the degree of protection the device offers. The executives should review any existing corporate policies, government guidelines, and industry recommendations prior to investing in this protection.

As previously mentioned, financial institutions are required by the federal government to install some type of holdup protection for their employees. Today, **hold-up alarms** are designed to send a silent signal to an organization monitoring the alarm. In many cases, these silent alarms are connected to the burglar alarm system. In previous years, hold-up alarms activated a bell or siren to notify people (inside and outside) of the robbery. The use of an audible alarm could also agitate or upset the would-be robber and greatly increase the possibility of personal harm. With the use of silent alarms, the employees inside the financial institution can have the appropriate authorities notified and not escalate the threat of violence.

The actual hold-up alarm has been designed in various capacities. The traditional **panic button** style can be placed by each of the tellers' windows, in surrounding offices, and near safes and vaults. Silent hold-up alarms can also be activated through the alarm systems keypad. If an employee is attacked when attempting to enter or leave the facility, he or she is able to use a secondary alarm code to activate or deactivate the alarm as well as send a silent signal known as a **duress alarm.**

A **money clip** (also referred to as a bait clip) is a device that is placed in the teller's cash drawer. Money is placed in the device and when removed, activates the silent alarm. With these hold-up devices, the goal is to activate the alarm without the would-be robber realizing the apparatus has been activated.

Some financial institutions utilize a proactive silent system, called a **dye-pack.** Unlike other silent alarm systems intended to notify authorizes that the robber is in the facility, the dye-pack in intended to apprehend the criminal after he or she depart from the facility. With this device, the "pack" is placed within a stack of money. Fake currency that holds the dye-pack can be surrounded above and below with legitimate money for authenticity purposes. The money with the dye pack is given to the robber along with other actual money. When the robber leaves the facility, the dye-pack is activated by an antenna or transmitter near the exit. At that point, the dye-pack is then programmed to activate within a pre-determined period of time. When the dye-pack activates, a thick, indelible ink explodes from the pack, covering the money, the robber, and anything else near the explosion with a colored ink. In some cases, the dye-pack may also include some form of CS or tear gas, rendering the robber helpless for a brief amount of time. With the use of these devices, the financial institution forfeits the money in the hope of apprehending the offender. Some banking organizations refrain from the use of dye-packs due to the threat of violence. In the event the dye-pack is programmed to explode immediately or malfunctions, the possibility of the robber returning to the bank and assaulting or shooting the employees exists. Financial institutions conduct research as to the positive and negative attributes with the use of any silent-alarm and security device. The training of the employee is an essential element for the successful use of these devices as well as avoiding unwanted or accidental activations, creating false alarms.

Closed-Circuit Television Systems (CCTV)

Even though closed-circuit television systems (CCTV) are not specifically required by the Bank Protection Act of 1968, many financial organizations understand the value of these devices. CCTV systems are a great asset to have in the event of robberies, burglaries, and thefts. These systems, when properly used, allow the organization the opportunity to see the events that previously took place. As stated earlier in the book, CCTV systems may be used in different applications. The organization must understand not only the operation of the system but what the cameras will be able to view (area) and the clarity of the recording. In the event of a criminal act, the financial institution and law enforcement authorities will rely on the recordings as a key element of the investigation. The images recorded cannot only assist to prove or disprove the guilt or innocence of a suspect but can be shared with other businesses in a proactive manner. These images can help other financial institutions, businesses, and the general public to possibly identify the suspect and contact the proper law enforcement authority for apprehension.

A key component of a CCTV system is the placement (location) of the cameras. The financial institution and their CCTV system supplier must work together in determining where the cameras will be placed to afford the best potential picture of the activities. Frequently, cameras will be mounted to record the activities at each teller's window. In addition, cameras may be placed at all entrances to view all individuals entering and exiting the facility. Cameras may also be placed in all rooms containing a safe or where the counting and transfer of cash takes place. If the facility has a vault, cameras may be placed outside the vault and if the device is constructed to permit the cabling and power supplies in the building, placed inside the vault as well. In larger buildings and facilities, the financial organization must also determine any other sensitive or critical areas that they may determine the need of CCTV cameras. If automatic teller machines (ATMs) are used (either on-site or off-site), cameras should be placed outside to view the activity at these machines and/or mounted inside the ATM to view the individual coming up to the device. Elevator lobbies, common areas, or hallways can be locations where cameras may be placed to record the events taking place.

Diligent and regular inspection of the camera systems is also essential. An inspection schedule should be developed and followed to ensure all components of the CCTV system are in proper working order. In the event that part of the system is malfunctioning, the immediate repair of the device must be a top priority. Because financial institutions experience a continuous threat of robbery and theft, the upkeep of the CCTV system is essential to properly record any and all criminal actions or activities.

Access Control

Maintaining a safe work environment in financial institutions is greatly enhanced by controlling the access into the building. As covered previously in the text, there are various methods of access control that can assist to deter unwanted entry into a facility. Financial institutions are no different. All employee and service entrances should be locked at all times. Depending on the location of the financial institution and the budget for security, protecting the non-public entry doors can be done with card access systems, electronic locking systems, or simple locks. Doors may also be required to have "crash bars" or "fail-safe" locking devices in the event of a fire. The facility needs to verify these life safety requirements prior to determining the locking and access devices that will be used on the non-public exterior doors.

Access control options are also available for the public entrances and the interior of the facility. At the entrance, normal glass or a Plexiglas-style door can be used, allowing normal entrance and exit. In some circumstances, revolving doors are installed that aid in maintaining an orderly flow of incoming and outgoing traffic. In some cases a second set of glass or Plexiglas doors are installed, creating a vestibule at the entrance. Vestibules are advantageous to help with climate control, offering access to an automatic teller machine (ATM) and the slowing of traffic to help with viewing customers on CCTV systems. In extreme cases, the vestibule can be transformed into a **man-trap**, in the event of a robbery. Man-traps involve an electronic access control system manually operated by the employees to lock both the interior and exterior doors. When the system is activated, the would-be robber cannot leave the vestibule or enter back into the building. Man-traps can be extremely hazardous if they are not properly designed, installed, utilized. Man-traps can be made of bullet resistant (BR) glass for the doors and any windows. In the event a criminal is detained in the trap, the BR glass can withstand the attack of the weapon depending on the construction and the manufacturer's guidelines. The frames of the doors and windows must also be constructed of steel that can also withstand an attack. These systems are not without fault or concern for safety. To properly activate the system, the bank employee must time the departure of the criminal before they reach the exterior doors. Another major concern is additional customer traffic entering or leaving the facility. If the man-trap is activated with an innocent customer also inside the vestibule, an unwanted assault or hostage situation may ensue. Many financial institutions avoid using man-traps due to the threat of innocent lives being injured. To control the access of the public entrance, it may be most beneficial to have an entryway designed to slow the incoming or outgoing traffic, allowing for the recording of the activity on the CCTV system.

Access control may also be used inside the facility to allow not only for an orderly progression to the employee's station or teller's window, but for the proper recording of the customer by the CCTV system. Portable crowd control stations with ropes, chains, or nylon straps can be used to direct the traffic leading to the teller's window. Although these devices are not solid and can be easily compromised, most customers will abide with the devices and follow the designated pathway to the counter. Again, these devices not only help to maintain an orderly flow of pedestrian traffic but can greatly assist with the recording of the customer's activity on the CCTV system.

A final concept of access control deals with the personal interactions of the bank employees. In some cases where a high threat of criminal activity exists, the financial institution may use bullet resistant glass to separate the employee and the customer at the teller window. A slot may be constructed to allow the passage of small items but not large enough for a firearm to fit. In these circumstances, the financial institution must also consider the protection of all employees working in the area of the teller line. If their threat of crime is great enough to encase the teller stations with BR glass, then receptionists, personal bankers, or other employees must also be physically protected from harm. The concept of interior access control and protection must be designed to ensure that the employee or another customer does not become a victim of a violent act.

Burglar Alarm Systems

Burglar alarm systems can serve multiple purposes in a financial institution. These alarm systems may incorporate the silent hold-up alarm systems as well as the anti-theft devices potentially installed within a safe or vault. The burglar alarm system can also be the mechanism for duress alarms that are activated from the keypad. The financial institution must decide the extent of the use of a burglar alarm system and what they wish to protect. The typical or common burglar alarm components can detect doors opening, movement, breaking glass, or sound. As explained earlier in the text, all of the components in the burglar alarm system can be monitored by an outside source. This source can be part of the security department working directly for the institution or a third-party contract agency. The system can also be programed to track when the alarm has been activated and deactivated. This ability to track the "opening and closing signals" can be beneficial to record the activities of the employees to ensure the facility is safe from criminal or illegal activities.

As with any electronic security component, all aspects of the burglar alarm system must be regularly tested and inspected to ensure proper operation. This inspection requires each component of the system to be activated, verified that the alarm signal is properly transmitting to the monitoring center, and then reset for use. If a component of the alarm system is not working properly, then a repair should take place as soon as possible. In some cases, if a component of the alarm system is inoperable, the employees will not be able to turn on the alarm. This allows the facility to address the malfunction as soon as possible. The financial institution will determine the frequency of the inspections. Even though these inspections can be time-consuming, it is a vital part of the security operation. The burglar alarm can be used as part of the outer defenses and inner defenses to protect the facility. The importance of this system, especially when combined with the hold-up, duress, vault, and safe protection, makes the burglar alarm system one of the primary defenses against harm or loss.

Security Personnel

Utilizing proprietary or contract security personnel can assist with the protection of financial institutions. Security officers dressed in a military style or a softer corporate style of uniform can present a physical deterrent against illegal or unwanted activity. Depending on the needs of the financial institution and the amount of crime in the area, security officers can be armed or unarmed. Many organizations frown upon arming security personnel based in part of the concern that an officer carrying a firearm could deter customers.

It is important for the institution to understand the pros and cons of arming security officers and the impact it may have on business.

Security personnel can also serve as customer service representatives, monitor alarms, conduct rounds of the facility (both inside and outside), be responsible for testing the security equipment, escort employees to and from their vehicles, and be the first line of defense against unwanted activities. For larger institutions, management may have security officers at their headquarters and then make the decision to staff branch locations as needed or have officers make vehicular rounds of the branches.

Perhaps the largest deterrent to employing security personnel is the cost. All security personnel must be properly trained, licensed, and insured. In addition, the cost for uniforms and equipment must also be taken into consideration. These costs are combined with the price for the security personnel's wages and benefits. It is extremely important that the security personnel show their value constantly. They must stay busy and productive at all times to prove their value. In far too many circumstances, when an organization looks at ways to save money and reduce expenses, the security personnel are often considered. Therefore, for security personnel to be maintained and valued by the organization (by any organization, not just financial institutions), the employees must continually "prove their worth" by working hard and contributing to the mission of the financial institution.

Cyber Defenses

Threats to the financial institution come from a physical presence but also from a virtual theat. Today's financial institutions are constantly threatened by cyberattacks. These attacks may come from disgruntled or disloyal employees or by outsiders seeking to profit from the financial institution. The cyber criminals may attempt to conduct illegal transfers of funds or steal client lists, as well as commandeer customer information that can be eventually used for identity fraud.

As stated previously in the text, it is essential for financial institutions to install and maintain the proper and essential cybersecurity methods and equipment. Routers, firewalls, and the most recent security software must be incorporated, updated, and maintained. The threat of a cyberattack is real in today's society. Criminals and deviants both inside and outside the financial institution are constantly seeking ways to break through cyber defenses and take information for their own person use or to illegally sell to a third party. Financial institutions must be constantly vigilant to maintain and ensure the protection of electronic data. Without management making these protective efforts a priority, the threat of becoming a victim of a cyberattack increases exponentially every day.

Employee Training

The training of employees so that they know and understand security procedures is mandated by the Bank Protection Act of 1968. It is the responsibility of the bank security officer (security executive) or their designee to ensure the training is conducted on a regular basis and meets or exceeds the requirements of the federal government. These federal requirements call for the employees to know "their responsibilities under the security program and in proper employee conduct during and after a robbery, burglar or larceny" (FDIC, n.d.). In addition to teaching the elements of compliance to the Bank Protection Act of 1968, the employees should also be trained in safety measures, observational skills, the use of the alarm equipment, and how to personally conduct themselves during a robbery. A robbery is a very stressful situation that can develop rapidly and without warning. Through the regular training of employees on how to conduct themselves in the event of a robbery, employees can potentially alert the authorities to a robbery in progress, obtain a physical description of the perpetrator, and most importantly, ensure their personal safety and well-being as well as that of their co-workers and customers.

Employees need to know proper compliance and procedures after a robbery, burglary, or larceny takes place. Employees will need to follow all internal and governmental procedures for notification and reporting of the incident. Through the efforts of the bank security officer and the local, state, or federal law enforcement agencies, the proper review of all first-hand accounts, written reports, and all CCTV footage can take place. With this information, other financial institutions can be notified of the event and the general public can be alerted in an attempt to identify the culprit and bring him or her to justice. This coordinated effort starts with the regular training of employees in security procedures in order to maintain safety, gather information on the perpetrator(s) and apprehend the criminal. The unfortunate reality is that these incidents cannot be avoided, but through proper training, education, and compliance, the employees and customers can remain safe and minimize the trauma of such an event.

Private/Public Partnerships

The need for private and public partnerships is never more apparent than with the protection of financial institutions. The mandates required by the

Bank Protection Act of 1968 call for bank security employees and law enforcement agencies to work together in the aftermath of a criminal incident or event. Regular communication and interaction between the bank security representatives and the law enforcement communities builds trust, discovers commonalities between the groups, and results in better working relationships. These positive attributes can be imperative when conducting investigations on incidents such as the circulation of counterfeit monies, fraud and embezzlement cases, and bank robberies and burglaries. The professional relationships developed by these interactions will help to better protect the community as a whole as well as the individual financial institutions.

Conclusion

Historically, financial institutions have been targets for criminals and criminal enterprises. These institutions hold a tremendous amount of currency and valuable items of their customers. Through the guidelines developed by the federal government, the efforts of the bank security officers, and continual cooperation with law enforcement authorities, financial institutions work to reduce the number of unwanted attacks. With the added threat of cyber criminals seeking to steal the institution's data for fraudulent acts, financial institutions must now be vigilant to protect against electronic attacks, as well as illegal activities by employees. These threats show no sign of slowing or stopping, making the need for security in financial institutions a continued priority today and for the future.

Case Study — The Duress Alarm

On a quiet Saturday morning, a bank employee walked up to the employee door of the building to get into the location and open for business. As she approached the door, a man came out from behind the bushes and threatened her with violence if she did not open the door, let him inside, and unlock the safe so he could steal the money. The employee remembered her security training and opened the door and deactivated the alarm using the silent duress code, alerting the company monitoring the alarm. In a short period of time, local law enforcement officials arrived on the scene and the perpetrator then took the employee as a hostage. After a few hours of tense negotiation, the trained law enforcement negotiators convinced the perpetrator to give up, leave the bank employee unharmed, and come out of the facility.

After reading this chapter on financial institution security, what else could the bank security officer and the banking corporation do to protect the employee and avoid this potentially tragic incident? Given your current knowledge of electronic security, what other types of security devices could be installed to protect and monitor the situation?

Discussion Question — The Use of Dye Packs

Dye packs are a device that can be used to apprehend criminals after they carry out a bank robbery. After reading the chapter on the use of dye packs to protect financial institutions, answer the follow questions:

- What are the positive aspects of the use of dye packs?
- What are the negative aspects of the use of dye packs?
- If you were a security consultant, would you recommend that financial institutions use dye packs at their locations? Why or why not?

Research Focus — The Bank Protection Act of 1968

Go onto the Internet and search "The Bank Protection Act of 1968," through the United States Federal Deposit Insurance Corporation (FDIC). After reading the act and the information, answer the following questions:

- What aspects of the act are the most relevant for the protection of modern-day financial institutions?
- Do you feel any of the details are outdated for today's society?
- If you were to testify before the United States Congress regarding the current relevance of this act, what would you tell the representatives? Would you make any recommendations for adding or deleting specific aspects?

Key Terms

The Bank Protection Act of 1968	Bank security officer	Robbery
Burglary	Employee theft	Fraud
Counterfeit currency	Vaults	Safes
Hold-up alarms	Duress alarms	Panic alarm
Money clips	Dye packs	

Sources

Avery, R. (n.d.). *America's first bank robber.* Retrieved from http://www.ushistory.org/carpentershall/history/robbery.htm, February 23, 2015.

Collins, P. A., Ricks, T. A., & Van Meter, C. W. (2000). *Principles of security and crime prevention* (4th ed.). Cincinnati, OH: Anderson Publishing Company.

Federal Deposit Insurance Corporation (FDIC). (n.d.). Part 326—*Minimum security devices and procedures and bank secrecy act compliance.* Retrieved from https://www.fdic.gov/regulations/laws/rules/2000-4900.html

Okomo, C. (n.d.) *Top 5 most notorious U.S. bank robbers.* Retrieved from http://www.mybanktracker.com/news/2011/03/05/top-5-notorious-bank-robbers/ http://vault.fbi.gov/barker-karpis-gang. February 25, 2015.

Underwriters Laboratories. (n.d.). *Our mission: Working for a safer world.* Retrieved from http://ul.com/aboutul/our-mission/

Underwriters Laboratories. (n.d.). *UL standards.* Retrieved from http://ul-standards.ul.com/standard/?id=687

United States Secret Service. (n.d.). *Mission statement.* Retrieved from http://www.secretservice.gov/mission.shtml

Chapter Ten

Helping the Healing Process: Hospital and Healthcare Security

Introduction

As the median age of the world's population continues to increase and people continue to live longer lives, the need for hospitals and healthcare facilities grows. The unfortunate reality is that these facilities can be ripe for crime and abuse. According to the American Hospital Association, in 2013 there were approximately 5,686 hospitals in the United States, offering over 914,000 staffed beds for patients (American Hospital Association, n.d.). The role of security becomes a vital aspect to protect patrons, visitors, and employees from harm or loss. Security departments and security-related services face continual challenges from a number of areas. The field of healthcare security can be considered one of the most complex and difficult areas to work within the private security industry today.

Learning Objectives

In this chapter, the reader will be introduced to challenges facing today's security professionals in the healthcare arena. In addition, specific areas of concern for security departments will be covered as well as protective measures to achieve a safe environment. The chapter will conclude with the role of training and certification for this field as well as a healthcare related case study, discussion topic, and research focus.

The Complexity of the Healthcare Environment

Working within a healthcare facility can be a stressful experience. Patients enter the facility for a variety of reasons ranging from wellness appointments to life-threatening conditions. With this wide range of reasons for coming into a healthcare facility also comes a wide range of emotions of the patients, their families, and visitors. These emotions can cause people to act out of character depending on the situation they face. People can be joyous at the birth of a healthy baby or the success of a medical treatment or procedure. People can be faced with great amounts of stress or anxiety when waiting for a diagnosis, the results of a complicated surgery, or for a patient's health to improve. Also, grief and despair may result from a terminal diagnosis, learning a friend or loved one is in the facility for treatment, or finding out that a patient passed away. These life events result in an emotionally turbulent environment on a continual basis. The events can also take a relatively calm and rational person and totally change his or her disposition and mind-set.

This highly emotional working environment can take a toll on the employees as well. Even well-trained workers can be affected by the constant ebb and flow of these ever-changing emotional environments. Employees can also be stressed by their personal working conditions. If the facility or department is understaffed, the increased work load can create pressure on the people working that shift. In the event there are labor issues or is unrest between the employees and the administration, attitudes may shift depending on feelings of loyalty or job security. Finally, healthcare facilities are continuously facing financial pressures to provide quality service for their patients while attempting to manage the ever-increasing cost of healthcare and managing a solvent and efficient operation. These financial stresses can result in changes in staffing and the equipment used to treat patients. These changes may not always be for the better but could force reductions in the equipment or staffing levels. These internal and external stresses can only worsen with the threat of acts of crime, violence, and dishonestly. For these reasons, working in a healthcare facility can be an emotional and mental challenge. Security employees must be aware of these factors and properly trained and supported to professionally handle these situations and be a help, not a hindrance.

Workplace Challenges

All working environments have challenges that security personnel must face. These challenges are frequently specific to that particular job, corporation, or industry. As previously stated, the healthcare industry can be an intense environment for anyone to work in. In addition to the institutional pressures, security employees must also be aware of specific challenges that can impact how these facilities are protected.

The first challenge revolves around privacy. Patients have legal rights to privacy under the Health Insurance Portability and Accountability Act of 1996, also known as **HIPAA** (U.S. Department of Health and Human Services, n.d.). Under this federal legislation, all patient information must be kept in confidence and cannot be disclosed without proper authorization. It is the responsibility for the healthcare institution to ensure that all employees understand the privacy rights of patients and the methods for keeping this information secure. In the event of a breach of a patient's privacy and their rights to privacy, the United States Department of Health and Human Service's Office for Civil Rights can become involved by investigating the claim. The agency can review the HIPAA compliance of the healthcare institution and recommend training and education to prevent future compliance issues. In the event of a possible criminal violation, the United States Department of Justice may become involved to investigate and seek formal charges (U.S. Department of Health and Human Services, n.d.).

Institutional politics may also create added stress on security departments and their efforts. Corporate missions, personal agendas, and individuals' mindsets can create a difficult environment for a security department that is entrusted to serve and protect. These corporate ideologies and personal opinions can have a direct and indirect effect on security operations. Some of these policies and opinions could make the enforcement of rules and regulations more difficult or challenging. The security department must work to remain diplomatic and professional when dealing with institutional politics. The security department must focus on their departmental goals and objectives and provide the best quality of protection to all within the institution. Institutional politics can derail and cloud objectivity and the professionalism needed to properly serve and protect. While it is highly important for security departments to understand their roles within the institution, they also need to know and understand the politics of the organization and adapt accordingly to ensure the proper protection of lives and property.

Another challenge frequently faced by security departments is the justification of their staffing, roles, and resources. The healthcare industry is under constant scrutiny to provide competitive services on an economical or tight budget. Because of this financial pressure, security departments may be forced to expand departmental services to justify their existence. Security departments may take on a "customer service" persona and oversee valet services, parking booth operations, and in some cases, receptionist or operator duties. The reason for this shift is to add additional duties and responsibilities that can coincide with and complement the security mission to protect lives and property. Healthcare facilities are continuously looking to streamline expenses and save money. Many individuals will look at the security department and not fully understand their proactive role of prevention or feel budgetary resources could be better spent in other areas. Because of this skepticism, the security managers and administrators must keep track of all activities and justify that their efforts are helping to create a safe and positive environment for everyone. This is not always an easy task to achieve when external departmental opinions can find fault in security practices or do not understand the benefits of the security department. Taking on additional duties and responsibilities which may coincide with traditional security duties can prove additional justification for a hard-working and highly professional security staff. Security employees must understand and accept that they are "continuously under the organizational microscope" and not let institutional politics dilute their professionalism. The managers and administrators must always be ready to prove and explain the benefits of their departments to the organization's mission so that unnecessary cuts to the budget, resources, and personnel do not take place.

Security departments and their services are vital and important elements of a positive healthcare environment. Members of the security operation must remain continuously professional at all times and be vigilant to provide the best protective services possible to the organization.

Areas of Concern

Healthcare institutions face numerous threats from inside and outside sources. Security departments must keep a watchful eye over these areas as well as receive the necessary training to respond and react to these concerns. The following is an overview that security employees may face while on duty.

Emergency Rooms

Emergency rooms are an area of high stress and potential danger. In many hospital emergency rooms, security personnel are on duty to help maintain a safe and orderly environment. Potential disruptions and threats can come from multiple sources. First, the patient coming in may be a threat due to his or her condition or mental capacity. Patients may come in for treatment and have possible communicable diseases that are highly contagious. Also, other patients may be under the influence of alcohol or drugs that can impede their judgment and influence them to become a threat to the well-being of those around them. Additionally, patients with mental illnesses or mental conditions can be very disruptive and a physical threat to staff, visitors, and other patients. For unruly or out-of-control patients, security personnel may have to assist hospital staff to restrain the patient so they can receive the proper and necessary care.

Visitors and families in the emergency room waiting area may also cause a risk. Due to stresses and anxieties caused by their family member or friend needing care, the visitors may act out and become a threat to those around them. In cases where the emergency room may accept trauma patients, the family members or friends could be under a high amount of stress. In addition, criminal activities that may have caused the patient to be sent to an emergency room could also become a threat to those waiting for other patients. In these cases, those involved in the potential altercation may want to force their way into the treatment area or physically confront others in the waiting area. Because of these threats and the concern for weapons entering the emergency room areas, the security staff may use metal detectors to screen all visitors as well as control access by only allowing immediate family in the waiting area. The threat of violence (either premeditated or unintended) is a real and continuous concern for security personnel. The security staff must be properly trained in restraint procedures, the use of metal detectors, and how to de-escalate potentially violent situations in order to maintain a safe environment.

Maternity/Neo-Natal Units

Maternity centers and neo-natal units are also an area for heightened security. Unlike the emergency rooms, where uniformed security personnel may be needed to maintain an orderly environment, maternity and neo-natal units may require physical security measures and solid access control methods to avoid an unwanted event. In these newborn areas, threats can come from unexpected sources. Mentally ill adults may try to come and take a child thinking that the baby is actually their own, as may non-custodial parents wanting unauthorized custody of the baby. In extreme cases, unauthorized adults may attempt to steal the baby for sale to black-market adoption rings or potential human trafficking conspiracies. No matter what the illegal, immoral, or unwanted rationale may be, healthcare facilities must take great care to limit the access into these units and ensure that only authorized personnel are allowed in the areas.

Hospital Pharmacies and Drug Distribution

Hospital pharmacies and the delivery and transportation of medications are other high-risk areas for concern. The United States Food and Drug Administration strictly regulates the distribution of drugs, many of which are used in a healthcare environment. Even with this regulation and administrative oversight, the actual pharmacy and the transportation of these medicines are a potential target for theft, loss, or illegal use. The pharmacy area can be equipped with access control equipment, alarm devices, and closed-circuit television systems to ensure proper access in the area and a continual recording of events. For the distribution of medications to the patient areas, well-constructed and secure carts may be used. These mobile storage units allow for the necessary transportation and distribution of the patient's medication but also provide the necessary security against the unauthorized appropriation of the substances. Tracking and distribution procedures must also be strictly followed and recorded in accordance with the facility and governmental regulations.

Patient Rooms

Patient rooms are also an area where illegal activities may take place. With the stringent governmental privacy regulations in place, security personnel may be instructed to only enter patient wards on an as-needed basis. Still, the patients can become a victim to the theft of their belongings or the presence of unauthorized visitors. Patient storage containers should be in place with a locking mechanism to prevent an unwanted theft while the patient is out of the room for testing or medical procedures or while they are unconscious or otherwise incapacitated. To prevent unauthorized visitors, the employees must be aware of any suspicious or unwanted activities. In the event an unwanted or unauthorized person or persons are on the floor, security should be notified immediately.

Visitor Access

Coinciding with the control of access within patient areas also comes the control of visitors within the facility. The security department may have a direct role with the access control of visitors and their guidance and assistance.

Security departments may be involved with the staffing of visitor information centers as well as visitor access stations. Depending on the policies of the specific healthcare facility, visitor access control can include the issuing of temporary access control or identification badges or removable stickers, escorting visitors to and from specific areas, providing wheelchair services for incapacitated visitors, and the locking/unlocking and monitoring of visitor access points at the predetermined time. Security must be aware of visiting hours as well as specific areas in the facility that may allow extended or continual visitation. Consistent and courteous customer service is vital for assisting visitors and maintaining a professional environment.

Employee Locker Rooms

Employee locker rooms are another area of potential loss and concern for security. In these areas, employees store personal belongings and valuables while on duty. Any and all authorized employees may have access to these locker rooms. Protecting these areas can be a challenging task. The security staff must respect the employee's privacy while in the locker rooms and avoid using electronic recording equipment. If the security staff desires to conduct patrols in these areas, they must ensure that the proper gender enters the designated areas. In most cases, employees are encouraged to use self-protective measures such as locking all doors with a padlock and avoiding bringing expensive items to work. Another concern for security in these areas is the potential threat of illegal activities by employees in these areas. Illegal drug activity and sales, harassment or abuse of fellow employees, and thefts may take place. In these situations, the security staff must wait until reports of the activities are made. Any attempt to conduct a prolonged investigation due to illegal or unwanted activities must be treated with extreme care and caution. Qualified legal representatives should be consulted as well as labor union officials if the employees are unionized. These areas should be locked with some type of access control system to ensure that only those with legitimate need and access may enter into the locker rooms.

Parking Lots and Garages

Parking lots and parking garages can be an area of concern for security personnel. These areas may be open to the public or limited for employee use only. Continual foot or vehicle patrols and the use of access control and closed-circuit television systems are recommended to help protect people, vehicles, and belongings. Since many healthcare facilities are a 24/7 operation, additional measures can be taken to help protect employees and visitors as they leave and enter. Emergency phones or call boxes can help to alert security personnel to an unwanted event. In addition, the security staff should offer escorts to and from parking areas for both employees and visitors upon request. Also, the parking areas should be very well lit during times of darkness or in all areas that do not have natural lighting. Parking lots and ramps should be considered a high-risk area for crime and violence. The proper patrol and oversight of activities in these areas must be a continuous and vigilant effort to avoid unwanted injury or loss.

Satellite Locations

Another important area that may be in need of protection are the healthcare facilities' off-campus or satellite locations. With the competitive growth of the healthcare industry, doctor's offices and treatment facilities may be located in numerous locations. These facilities may not be in close proximity to the main medical center and the security staff. Policies need to be in place determining how the healthcare organization will protect these locations. Some of these sites require little or no assistance for protection while others are constantly under the threat of danger. The healthcare institution will need to determine how to protect these facilities and to what extent. Some locations will require full-time security personnel and electronic security systems, others may only require a routine patrol stop by a security officer to maintain a visible presence, and some can rely solely on basic access control and security measures to protect lives and property. These locations cannot and should not be ignored or discounted. Any unwanted or illegal event can still be the responsibility of the healthcare organization and facilities are in need of proper security policies, procedures, and protective measures.

The threats to healthcare facilities are numerous and distinctive. The security department must take great care to identify and protect against these concerns. Security personnel and their professional colleagues must remain proactive and ever vigilant to deter these deviant acts that can harm patients, visitors, employees, and the infrastructure of the organization.

Protective Measures

Training

The concept of training employees to be aware of potential threats and dangers must be an ongoing effort. The security department and their employees should have regular training and review of any issues that may pose a threat to lives and property. All new employees should receive training, which includes formal classroom education as well as training with qualified employees throughout the facility. This new employee training is critical not only to provide the basic education of the employee but to set a positive tone for professional demeanor, conduct, and expectations.

The continual training of the security staff can be maintained through smaller educational segments during a pre-shift briefing or formally during department meetings. Policies, procedures, legal concerns, and medical conditions should be reviewed. With the wide-scale list of threats and concerns that the security department may encounter while on duty, employee training becomes the cornerstone for quality service.

Another area of importance is the training of the healthcare facility's employees on basic security methods and procedures. Employees should be encouraged to maintain a diligent demeanor to protect against the threat of loss and the possible violation of the patients' rights, as well as visitors' rights. This training should be designed to create an environment of positive awareness for the employees and not general fear or panic. Employees can be briefed on how to contact security for assistance, where emergency call boxes may be located, and how to recognize potential concerns. This attitude of "total security responsibility" is a proactive measure that is intended to protect all personnel in the facility and keep them safe from harm. This is intended to be a proactive method of protection that can raise positive awareness to protect lives and property. All training (of both security staff and employees) needs to be well developed, professional, and in accordance with the mission and legalities of the healthcare institution.

Security Staffing

The role of security staffing has evolved over the past twenty years. Security professionals in the healthcare industry still have the primary mission of protecting lives and property but the addition of customer service responsibilities offers added benefits for staffing and budgets. The primary role of security to "observe and report" does not necessarily apply to the healthcare industry. Depending on the location and risk factors within the facility, the security leadership and administration may decide to have officers equipped with firearms as well as empower them with limited abilities to detain and arrest. These added security enforcement measures can be very controversial with the leadership and employees of the facility. To some, having armed security personnel or a quasi-police force can be a deterrent and set a negative tone for employees, patients, and visitors. Yet others will argue that these security officers are necessary based on the location of the facility and the potential for violent incidents that could occur. If a security department and the administration make the educated decision to arm security officers or afford them limited powers of arrest, the institution must ensure that all legal conditions are met, the proper liability protections are in place, and the officers are well trained. Any and all training must be conducted by qualified instructors and detailed training documentation must be kept in the security administrator's office.

For some healthcare institutions, the use of a proprietary security staff (in-house) remains the norm. These institutions believe that the officers working directly for the institution offer a higher level of personal service, employee loyalty, and lower employee turnover. These proprietary security staffs may pay a higher wage for their security staff but also require high levels of training for all employees. For some institutions, qualifying employees may be eligible for paid time off as well as healthcare or retirement benefits. These added benefits can help to improve employee morale but can be extremely expensive for healthcare institutions that are continuously under budget constraints.

Contract security officers can be a major budgetary advantage for healthcare security departments. For some healthcare facilities, all members of the security department, including supervisors and managers, can be outsourced to a security company. When a contract security agency is used, all of the payroll, insurance, and tax responsibilities are the obligation of the contract security agency. The healthcare facility and the contract security agency will approve a contractual agreement that can include the hourly rates for the contract officers, supervisors, or managers; the number hours of staffing to be supplied per week; and in some cases, the defined pay scales for the security employees. Another area of concern is the required training of contract security employees. This can be another point of negotiation and contractual agreement between the healthcare facility and the contract security agency. Security personnel can be expected to have particular training prior to working in the healthcare facility (such as basic first aid and CPR certifications). Other areas of training can take place at the healthcare facility and can include classroom and on-the-job training. The largest benefit to contracting employee security services is the cost savings afforded to the healthcare institution. At the same time, the healthcare institution must clearly define all expectations of the contract security service, including staffing levels, training expectations, supervision and oversight (also known as quality control), and any other services or equipment to be provided by the agency.

Over the past ten to fifteen years, healthcare organizations have been utilizing a hybrid security staff, comprised of both proprietary and contract security personnel. In these security departments, staffing levels of in-house versus contract officers can be determined by position. For example, the security department management and supervision may be staffed by full-time hospital employees and the security officers are supplied by a contract security agency. In other circumstances, all security management, supervision, and officers protecting the internal facility are hospital employees while the protection of parking lots and ramps are outsourced to a security agency. These hybrid departments can provide expected levels of oversight by the internal security employees while assisting to reduce costs by employing more affordable contracted employees. It is essential that all individuals and both organizations have detailed and well-documented expectations of duties, responsibilities, training, and oversight. As the healthcare industry continues to seek ways to provide reliable services in the most cost-efficient way possible, the security department will be asked to find new and innovative ways to meet these organizational goals.

Physical Security Measures

Physical security plays an important role in the protection of healthcare facilities. Closed-circuit television systems, access control systems, radio frequency identification devices, and metal detectors can assist in avoiding unwanted occurrences. Alarm systems can also be of assistance to detect unwanted entry or exit. Primarily, many alarm systems are monitored by the security staff at a central station area. For satellite locations, the administration may decide to have those facilities monitored by a contract alarm company. This rationale is because the security staff may not have adequate staffing to respond to alarms and their duties and responsibilities may be confined to the immediate campus of the hospital. The outsourcing of alarm services allows the local police to be notified in the instance of a legitimate alarm signal, providing a potentially faster response time.

There is no "one-size-fits-all" standard for electronic security systems for healthcare facilities. The type of device to be used will be determined by the need of the department or location in the facility. The determination may be decided by multiple departments including security, facilities management, and the specific department needing the physical security protection. It is important that all employees understand the operation of the devices and who to contact in the event of an alarm. Even with continuous activities and twenty-four-hour personnel on duty, physical security systems can be an enhancement to protect against unwanted occurrences such as the theft of pharmaceuticals, the abduction of infants, the accidental exit of patients with mental health issues, the theft of belongings, and the physical assault of em-

Person Going Through Metal Detector © Monkey Business via fotolia.com

ployees, patients, or visitors. It is vitally important for the security department to work with all potentially affected departments to design physical security controls that are appropriate, effective, and cost efficient.

Professional Organizations and Certifications

As highlighted in the chapter, training and education are extremely important in the field of healthcare security. Security departments must remain vigilant to ensure their employees are properly trained in all necessary rules, regulations, and procedures that impact duties and responsibilities. The leadership overseeing the security department must also stay abreast of any changes or enhancements to healthcare security education.

Many healthcare establishments or corporations seek accreditation from an oversight organization to maintain quality, professionalism, and proper care. When an organization seeks accreditation, it is looking to earn approval or certifications to the standards and policies set forth by that professional entity. In the healthcare industry, many organizations and hospitals seek the approval from the Joint Commission on Accreditation of Healthcare Organizations, better known as **JCAHO**. Established in 1951, JCAHO is an independent and non-profit organization dedicated to quality healthcare in a safe, professional, and well-managed environment. The organization offers numerous accreditations and certifications, along with industry standards and guidelines (JCAHO, n.d.). These standards also have an impact on the security department. JCAHO also reviews emergency procedures and policies as well as safety standards. These are areas in which the security department has a direct involvement for the betterment of the healthcare organization as a whole (JCAHO, n.d.). Certification and accreditation from JCAHO remains a coveted and highly sought credential in the United States.

A valued organization pertaining to professionalism and training in the healthcare security industry is the International Association for Healthcare Security and Safety, referred to as **IAHSS**. The mission of this organization is to provide training and credentialing opportunities to both security officers and security administrators. These training and credentialing opportunities include basic and advanced training for security officers, basic and advanced training for administrators, and certifications for security personnel. The training and educational process calls for detailed knowledge in a myriad of healthcare security areas such as patient interaction, methods of patrol, liability, and critical incident response for security officers, as well as topics for supervisors that include leadership, authority and control, and employee relations (IAHSS, n.d.). Healthcare security administrators can apply for and take the proper testing to become a Certified Healthcare Protection Administrator, or **CHPA**. Those achieving and earning this distinction illustrate a high level of knowledge and efficiency in healthcare security and safety (IAHSS, n.d.). These exams can be a tremendous benefit to the security employee and their healthcare institution. These individual exams and certifications should be welcomed and accepted as a part of the security education process but not relied upon as the only method of continuing education for the department as a whole.

Continued training and education is essential for any security employee, program, and organization. These healthcare industry-specific training and certifications illustrate a high level of commitment and professionalism in the mission to provide excellent care for all patients and a professional environment for visitors and employees.

Conclusion

Security in the healthcare industry can be an essential component of the mission to deliver quality patient care. Working within an extremely volatile and potentially stressful environment, security personnel must remain vigilant, patient, and professional when working in this field. It is essential for security professionals to stay up to date on any threats or concerns within the healthcare facility and do whatever they can to assist and show their value to the organization's administrators.

Avoiding complacency and working hard every day and every shift is a necessity. Because of the constant concern of budgetary constraints, the security managers must not take anything for granted. They must work hard to prove the value in their department and be efficient with any budgets granted to them. Security leaders must look for efficient ways to manage their departments, including through staffing, training, and equipment. If security leaders attempt to continue with a "status quo" approach in their management styles, they may find themselves losing funding and resources. This fiscal reality must be realized and accepted in this highly competitive industry.

Even with all the stresses and pressures that are continuously present in this environment, the job can be extremely gratifying and humbling. Working to protect people who may be facing either joy, uncertainty, or despair can take an emotional toll on any employee. The healthcare security employee must remember that not only are they there to protect lives and property but to serve as a goodwill ambassador by exercising superior public relations. These challenges and rewards make the field of healthcare security different from many other industries. The challenges will continue to grow and change as the healthcare field advances to provide the best care possible to a growing client population.

Case Study — The Confused Patron

A mid-sized medical center was faced with a continuous problem. An elderly woman was regularly coming into the facility and trying to go to the maternity floor to see "her baby." The gentle and unassuming woman would talk to employees, trying to convince them that her baby was in the nursery department and she needed to take the child home. As time went on, the staff at the maternity center and the security department learned that the woman was a former volunteer at the facility and did indeed give birth to a child there years previously. The elderly woman was suffering from mental impairment and believed she was living in the past. To complicate matters, she would wear her volunteer's uniform and was often unnoticed coming into the facility. After thinking about this problem, answer the following questions:

1.   What kind of a threat or risk does this elderly woman pose to the healthcare facility?
2.   What type of problems could she pose to the maternity center?

3. How should the security department confront and deal with this woman?
4. How can this problem and distraction be stopped and avoided in the future?

Discussion Topic—Security or Customer Service?

Throughout this chapter the term "customer service" has been presented. For some working in the security field, this concept may be difficult to grasp and understand. Some people believe that the role of security is to protect, be a deterrent, and intervene when there are problems. If you were serving as a security manager for a healthcare facility how would you explain the following concepts to your security staff:

1. The importance of customer service
2. The need for tactful enforcement methods
3. How customer service and tactful enforcement could make their jobs easier

Research Focus—The Emergency Room

In this chapter the very complicated, difficult, and volatile area of emergency rooms was discussed. Logging onto the Internet, search the phrase "emergency room security." After looking at multiple web sources, answer the following questions:

1. What kind of challenges or incidents within an emergency room were found?
2. What type of physical security devices could be used to help protect those in an emergency room or emergency center?
3. How can security departments better protect the patients, visitors, and employees working in this area?

Key Terms

HIPAA	JCAHO	IAHSS
CHPA		

Sources

American Hospital Association. (n.d.). *Fast facts on US hospitals—2014.* Retrieved from http://www.aha.org/research/rc/stat-studies/fast-facts.shtml

International Association for Healthcare Security and Safety. (n.d.). *IAHSS mission and goals.* Retrieved from http://iahss.org/About/Mission-Goals.asp

International Association for Healthcare Security and Safety. (n.d.). *IAHSS training: Our training programs.* Retrieved from http://iahss.org/Training/Default.asp

United States Department of Health and Human Services. (n.d.). *Health information privacy.* Retrieved from http://www.hhs.gov/ocr/privacy/hipaa/understanding/index.html

United States Department of Health and Human Services. (n.d.). *Enforcement process.* Retrieved from http://www.hhs.gov/ocr/privacy/hipaa/enforcement/process/index.html

The Joint Commission. (n.d.). *About the joint commission.* Retrieved from http://www.jointcommission.org/about_us/about_the_joint_commission_main.aspx

Chapter Eleven

Protecting the K-16 Process: School, College, and University Security

Introduction

According to the advocacy website stoptheshootings.org, there have been 387 shooting incidents at schools, colleges, and universities in the United States. During this period of time, 59% of the victims were between the ages of 10 to 19 and 69% of the shooters were between the ages of 12 to 19. Two of the youngest shooters and youngest victims were at the former Buell Elementary School in Mt. Morris, Michigan. In this tragic event, a six-year-old brought a handgun to school and shot another six-year-old in front of a teacher and 22 students (stoptheshootings.org, n.d.).

Schools, colleges, and universities were at one time viewed as safe havens from violence and crime. The unfortunate reality is that these educational facilities are just as vulnerable to crime and violence as any other geographic location in our society. These buildings present an opportunity for crime and violence from students, parents, employees, and community members. The days of looking at schools as community centers which are safe from violence are now over. The challenge upon today's society and the security industry is how to protect these students, educators, and employees from becoming the next tragic story on the news.

Learning Objectives

In this chapter the reader will be introduced to an abbreviated history of school violence in the United States, the complexities of protecting educational buildings, the challenges and threats being faced, and protective measures to deter these incidents. The educational system will be divided into two groups,

K-12 and **higher education** (colleges and universities). The combined groups will be referred to as the K-16 system (kindergarten through a college bachelor's degree). All of these facilities face common threats and concerns but have to approach their protective methods and security procedures in different ways. The chapter will conclude with a case study, discussion topic, and a research focus pertaining to the violence in our K-16 schools and how to better protect the students, educators, staff, and visitors.

The Horrific Past

Recent history shows a dramatic increase in horrifically violent acts in today's education facilities. These terrible events are not a new phenomenon, but rather a problem that has taken place for years. With the shifting of morals and norms among members of society, schools, colleges, and universities no longer appear to be safe havens. In fact, history shows just how these building have devolved from a safe environment to becoming targets. The following is an overview of some of the startling and tragic incidents that have taken place in the American educational system.

Bath, Michigan, School Bombing

In 1927, Andrew Kehoe enacted a plot to protest the potential taxation of the community to raise funds for a new school. Kehoe, a trained electrician, volunteer school handy-man, former town clerk, and member of the school board, reported being very upset that the additional taxes could force him to lose his 80-acre farm. Because of these factors, Kehoe planted hundreds of pounds of dynamite in the basement of the Bath Consolidated School. When Kehoe triggered the explosion, thirty-seven children and one teacher were killed with many more wounded. In addition to the bombing of the school, Kehoe also killed his wife in their home, and set off another explosion, which killed the district superintendent, other officials, and Kehoe himself (Biography.com, n.d.).

West Paducah, Kentucky, Shooting

On December 1, 1997, Michael Carneal, a fourteen-year-old freshman, entered Heath High School with two shotguns, two rifles, and 22-caliber revolver. Carneal wrapped the shotguns and rifles in a blanket, telling people the bundle was a school project. Inside the building, the boy opened fire on a student prayer group. Firing a total of eight shots, he killed three students and injured five others (Stoptheshootings.org, n.d.). He quickly surrendered and was convicted of the crime. The following year, Carneal reached an agreement with prosecutors for the charges and was found guilty but mentally ill (*NY Times*, 1998).

Columbine High School Shootings

In Littleton, Colorado, on April 20, 1999, Eric Harris and Dylan Klebold entered Columbine High School and set down two duffle bags containing bombs. The two left the school and waited for the bombs to detonate. When the bombs failed to activate, Harris and Klebold reentered the school to open fire. The two students killed a total of 13 people and wounded 20 others. They both committed suicide, ending the tragic massacre (History.com, n.d.).

Virginia Tech University

On April 16, 2007, a Virginia Tech senior named Seung-Hui Cho went on a shooting spree at the Blacksburg, Virginia, campus. At 7:15 AM, Cho first shot two students in Ambler-Johnston Hall, a resident living facility. Approximately two and a half hours later at 9:45 AM, Cho again opened fire during a class in Norris Hall, killing thirty-two students and faculty members. The shooter also sent a video tape to NBC News prior to the event with a video manifesto giving his rationale for his actions. The package was opened by NBC employees in the time frame between Cho's first and second round of killings (CNN, 2015). The rampage ended when Cho turned a gun on himself and committed suicide.

Northern Illinois University

On February 14, 2008, Steven Kazmierczak, a former graduate student at Northern Illinois University, entered into a lecture hall and walked onto the stage. He opened up a guitar case and immediately shot the professor next to him and then opened fire on the approximately 150 students in the introduction to geology class. When the shooting ended, six people were dead and 18 were wounded. Kazmierczak took his own life in the lecture hall of the DeKalb, Illinois, university (Gray, 2008).

Sandy Hook Elementary

Mayhem erupted in Newtown, Connecticut, on December 14, 2012, when a mentally ill 20-year-old man named Adam Lanza went on a shooting spree.

Lanza first killed his 52-year-old mother, Nancy, in their home. He then went to Sandy Hook Elementary and shot his way through locked doors equipped with an intercom system for access control into the school. Lanza walked into the school and within eleven minutes killed 20 children and six adult members of the school's staff before taking his own life (CNN.com, 2014).

These horrific and unthinkable killings of innocent lives represent the continuous threat posed in schools, colleges, and universities. Numerous lesser events of violence and anger take place in educational buildings on a regular basis. The past history of these events needs to be treated as a continuous reminder of the threats facing our educational facilities and the need to improve and enhance how these facilities are protected.

The Complexity of the Education Sector

The threats to our schools and educational facilities are vast and ever growing. The security industry must work to lead the effort of protecting the sanctity of our educational institutions. In order to achieve these goals, our society must admit there are dangers that can occur at any moment with all schools and educational institutions and work to keep these lives safe and secure.

One of the first goals and objectives in the protection of our educational facilities is to work to change the **mental mind-set** of our community. This can be a daunting task. In our busy lives, too many people ignore or cannot accept that these facilities can be threatened by an internal or an external attack. Our society must understand that our beloved schools and institutions of higher education are not only sources of knowledge, activities, and community pride but a potential target of violence. The acceptance that these facilities are a potential target of violence will help to motivate and achieve the proper protection of all lives and property.

Another key component to properly protect these facilities is for all internal stakeholders to adapt a proactive approach to the protection of these lives and properties. In the horrific event of a violent incident, our local law enforcement agencies provide stellar response from the calls for help. In addition, the school districts, colleges, and universities have diligently worked with the law enforcement sector to develop appropriate responses to protect innocent lives, if violent acts take place. These well-developed and appropriate responses work to minimize additional potential injuries or loss of life. The unfortunate reality is that these unwanted acts were allowed to take place. Through the development of a preventative or proactive approach to deter these events, the possible incident could be deflected or deterred, thus not requiring the need to initiate the intruder procedures. Our schools' employees are responsible for an enormous amount of duties and responsibilities. We must continue to strive for a mental shift in the mind-set from reactive methods to a proactive approach to protection. This change of mental mind-set puts all of those involved in the educational process on a path to keep the facility safe and does so with the understanding that it is everybody's responsibility to protect these lives.

Another dilemma that takes place in our society can be referred to as the "not in my backyard" attitude. This potentially detrimental frame of mind allows naïve individuals to believe that these school violence issues will not take place where they reside. These individuals may have empathy and feelings of sorrow for other victims, but fail to accept that these horrific occurrences can happen at their educational institutions. This attitude of ignorance or denial greatly weakens any attempt to develop a preventative or proactive approach to protecting these facilities. The reality of the situation is that these events are not a problem solely within inner-city schools or facilities without active law enforcement protection but are systemic to our society as a whole. An attitude of denial only increases the chances that an unwanted or tragic event could occur. Simply stated, the threat to our educational facilities is real and in every community.

Concerns about the number of adults and children with mental illnesses, issues with diagnosis, and the proper care for those afflicted with these conditions is a concern for all segments of society. After reviewing the horrific massacres that have taken place at our schools, colleges, and universities, it is all too easy to say that many of the perpetrators of these events had some form of mental issues. At times, our society ignores the fact that there are millions of people who suffer from some type of mental illness or disorder. According to the National Institute of Mental Health (NIMH), in 2012, it was estimated that approximately 43.7 million adults in the United States (18.6% of the population) suffered from some form of mental illness. The NIMH also reports that according a survey conducted by the Center for Disease Control and Prevention, 13% of children aged 8 to 15 had a diagnosable mental illness. In fact, the NIMH also claims that 46.3% of children aged 13 to 18 will have some prevalence of mental disease in their lifetimes (NIMH, n.d). This information can illustrate the problem mental illness in today's society and the potential concerns, problems, and unwanted acts caused by these individuals (either intended or unintended). With public and/or open access to many of our schools, colleges, and universities, adopting a proactive approach to protecting our students, staff, and visitors can become a vital component to reducing unwanted incidents caused by those suffering from mental illnesses.

For many people in our society, the thought that a violent act could take place in their life does not occur on a regular basis, if at all. While this is an admirable and understandable trait, the unfortunate reality is that those individuals in a position of responsibility within a school, college, or university need to accept the fact that at any given time an unwanted event can occur. Because of this fact, our teachers, instructors, professors, and staff need to become increasingly aware of outside threats and adopt a proactive/preventative mind-set. These people in positions of responsibility should adopt what can be described as "a healthy paranoia." This is not intended to be disrespectful to those suffering from mental illnesses but rather it means keeping a watchful eye out for any irregularities and possible problems while conducting their daily tasks. This awareness can also be referred to as "a gut feeling" when things do not look or seem normal. These individuals in charge are literally the first line of defense to protect the lives with which they are entrusted. Staying vigilant in the event of a potential issue can be a great asset and help them to take immediate action, thereby protecting the lives around them and notifying security or law enforcement officials.

Finally, school districts, colleges, and universities should strongly consider making adjustments to their employee training regarding school security and safety. The current policies and procedures on reacting to potential violence should also include a systemic, proactive component to their training. There is no contesting or questioning the need for emergency procedures to respond to a violent act as well as notify and evacuate the facility. Yet, if employees are regularly trained to understand the importance of a proactive security approach, additional eyes and ears can be conditioned to notice potential problems before they occur. Employee training of this nature should be positive and work to motivate the employees to employ the mind-set of both prevention and reaction. If it is said that "it takes a village to raise a child," then it can be also said that "it takes a village to protect that same child." The security and well-being of these educational facilities is everyone's responsibility and not just that of security and law enforcement personnel.

Primary Educational Facility Protection

In the field of criminal justice and criminal prosecution, it is a belief that children under the age of seven do not have the mental capacity or the ability to distinguish right from wrong. It is also accepted that children between the ages of seven and thirteen have a limited mental capacity to distinguish between right and wrong. Even though this could be argued, the reality is that any person is capable of causing an unwanted or dangerous incident, whether they understand the ramifications or not. The protection of **primary school facilities** (also known as elementary schools) provides certain challenges that middle or junior high schools, high schools, and colleges or universities do not face. While the internal threats of violence from the children are reduced, the threats from the outside are constant. A primary concern and challenge is the need to fight complacency and the mind-set that problems cannot occur. This lack of vigilance opens up opportunities for unwanted events to take place. These sentiments are echoed by university professor and educational scholar Dr. Anne Tapp. Dr. Tapp states, "Our priority needs to always lie with students' safety. Above political correctness, convenience, etc., we need to continuously work toward the best plan and educate our students, school employees, and families on proper protocol" (Anne R. Tapp, personal interview, November 2015).

Threats

Threats to primary schools can come from internal and external sources. As stated above, even though internal threats are few in comparison to middle and high schools, the activities of the children must be monitored and watched for signs of possible violence and unwanted conduct. Students at this age may be inclined to act out or respond to situations from their own personal experiences. These experiences include the actions of their parents and guardians, examples from the media, and behavior learned through electronic or video games. These external influences may influence a child to act in a violent or unwanted manner. Another internal threat may also come from those working with the children in the classroom or as support staff. Even with policy guidelines in place to conduct background checks on school employees, these often minimal investigations may not be able to detect all concerns. Outside influences and stresses on the teachers and staff can also influence behavior and actions. While many would not like to believe that the people who are hired to educate and take care of a student could be a threat, it must be noted that proper and detailed due diligence must take place to ensure that children and other members of the staff are not threatened or harmed by a member of the staff.

External threats in primary schools must be viewed as a constant and potential concern to the well-being of the students and staff. These threats may include individuals like parents or guardians, school volunteers, vendors, other employees of the school district, invited visitors to the school, and members of the general public using the facilities for events or after school activities. Violent or unwanted acts can take place either directly targeting the students and staff or indirectly as a result of other outside issues. Parents involved in custody battles could end up on school property engulfed in a personal conflict, volunteers or visitors could act inappropriately, therefore negatively influencing or disrupting the educational process, and members of the general public may enter for what could be viewed as a legitimate reason then create a harmful or distressing situation. Finally, outsiders with social or mental issues may attempt to gain unauthorized entry into the school to act out in a negative way that can directly or indirectly harm students either physically or psychologically.

It is imperative for the schools and the district's leadership to understand what types of threats may occur and the potential sources of these unwanted acts. The school should be looked upon as a fortress that needs to be protected at all times, thus adopting a **"fortress mentality of protection."** School leadership must accept this reality in order to properly prepare and deter unwanted acts from occurring. While these examples of internal and external threats are not a complete list of possible problems, each school and each district must work to understand the potential sources of unwanted acts that can affect their buildings. Even if a school is located in what is believed to be a safe area, the leadership and staff must understand that these threats are a reality and can occur anywhere at any time. This acceptance of the possibility of problems and their source can reduce the threats and the unwanted acts of violence within the facility.

Preventative Measures

Many schools are already equipped with primary security devices that can be used to help protect the facility. These include locking doors and windows, communication systems such as intercom systems and telephones, as well as lighting for the inside and outside of the building. Continuing with the mindset that the school is a fortress, school leaders and administrators must decide what areas are at risk from an unwanted intrusion or act. The following are examples that can assist in the protective process of these facilities.

The first area of protection is the development of well-thought-out and well-researched policies and procedures. These policies and procedures need to inform the employees on the use of protective devices, and provide notification of possible emergencies, as well as the proper response to an emergency situation. These guidelines and practices must be reviewed at regular intervals to ensure proper understanding of the information, raise awareness to observe potential threats, and teach how to respond to emergencies. The redundancy of the training will assist an appropriate response in the unfortunate circumstance of a threatening situation or attack. The policies and procedures need to be detailed enough so the reader will know how to operate a system or react to a situation but general enough so they are not confusing to the reader. A detailed and user-friendly policy and procedure guide will become the cornerstone for successful protection of lives and property.

Additional physical security measures can enhance the protection of the educational facility. Closed-circuit television systems (CCTV) may be useful as a visible deterrent to a potential perpetrator as well as an avenue to record and capture images of unwanted activities. The difficulty with CCTV systems is not the operation of the devices but the way they are utilized. Without regular and consistent monitoring of the cameras (which schools may not be able to financially afford), the devices fail to be a proactive system and become a reactive system. If the cameras are recording (which is strongly recommended) then the images can be used in internal or external investigations.

Access control systems and the development of controlled entry points can be a great method to deter or delay unwanted acts of harm. Schools should consider incorporating the vestibule access concept used by financial institutions. Visitors enter through designated areas and must be allowed access into the school. This visitor control method can incorporate the use of mechanical locking mechanisms control at a central location as well as formal access control systems. Another key component is the use of doors and windows that can delay or deter forceful entry into the facility. Steel doors combined with bullet resistant glass (or similar components that delays firearms such as glazing or laminates) will allow for school employees to activate appropriate emergency procedures and notify law enforcement authorities. If a vestibule system is used by the school, the perpetrator or unauthorized visitor will not be able to enter into the school or exit in order to find another entry point. While this type of access control system may seem extreme, it can be beneficial to protect the students, teachers, and staff. In addition, other external doors should also be made of components that can delay and deter entry. The use of closed-circuit cameras, automated locking devices, communication systems, and access control components can deter or delay easy entry into the school away from a main entrance.

Alarm systems are recommended to protect the facilities after hours. Many schools (both primary and secondary) have expensive equipment in multimedia or computer rooms as well as the individual class rooms and offices. Alarm systems can also incorporate emergency notification devices that will send a silent signal for emergency assistance. These may be placed in the office areas and in proximity to entrances. Alarm points of protection include all exterior doors, hallways, or intersections and rooms where large amounts of

Smart Lock on Door © chesky via fotolia.com

valuable equipment is placed. Depending on the physical location of the school, the amount of security equipment may vary. In high crime areas, additional equipment may be installed to detect any illegal or unwanted entry to the school. This can become an expensive investment, so school officials should review in detail the possible risks and the need for the location of alarm components.

For some elementary schools, the use of paid security staff may be a viable option. Security staff members can physically operate access control points or in some cases act as greeters working to allow authorized entry and exit into the school. The security staff can also conduct patrols of the facility (both inside and outside) looking for possible violations of security procedures as well as the observation of potential threatening circumstances. Security staff members can be a great assistance to the protection of the school, but it is a very expensive method in comparison to other forms of physical security. The school and the school district must appropriately research the degree or possibility of threats to the facility and determine if the use of security officers is appropriate and cost effective.

The final measure used by many schools is working with local law enforcement officials to develop notification and response procedures in the event of an unwanted visitor or a violent incident. Law enforcement agencies have worked diligently to develop and practice methods to respond to unwanted situations and assist in the rapid evacuation of students and staff, while seeking to isolate and capture the perpetrator. Working agreements and understandings need to be developed and adopted between the school districts and the law enforcement agencies in order to maintain these proactive efforts. While the school districts work with law enforcement agencies for emergency response assistance, the district leadership must understand that the use of police agencies is the last or "worse case" method for protecting the students and staff. The proactive methods and procedures must be established as a first line of defense to deter and delay unwanted aggressors. Continued development of a proactive approach to protecting the school "fortress" can result in safer learning communities and reduce or detect any unsafe conditions.

Secondary Educational Facility Protection

Secondary educational facilities, also known as middle schools, junior high schools, and high schools, have many commonalities with the primary schools. Many of the internal and external threats are the same and the protective methods can be similar. This allows for consistent development of policies, procedures, and security devices or protective methods throughout the entire school district. Even with the commonalities between the primary and secondary facilities, there are some very different threats to students and staff. In additional, differing preventive methods from primary schools can be expected in these facilities. These challenges create additional concerns for the school staff to maintain a safe learning community.

Threats

The defined threats in primary schools also exist in the secondary buildings. Threats from outsider such as parents, guardians, and members of the community continue to be areas of concerns. In addition, secondary schools also face threats from those with undetected, untreated, or improperly treated or diagnosed mental health issues.

A primary difference between potential concerns posed by primary and secondary educational facilities exists with the internal threats. In secondary facilities, the student population becomes a regular challenge for school staff. As the students age and progress into the secondary facilities, they are going through physical and emotional changes. In addition, these students are exposed to various positive and negative influences that can motivate them to act out verbally or physically. The maturing student population becomes one of the primary threats in secondary schools. Students are willing to act out and cause disruptions, harm classmates either physically or emotionally, and destroy property, as well as bring banned or illegal items into the school. It needs to be noted that not all students will behave in a deviant or inappropriate manner, but these potential threats are real and can occur. Secondary schools should spend time and effort understanding the threats that can occur, their potential sources, and potential signs of unwanted activities.

Preventative Measures

As with the commonalities between the potential threats of primary and secondary educational facilities, there are similarities with preventative measures between these classifications of schools. Physical security equipment used in primary schools is also recommended for secondary schools. The design of the security systems will need to be customized for the respective buildings' physical design.

The primary difference with protective measures centers on the use of personnel to protect the students, staff, visitors, and buildings. In secondary school buildings, teachers and staff frequently have an elevated role dealing with issues and problems in the schools. Teachers and staff need to be trained on appropriate and effective skills to recognize, report, or possibly deter unwanted activities. In addition to a heightened state of awareness by teachers and staff, security or police personnel may be widely used to maintain order and respond to incidents in these schools. Security personnel can maintain access control into and out of the school, patrol the halls for truant students, monitor activities in halls and corridors, and ensure the perimeter of the building is locked and secure. Security personnel may be used to monitor CCTV systems and local alarms, as well as operate handheld or stationary metal detectors. For many secondary schools, additional budgeting is allocated for police officers to be stationed in specific schools or patrolling between school buildings. This law enforcement presence acts as an additional deterrent from unwanted acts and provides potentially a faster response to serious incidents. Law enforcement personnel often take on the role of a community police officer within the schools where they are assigned. These interactions with the students, staff, and visitors can be a positive experience as well as serving as a deterrent against unwanted acts. Additional police presence may also be utilized to help school personnel conduct appropriate searches of school property. Depending on the resources available to the police department, drug sniffing or bomb sniffing dogs may be brought in for inspection of school buildings. This proactive approach to deter and detect unwanted events can greatly assist to keep the schools and their occupants safe.

Additional areas of concern and protection for school districts can include administrative offices, facilities where extracurricular activities occur (such as athletic fields or gymnasiums and auditoriums) and transportation facilities or warehouses. Any property owned by the school district needs to be considered for protective measures. These measures may include physical protective devices as well as a security and law enforcement presence. With the growing number of reported violent or deviant events occurring in both primary and secondary school facilities, the use of security policies, procedures, and equipment needs to become a common occurrence. These continuous threats of violence are now on the minds of middle school and high school students, according to secondary education professional Mr. Gregory C. Kovel. He also adds that lockdown drills are now as commonplace as fire or severe weather drills. In addition, students now think about how to escape from a room in case of a violent act and how to avoid becoming a victim to school violence (Gregory C. Kovel, personal interview, November 2015).

When school districts adopt a proactive approach to protecting students, staff, visitors, and property, the financial investment becomes a viable and acceptable use of funding. Detecting and deterring violent acts needs to be a priority in all schools, both public and private, to ensure a positive and productive learning environment for all students.

Colleges' and Universities' Challenges

Protecting colleges and universities can be a very complex issue. Colleges and universities range in size from "store front" satellite locations in shopping centers or strip malls to extremely large campuses with thousands of students, faculty, and staff. **Higher education institutions** (colleges and universities) may be privately or publicly funded and offer a full range of academic, cultural, political, and athletic programs. The complexity of the public integration of these facilities is unlike primary and secondary education facilities, where access can be limited. Unlike the K-12 educational system, higher education institutions are a vibrant and continually engaged environment. Because of this complexity, the protection of these campuses can vary depending on the type of building, the location, and the resources available.

Threats

Similarities exist between the K-12 educational system and higher education when it comes to potential threats. Both educational systems have internal and external threats, but the typically open design of many colleges and universities and the advanced level of stress faced by students creates nuances that apply to the higher educational system.

Internal threats for employees may include undiagnosed or untreated mental or emotional impairments, family issues or concerns which are brought into work, and employees upset with their working conditions. In addition, employees can also steal from their employer, sell or buy illegal drugs, and act out inappropriately to their coworkers and those around them. The larger the institution the greater risk of problems from employees, which must be addressed by human resource departments, security, or police staffs. The student population creates concerns which may impact the safety of the campus. Undiagnosed or untreated mental health issues, acting out while under the influence of drugs or alcohol, dealing with depression due to the radical change in their living environments, or facing large amounts of stress can easily impact how students act out in the college or university environment. Students can also initiate incidents of damage, destruction, violence, and property crime, and the use or distribution of illegal substances. These internal factors can arise at any moment and under any circumstance.

External threats are equally important to understand how to properly protect a college or university. External threats may come from the surrounding community; those looking to prey upon the student population; visitors on campus acting out during athletic, cultural, or academic events; groups or organizations with radical social agendas looking to protest or sway the minds of students; and family members or friends of students acting inappropriately. Both internal and external threats can occur at any time due to the continuous operation and activities at many colleges or universities.

In order to properly protect against the multitude of potential threats, administrators and protective service departments must study and understand the possible dangers and risks that surround them. Upon determining and understanding these perils, decisions can be made on how to best work to prevent these circumstances.

Preventative Measures

The reality of protecting colleges and universities is that there is not a one-size-fits-all method to protect lives and property. Smaller satellite campuses can be protected like a business facility. Many of these smaller locations have limited hours of operation and limited access into the building. This allows for the use of industrial-grade locks and doors, access control systems, closed-circuit cameras, recording devices, and burglar and panic alarms to protect the building's contents in addition to notifying the proper authorities in the event of a disturbance.

Larger colleges and universities must learn to understand the potential threats which may occur and protect the facility accordingly. The reality is that the larger the campus, the greater the need for security methods and procedures to protect lives and property. Different buildings may need general and specific security policies and procedures depending on the activities within each individual structure. Common protective devices include (but are not limited to) permanent industrial designed doors and locks, access control systems, internal and external lighting, and cameras and alarm systems. Another key protective component is communication systems, both for internal and external use. For many buildings, internal phone systems with emergency phone numbers posted by the phone can be used. For areas that do not have phone systems, emergency notification systems can be placed internally and externally. These "call boxes" can be connected directly to the appropriate emergency response staff on the campus. Also, for short-term needs to protect events, devices such as temporary lighting and portable CCTV cameras may be used to enhance protection.

Another distinguishable difference between K-12 and higher education facilities is the use of full-time police, public safety, or security departments. Depending on the size of the campus and the potential threats or issues that may take place, administrators can employ full-time security personnel to patrol the grounds and respond to incidents or hire public safety, use police departments for patrolling and protection, or use a hybrid system combining police and security personnel. These individuals must be well qualified and trained to understand and properly respond to the incidents which may occur twenty-four hours a day, seven days a week. Determining between a security force, a police department, or a combination of both services must be determined according to need and budget. Employing and housing these professional departments can be a major cost center for the college or university. With a proper needs analysis of potential threats, staffing, training, and purchasing of necessary equipment, these departments become a vital component for both proactive protection as well as necessary reactive measures to protect lives and property.

The protection of colleges and universities is a very complex task. A tremendous amount of time, effort, and study is needed to properly understand the threats and the preventative and reactive methods needed to ensure and safeguard all those who attend, work at, or utilize the resources in these institutions.

Conclusion

The abundance and magnitude of potential threats to the **K-16 educational system** (kindergarten through a four-year college program) creates a very important need to protect these facilities. For many schools, it could be beneficial to study and adopt an "**urban mentality**" used to protect inner-city schools. Schools, colleges, and universities that operate within highly populated and potentially dangerous geographical areas understand and adopt the "fortress approach" of protection. The understanding of these schools is that the threat of violence, crime, and peril is surrounding their buildings. Because of this, a very proactive approach is used to protect lives and property. Strict adherence to access control policies and continuous supervision of activities, both internally and externally, work to limit the amount of crime and deviant behaviors that may harm the occupants of the buildings and detract from the educational process. Even though many schools, colleges, and universities are not located outside urban centers, adopting the mentality that potential threats may occur at any time (both inside and outside) can greatly assist in the development of policies, procedures, and security methods to detect and deter unwanted acts of violence or deviance in and around these buildings. The worst thing that can occur is for school administrators to adopt an attitude of denial, falsely believing that acts of violence will never happen "in their backyard." As stated multiple times in this chapter, these education buildings are not immune to violent acts. The threat of violence is continuously around us—in all segments of our society. In order to protect the sanctity of our educational process, we must adopt a "real world" mentality, knowing that it takes a great amount of time and resources to protect lives and property within the educational sector.

Case Study — The Bath, Michigan, School Bombing

In 1927, community member and local leader Andrew Kehoe committed one of the most heinous crimes against the American K-12 school systems. For this learning exercise, look up "The Bath, Michigan, School Bombing of 1927." Carefully read the accounts and details of the attack and answer the following questions:

1. Why did Kehoe bomb the school building in Bath, Michigan?
2. How did he gain access to the school building?
3. Do you believe that this type of an attack could occur in our modern-day K-12 school buildings?
4. If so, what can administrators and security professionals do to prevent such an occurrence?

Discussion Topic — Public Access vs. Public Safety

In this chapter, the concept of treating a school building like "a fortress" is addressed. In this protective model, access to the school building is limited with the intention of protecting the students and staff inside. If the school is publically funded, community members and taxpayers may want access to the school for organizational functions (both school related and non-school related).

A major suburban school district has hired you as a security consultant to assist the administration to develop policies and procedures to protect their educational facilities. After reading the chapter and applying the contents to your new consultant role, answer the following questions:

1. Can you allow public access to the educational facilities and still protect the students and staff members?
2. What types of threats do you potentially foresee with the access of the public to the school buildings?
3. What type of access control policies would you recommend to the school district?

Research Focus — Violence on the College Campus

Research the Virginia Tech University massacre of 2007. Focus particularly on the perpetrator's method and pattern for committing the shootings. After reviewing the details of this atrocity, answer the following questions:

1. How did the shooter gain access to the buildings?
2. Was the shooter denied access into any of the facilities?
3. In an open-access and publically funded college or university, can strict access control be implemented?

4. In addition to the response by the local law enforcement officials, what types of security equipment or procedures could be implemented to combat or deter another event such as this?

Key Terms

K-12	Primary school facilities	Fortress mentality
Secondary school facilities	Higher education institutions	K-16 educational system
Mental mind-set	Urban mentality	

Sources

Biography.com. (n.d.). *Andrew Kehoe biography*. Retrieved from http://www.biography.com/people/andrew-kehoe-235986

CNN.com. (2014). *Connecticut shootings fast facts*. Retrieved from http://www.cnn.com/2013/06/07/us/connecticut-shootings-fast-facts/

CNN.com. (2015). *Virginia Tech shootings fast facts*. Retrieved from http://www.cnn.com/2013/10/31/us/virginia-tech-shootings-fast-facts/

Gray, S. (2008). *How the NIU massacre happened*. *Time Magazine*. Retrieved from http://content.time.com/time/nation/article/0,8599,1714069,00.html

History.com. (n.d.). *Columbine high school shootings*. Retrieved from http://www.history.com/topics/columbine-high-school-shootings

National Institute of Mental Health (n.d.). *Any mental illness among adults (AMI)*. Retrieved from http://www.nimh.nih.gov/health/statistics/prevalence/any-mental-illness-ami-among-adults.shtml

National Institute of Mental Health. (n.d.). *Any disorder among children*. Retrieved from http://www.nimh.nih.gov/health/statistics/prevalence/any-disorder-among-children.shtml

Stoptheshootings.org. (n.d). *U.S. statistics*. Retrieved from http://www.stoptheshootings.org/

The New York Times. (1998). *Teen-Ager Pleads Guilty in Fatal Shooting at Kentucky School*. Retrieved from http://www.nytimes.com/1998/10/06/us/teen-ager-pleads-guilty-in-fatal-shooting-at-kentucky-school.html

Chapter Twelve

Ensuring Items Get from Here to There: Transportation and Cargo Security

Introduction

A tremendous amount of freight and cargo enters, travels within, and exits the United States on a daily basis. Goods and products are transported by road, rail, air, and waterways. This astronomical amount of items is continuously susceptible to theft or damage. Miscreants, criminals, and those with illegal or immoral intentions prey upon these shipments for their own benefit. According to the Federal Bureau of Investigation (FBI), it is unknown just how much loss is actually incurred from cargo theft. The FBI estimates that approximately 30 billion dollars of losses occurs from cargo theft rings alone (FBI, 2010). These estimates do not include losses due to other theft, damage, or falsified documents. The cost of theft and losses suffered while goods and cargo are in transit is ultimately passed down to the consumers through higher prices for products and higher insurance rates.

Learning Objectives

In this chapter, the reader will be introduced to the basic concepts, threats, and potential solutions of protecting the transportation and cargo industries. Concepts such as pilferage, hijacking, and supply chain management will be covered. In addition, specific areas of concern addressed will include ports, shipyards, airports, and distribution and transportation centers as well as the various methods of transit used to move people and cargo. The chapter concludes with a case study on the emerging drone industry, a discussion topic pertaining to pilferage, and a research focus on airport security.

The Impact of Protecting Cargo

To see how important it is to protect the transportation of cargo, stop and take a look around you. What is in front of you? A textbook, computer, pen, highlighter, food, beverage, table, and chair—everything you are using or that is around you is transported and shipped at one point or another. In fact, everything that we use and purchase is transported from a starting point to its final destination. If the transportation of goods and cargo is interrupted or disrupted, huge amounts of money will be lost and multitudes of potential customers will be disappointed. What may sound overly simplistic is actually a very real and legitimate concern for producers, suppliers, retail establishments, and customers.

In the course of distribution and delivery, cargo travels thousands of miles and can be stolen, lost, delayed, or deterred at any point in this process. This potential loss can force companies to close or go into bankruptcy as well as have a negative impact on the national or global economy. The ability to track cargo and ensure unimpeded or undisrupted delivery takes a great amount of time and resources. What many people may take for granted can create a major disruption to our everyday chain of events if the process fails. This is why companies and organizations invest time, money, and resources to protect the transportation and delivery of these products.

Pilferage—"Public Enemy Number One"

In chapter 8 of this text, the term pilferage is introduced. Defined as the act of employees stealing from employers, **pilferage** is a serious concern with those involved with the transportation of products. In these situations, theft from employees can come from numerous sources. Items can be stolen where the product is produced, taken by employees transporting the goods, or stolen when stored in a warehouse or distribution center. The motivations for stealing products by distribution employees can be similar to those of employees working in a retail environment. Inadequate wages, limited opportunities for promotion, or selling items to family or friends at a discounted rate, as well as re-selling the items to others in order to support habits or pay off debts are just a few of the reasons why employees steal from their employers. Left unsupervised or undeterred, pilferage can be a major source of loss for the producers of the goods, the transportation companies, and the intended recipients of the items or the companies insuring the items. In addition to employee theft, organized crime rings may attempt to steal items for illegal sale or distribution.

These criminal activities can involve employees working for the organizations responsible for the production, distribution, and sale of the items. Also, organized crime rings can work independently and steal large quantities of items. In either case, the crime ring (or criminal syndicate) gains knowledge and information on the products to steal and redistribute illegally.

Another form of theft occurs when companies produce fraudulent or **counterfeit goods and products** and attempt to distribute them openly or subversively to unaware retail or commercial buyers. The fraudulent or counterfeit goods may be produced using sub-standard materials that do not meet the quality standards of the corporation or organization. To the purchaser, the items appear to be legitimate. They may have similar packaging and identifying markings (such as a logo or company insignia) printed on the item, the box, and container. These false goods are produced at a fraction of the cost of the actual item and can be sold at the normal wholesale rate. These items can come into the supply chain presumably from legitimate or unknowing sources or be integrated through other, unscrupulous methods. These items cannot only defraud the buyer and the end user but also have a negative impact on the economy. When the fraudulent items are intercepted, discovered, or recovered there may be no method to get a refund for the investment.

Ports and Shipyards

With millions of tons of cargo entering and exiting the hundreds of ports in the United States, the protection of these facilities is a priority of their owners and the government. Ports and shipyards generate millions of dollars of revenue in taxes, fees, and profits. In the event of a work slowdown or the closing of a port, money is lost and the transportation of goods becomes strained or crippled.

Risks

Ports and shipyards can range from minor facilities to major points of commerce. The threats to these facilities can be caused by natural as well as man-made reasons. **Natural threats** include storms or hurricanes that can force the temporary closure of the facilities due to high winds, tremendous amounts of precipitation, and damaging storm surge (an immense shifting of water toward the shoreline). These natural threats can last for hours depending on the size of the storm and how quickly the storm is moving. While the storms are passing through, catastrophic damage to ports and shipyards may occur due to the battering from the elements and the massive flooding damage caused by the salt water surge.

Man-made threats are a continuous concern and battle for port employees as well as governmental authorities. The threats to the ports can come from the incoming cargo and ship personnel or cargo exiting the port, as well as illegal or unwanted activities from those involved in the shipping process. Port authorities wage a continuous war against illegal or unauthorized items entering and leaving the ports. With the tremendous amount of items shipped by massive containers, illegal or unauthorized cargo can be shipped in numerous places. Another threat is the theft or loss of items as they enter or exit the facility. These threats can come from established organized crime rings, local crime rings, individuals looking to profit from the illegal activities, or careless transport and unintended damage of the products. Any loss of cargo results in financial losses for the manufacturers, the shipping companies, and the potential recipient of the cargo. These illegal or accidental incidents can create multimillion dollar losses for those involved with the cargo.

Ports and shipping yards must also be aware of potential terrorist threats from domestic and international groups or a singular/independent "lone wolf." Knowing that the disruption in the supply chain can create chaos and harm to American businesses and the economy, terrorists may attempt to infiltrate the property to cause harm or even attempt to import or export devices that can cause damage to lives and property.

Losses may also be created due to improper documentation of the shipping paperwork that lists and tracks the movement of the cargo. Much like the physical losses of cargo, the administrative errors can be intentional or accidental. Intentional errors may attempt to defraud the recipients of part of the amount of cargo in the container or the exact items that are shipped. Accidental administrative errors can cause products to be sent to wrong locations, lost, or never recovered. With the enormous amount of items shipped into and out of these facilities, the potential risks and threats of loss force the shipyard and port owners, as well as governmental law enforcement agencies, to invest tremendous amounts of time and effort to protect these locations.

Preventative Measures

With such a vast myriad of potential threats facing ports and shipyards, the facility management, security, and governmental authorities must work together to protect the property, its cargo, and human lives. Working toward the protection of these facilities needs to be outlined and explained in appropriate policies and procedures manuals. These documents must contain directives about responses toward viable threats, who to contact for assistance, and proper reporting procedures. These policies and procedures must be continuously reviewed and updated to ensure that the information they contain is relevant and appropriate. In addition, the information and details in the manuals need to be taught to and reviewed by all appropriate personnel working on the property. This training will assist employees to recognize and deter incidents and how to properly respond if an emergency takes place.

The protection and response to natural and man-made threats will be determined by the owners of the port or shipyard as well as the local, state, and federal authorities. The protection and response to emergencies may be the responsibility of all entities involved or of a specifically designated group. For example, a security force may be used to protect the grounds and the access control into the facility. Governmental authorities may be responsible for the inspection of items entering or leaving the port or shipyard, while other groups, such as a port authority, may also have access to the area for law enforcement and disaster response.

With these different groups also come different physical security devices needed to keep the property safe. These may include communication systems; professional lighting, fencing, and locking devices; closed-circuit television systems; sophisticated access control systems; computerized shipment tracking systems; and state-of-the-art scanning and surveying devices. In addition to these devices, computer and software protection will need to be integrated to protect against manipulation of the computerized records and documents as well as any protective device using computer or information technology. Even though this is a basic list of protective devices, the importance of the proper use of this equipment plays a highly important part in the protection of the workers, authorized visitors, equipment, and the cargo on the property every day.

Airports

According to the United States Department of Transportation, there are approximately 19,453 airports in the United States. These include 5,155 public airports and 14,009 private airports (U.S. Department of Transportation, n.d.). The International Air Transport Association (IATA) reports that in 2013, approximately 8 million people flew each day, averaging 3.1 billion people flying in that year. Also, approximately 50 million tons of cargo is legally transported by air each year (IATA, n.d.). These staggering numbers illustrate the high use of airline transportation for people and cargo. For the airports, these average

Barbed Wire Fence and Camera © schafar via fotolia.com

numbers for use also create continual threats and the need to implement various forms of protective measures.

Risks

Commonalities exist between the risks faced at ports and airports. The obvious difference is that one venue is water-based while the other is air-based. In the case of airports, natural and human risks are systemic threats. Natural and weather-based events cannot only hamper activities at one airport but at all other locations that are trying to fly into or out of the affected location. Natural and weather-based threats create a chain effect to segments of the airline transportation system. Winter storms, severe thunderstorms, tornadic activity, and tropical storms or hurricanes, as well as dense fog can hamper or delay activities at an airport. When these events occur, the airports must do what they can to remove snow or ice or wait for the other weather conditions to subside. Until the runways are cleared or the weather systems subside, flights in or out of an airport are delayed or cancelled. These natural events create a backlog of flights, delaying or shutting down air travel to and from the location. Depending on the size, length, and severity of the storm, the airport activities can be temporarily delayed or closed down for a prolonged period of time. When this happens, passengers are stranded and the transportation of cargo stops.

Human threats to airports, which may include the facilities, aircraft, passengers, employees, visitors, and cargo, are very real and must be recognized. The protection of airports can include various security and law enforcement agencies. This protection may involve proprietary or contract security personnel, airport police authorities, local police or sheriff organizations, state police, and numerous federal organizations including the **Transportation Security Authority** (TSA), and **U.S. Customs and Border Protection**. All of these organizations must work diligently to understand and accept each other's role and jurisdiction as well as coordinate all activities for proactive protection and reacting to unwanted events.

Criminal activities in airports may include common street crimes such as larceny, robbery, or assault. Airport-specific criminal activities may include tampering with cargo or luggage, the transportation of illegal cargo or contraband, or potential terrorist activities intended to disrupt air travel, destroy aircraft, taint or ruin cargo, and injure the lives of travelers, visitors, or employees. The threats can originate from opportunistic criminals, unruly employees or guests, or organized crime rings, as well as domestic or international terrorist organizations. Because of the continuous threat to all airports, both large and small, diligent protective measures and procedures must be in place and maintained.

Preventative Measures

As with the protection of ports and shipyards, airports must have detailed policies and procedures in place to direct and guide employees in how to protect lives and property. Depending on the specific organizations working to protect the airport, these policies and procedures will vary based on the mission and responsibilities of the protective agency. These differences in mission and responsibilities must be regulated by each individual agency. This regulation can come from separate security organizations, local law enforcement entities, and governmental agencies. The airport management (also referred to as the airport authority) will need to understand each enforcement agency's role and work to coordinate activities in the event of a sizeable incident or disaster. The size and activities taking place at an airport will also dictate what protective agencies will be represented on-site and the number of employees needed to protect lives and property.

Because of the complexity of airport travel, a vast array of protective devices or protective measures can be integrated and implemented. Physical security measures such as fencing, lighting, emergency communication systems, closed-circuit television systems, alarms, and access control and locking systems are integrated to control access and protect airport assets. Specific scanning devices intended to detect illegal items or contraband can also be utilized by airport security. These systems may include metal detectors, human body scanners, detectors used for luggage inspection, and the scanning of imported or exported cargo. These devices are designed to detect specific items carried on by people or hidden within luggage, packages, or cargo. The complexity of the protective items is directly dictated by the potential threats at the location. Also, animals trained to detect drugs, explosives, or illegal contraband may be on hand or called in to inspect people or items. It is crucial that each agency and the airport managing authority understand not only the proper use of these protective items, but also what specific items they are designed to detect and under what circumstances the equipment is to be used. As criminal and terrorist activities evolve, so too must the protective policies, procedures, and equipment in order to properly prevent and apprehend these items and activities. Airports and their managing organizations must understand and accept that they are constant targets for criminal or terrorist activities and must remain vigilant to protect lives and property at their locations.

Distribution and Transportation Centers

Distribution and transportation centers present a unique set of circumstances and potential problems that must be protected against. These facilities can temporarily store goods and products before they are shipped to their final destinations. The products in these locations can be stored for a matter of hours up to weeks or even months. The cost of these products sitting in these facilities can be valued at billions of dollars and are vital for the organization or corporation to profit and stay in business. These facilities may operate during traditional business hours or be open 24 hours a day with the products entering and departing via truck or rail. The owners of these centers must invest time, effort, and equipment to protect the items they store. Failure to protect the products can be detrimental or disastrous to all entities involved in the transportation process.

Risks

In the past, these facilities were disregarded or even ignored as a risk for potential loss. As time went on, the facilities became fertile locations for theft and loss. The risks to these facilities can come from internal and external sources. Internal threats may come from unethical employees looking to either profit by selling stolen items or keeping them for personal use. This employee pilferage can be secretive and calculated or brazenly take place in the open. Employees may take the items to be resold on Internet auction and sales sites, taken to local pawn shops for potential resale, or "fenced" (distributed) through illegal means or operations. Another source of loss created internally is accidental or intentional damage to products. Careless transportation of the goods and products throughout the facility can lead to drops, spills, or crashes involving the items. When these events occur, the products may be partially damaged or completely destroyed. In either situation, the organization or company will suffer a financial loss. Products may also be lost through administrative errors and misplaced within the facility. When these mistakes occur, additional time and effort must be invested to relocate the items, creating production and distribution slowdowns. Additionally items can also be miscounted or mislabeled when departing to their next destination. Whether intentional or unintentional, these clerical errors can lead to inaccurate deliveries and delays of the intended products to be distributed or sold.

External threats can also be a major concern for companies and organizations looking to protect their products. Criminals may attempt to illegally enter the facility to steal items. These thefts may be random crimes or well-planned and well-orchestrated operations. In either case, these events can create a high level of loss as well as potential damage to the facility. The end result is a loss of profit by the organization or corporation. Another threat of loss can come from external or contract employees used to transfer the products to other locations. When these contract employees are careless with the delivering or departure with the products, they may cause unintended damage or loss to the items. Finally, much like the internal administrative process, external sources used to transport goods can also create recording errors on the amount or type of products entering or exiting the facility. Some of these errors may actually be initiated by the primary company or organization but the contracted carrier is responsible for the items once they leave the facility.

At any time, some or all of these potential risks can damage items or property, if left unprotected and unsupervised. These internal and external threats must be taken seriously by the company or organization and properly addressed to avoid loss or to deter future losses.

Preventative Measures

The protection of distribution and transportation facilities must address and reflect the potential threats they face. Any and all protective measures must be detailed in a policy and procedure guide to ensure consistent enforcement of all procedures. These policies, procedures, and devices must be inspected or reviewed on a regular basis to ensure applicability and proper operation.

The external protection of these buildings and complexes should include reliable lighting, clear zones inside and outside the property line, closed-circuit television systems where the images are recorded, and industrial-grade locks on all external doors. Depending on the location of the facility and the value of the items inside, additional exterior protection may include industrial-grade fencing encompassing the facility, advanced access control systems to record all vehicles and personnel entering and leaving, and the potential use of security personnel to inspect paperwork, and vehicles and maintain a record of all entering and exiting vehicles. One specific item that can be inspected and administered by security personnel is the plastic or metal bands applied to trailers leaving the facility, known as "truck seals." These bands are imprinted with a specific number that can be recorded and tracked from one destination to the next. If the band is cut, missing, or replaced the driver must be held accountable as to the reason for the change. These seals help to ensure that the items in the trailer have not been potentially compromised, tampered with, or stolen. These seals can be applied at the dock or bay doors where shipments are loaded or attached by the security personnel after the trailer is inspected, prior to its departure from the property. The seal number can then be recorded on the cargo paperwork for verification at the next destination.

Internal protective measures include proper locking devices, professional-grade lighting, closed-circuit television systems, and access control systems. An essential component to the protection of goods entering and leaving the facility is a tracking system that allows for the recording of all incoming items, the location of these items, and the departure and destination of the product. In addition, the ability to track which employees "checked in and checked out" the products and placed the item into its temporary storage area can also be beneficial. This allows the organization to record all activities related to the product from the time it enters to the time it leaves the facility. With the advancement of computerized tracking systems and the software programs associated with the logistic devices, the recording and data storage for these activities has greatly improved. With any and all computerized systems, it is essential that all employees are trained to understand and properly use the equipment. In addition, internal controls such as well-composed and well-enforced policies and procedures must be maintained to ensure the successful distribution of the property. Also, supervisors, managers, or security personnel must physically inspect the overall process on a regular basis to ensure that all policies and procedures are being met. The data compiled from these logistic management systems must be properly maintained and protected from intentional or unintentional compromise.

Distribution and transportation centers are a critical aspect and component of the shipping of goods and products. Millions of tons of cargo can pass though one or more of these facilities during transit. In order to ensure the well-being of goods and products, these facilities must be protected and treated as vital aspects of the cargo security process.

Cargo in Transit

The protection of cargo in transit can be a daunting task. The suppliers and the recipients of the goods must rely on employees of either their own organization or outsourced personnel to transport the goods safely. Delivery of the goods can take place via multiple methods from start to finish. The unfortunate reality is that the longer the delivery route, the greater the chance for the loss or damage of the product.

The concept of the protection of the goods and products is referred to as **supply chain management**. Organizations and corporations invest significant amounts of money and resources to ensure that products travel unimpeded from start to finish. This can be interpreted to include the successful transportation of goods without loss or damage as well as denying unauthorized products from being shipped and integrated into the supply line. Without proper oversight and protection of transported goods and products, the logistical component of supply chain management can fail and cost the organization and consumers massive amounts of money in preventable losses.

According to the United States Department of Transportation, the shipping and moving of freight takes place over 4.1 million miles of roads and highways, 139,000 miles of railroads, and 12,000 miles of ocean and inland waterways, and within 5,000 airports or approximately 170 water ports. Of these transportation methods, over one-half to three-quarters of all the goods and products are transported 250 miles or less. Trucks transport the largest amount of delivered goods and products, followed by railroad lines and waterways, and then air transportation methods (United States Department of Transportation, 2012).

Similar risks to the transportation of all deliverable goods can be found in all modes of transit. Items can be damaged while en route, delivered to the wrong location, improperly marked or labeled, or stolen. As previously stated, employees and organized crime groups can blatantly steal items for resale. Another method of loss that can take place is the hijacking of goods and products. According to transportation professional James T. Block, organized groups or random individuals can target specific items while they are being transported.

In addition to the unwanted interception of the shipment, physically harm or a forced detainment could happen to the driver of the truck. These items may include highly sought or in-demand products such as newly released electronic or video gaming systems or popular items of apparel. Where this type of threat is not commonplace, it still remains a risk for those transporting goods and products (James T. Block, personal interview, June 2015).

In addition to the securing of the containers the items are transported within the locked semitrailers, railcars, and cargo holds on ship and planes, and the protection of the items can be greatly enhanced with communication and technology. Regular communication between the drivers, engineers, ship captains, and pilots to dispatchers or logistics centers allows the tracking of the cargo from the point of departure to final destination. Tracking devices can also be attached to the transportation vehicle or vessel, allowing for satellite tracing of the cargo. These devices, if properly maintained, can offer a real-time location of the vehicle. Finally, the use and incorporation of computerized shipping systems, hardware, and software can provide the departure and delivery of the items. This combination of traditional security measures (locks and identification seals/bands) combined with modern computerized tracking systems can greatly assist the oversight and the safety of the cargo as it is transported via road, rail, water, and air. The work to protect the logistics and transportation of goods and products has become a priority of the companies and corporations buying and selling the items as well as the third party or independent organizations tasked with moving the cargo. These protective methods and the use of tracking devices also creat new opportunities for electronic security providers to expand their services and abilities to secure transported property.

Conclusion

The protection of items while in transit can be a difficult and daunting task. With the multiple organizations and individuals who can become part of the transit and storage process of goods and products, the amount of resources and personnel needed to ensure a successful transfer can cost billions of dollars. In addition, the threat of fraudulent goods entering into the supply chain can also cost manufacturers and sellers huge sums of money. While concerted efforts are taking place to slow the process of loss, additional resources and consistently enforced policies and procedures are needed. Without a systemic effort to deter or eliminate these threats, the consumer and the general public will ultimately become the victims through higher prices, limited availability in quality items, and a negative impact to the overall economy.

Case Study — Delivery Drones

Large distribution and resale organizations are researching and reviewing the viability of using unmanned flying devices (drones) to deliver ordered goods. Currently the organizations experimenting with these devices believe that they can be used effectively in a limited distance or capacity. The drones will be programmed by the distributor to fly to a specific destination, drop off the package, and return to the distribution center. With this concept in mind and after reading chapter 12, answer these questions:

1. What type of threats do you envision that could take place to prevent the parcels from being delivered successfully by the drones?
2. Do you foresee any personal safety hazards or liability concerns if these organizations use unmanned drones?
3. In your personal opinion, is this form of delivery a good idea or a bad idea?

Discussion Topic — Justifying Theft

Certain employees believe that "they have the right" to steal from their employers. Even though these acts are illegal and unethical, it does not act as a deterrent to stop these thefts. With the knowledge you have gained in the chapter and the text as a whole, brainstorm what kind of employees would be motivated to steal and how they could perpetrate these acts within the following environments:

1. Water ports and shipyards
2. Airports and airfields
3. Transport and distribution centers

(Note: The rationale behind this activity is not to promote the pilferage of goods but instead, to teach how to recognize these potential threats and work to prevent these events from occurring.)

Research Focus — The Screening Process

Since the horrific attacks on September 11, 2001, our country has invested a tremendous amount of personnel, time, resources, and money to deter and apprehend those who desire to attack our airports and airlines. The screening of individuals, their belongings, and the cargo being transported has become a primary focus to protect lives and property. Go onto the Internet and research the devices used to detect illegal or unwanted devices or goods in airports. Specifically, investigate the following tools used for detection, how they operate, and what they specifically detect:

1. Detection items used on people
2. Detection devices used for luggage
3. Detection devices used on cargo

After discovering the various detection systems, do you believe that these systems are necessity or are they an invasion of personal and individual rights, privileges, and liberties? Also, do you believe there can be a "middle ground" between effective airport security and not violating patrons' personal rights and liberties?

Key Terms

Pilferage	Counterfeit products	Natural threats
Man-made threats	Transportation Security Authority (TSA)	U.S. Customs and Border Protection
Distribution and transportation centers	Supply chain management	Hijacking

Sources

American Association of Port Authorities. (n.d.). *Supply chain flow chart*. Retrieved from: http://aapa.files.cms-plus.com/PDFs/supply_chain_security_example.pdf?navItemNumber=1100

American Association of Port Authorities. (n.d.). *U.S. port industry*. Retrieved from http://www.aapa-ports.org/Industry/content.cfm?ItemNumber=1022&navItemNumber=901

Federal Bureau of Investigation. (2010). *Inside cargo theft: A growing, multi-billion-dollar problem*. Retrieved from http://www.fbi.gov/news/stories/2010/november/cargo_111210/cargo_111210

Transportation Security Administration. (n.d.). *Maritime*. Retrieved from http://www.tsa.gov/stakeholders/maritime

United States Customs and Border Protection. (n.d.). *CSI: Container security initiative*. Retrieved from http://www.cbp.gov/border-security/ports-entry/cargo-security/csi/csi-brief

United States Department of Transportation. (2012). *Transportation statistics annual report.* Retrieved from http://www.rita.dot.gov/bts/sites/rita.dot.gov.bts/files/publications/transportation_statistics_annual_report/2012/chapter3.html

United States Government Accountability Office. (2014). *Maritime security: Progress and challenges with selected port security programs.* Retrieved from: http://www.gao.gov/assets/670/663784.pdf

United States Department of Transportation. (n.d). *Table 1-3: Number of U.S. airports (a).* Retrieved from http://www.rita.dot.gov/bts/sites/rita.dot.gov.bts/files/publications/national_transportation_statistics/html/table_01_03.html

Chapter 13

Protecting a Crowd: Lodging and Entertainment Security

Introduction

In 2013, the United States Department of Labor's Bureau of Labor Statistics reported that the average American spends approximately $2,482.00 per person on entertainment (U.S. Department of Labor, 2014). This fact alone illustrates that the lodging and entertainment industries are a combined multibillion-dollar locus of consumer spending. With millions of people each year dining out, vacationing, or attending concerts and sporting events, the need to protect these venues and establishments is easily apparent. At any given moment, these patrons as well as the employees of the venue are a target for a criminal act. While people are attending these events and enjoying themselves, continuous efforts must take place to ensure the safety of the patrons and avoidance of any criminal wrong-doing. This massive effort takes a well-coordinated and well-executed plan that can involve security departments, law enforcement personnel, and a multitude of physical security measures.

Learning Objectives

In this chapter, the reader will be introduced to multiple facilities, venues, and events that require formal protection. These facilities, venues, and events can be modest in size or include thousands of customers and patrons in one place at the same time. The entertainment locations covered in this chapter include casinos, sporting events, concert venues, amusement parks and resorts, hotels, motels, and cruise ships. The chapter will also define the risks these venues face and an overview of preventative measures that can reduce the threat of unwanted acts. The chapter will conclude with a case study highlighting cruise ships, a discussion of the role of customer service in security departments, and a research question on the protection of casinos.

Casinos

According to a report from the American Gaming Association (2013), approximately 37.34 billion dollars was spent in American commercial casinos in 2012. On the website GettoKnowGaming.org (n.d.), it is stated that the casino and gaming industry has added 240 billion dollars into the United States economy, provided 1.7 million jobs, paid 73.5 billion dollars in wages, and contributed 38 billion dollars in tax revenue. Legalized gaming establishments and casinos can be small venues or massive facilities with entertainment facilities and hotels. Activities in these establishments include various forms of gaming, such as slot machines, card games, dice games, roulette wheels, bingo games, and wagering on live or upcoming sporting events. The larger facilities can also host concerts, sporting events, and meetings, in addition to offering multiple restaurants, bars, clubs, and formal hotels. These establishments can be located in large cities, smaller communities, riverboats, or cruise ships, and have numerous, smaller operations in transportation centers and other public venues. With all of these entertainment options, threats to gaming and casino establishments are a constant concern to the organizations that own and operate these venues.

Risks

Gaming venues and casinos face many continuous threats from visitors, employees, contractors, and patrons. These threats can be targeted to various aspects of the organization of these establishments. **Gaming manipulation** is a threat where people attempt the cheat a game in order to illegally win. These threats can come from devices placed on slot machines attempting to force winning combinations, counting cards during blackjack games, (where players work to keep track of the cards dealt to better their chances for winning), signaling by two patrons (when one person tries to watch which cards are being played or dealt and notify their partner), intentional diversion by the players to gain an advantage, the stealing of betting chips, or possible misdealing or misdirection by employees when passing out cards to the players.

Additional threats can come from potential stealing of money in these facilities. Gaming venues and casinos have the potential to generate huge sums of cash. This cash can be in the form of public currency or venue-specific monetary items like traditional betting chips or the modern electronic cash/debit cards. These forms of currency used in an establishment create concerns of internal and external theft, robbery, or possible manipulation of the electronic monetary cards. Additionally, the theft of property by employees or patrons is also a concern to the establishments. Items such as alcohol, unprotected property, or even expensive pieces of art are at risk of theft for personal use or monetary gain.

Other threats to these establishments include public acts of violence such as fighting between individuals and employees or rival groups and organizations. These activities could be an attempt at diversion to gain a monetary advantage or personal outbursts and/or vendettas that have no direct bearing to the gambling on-site. In addition, terrorist threats from domestic or international terrorist groups or their supporters could occur to derail the casino's operation or cause harm to the employees and patrons of the establishment.

Preventative Measures

Due to the high risk of loss of money and assets, gaming venues and casinos often invest large amounts of money and resources to keep their employees, patrons, and property safe. In many gaming establishments, the responsibility of security is divided into different sections. First is the security force comprised of security officers and attendants designated for interacting with the patrons and employees within the building. The second group can be labeled as executive protection of high-stakes games (utilizing large sums of money) or to escort VIPs within the facility. The third section of personnel is the group of employees who work in a loss prevention capacity. These individuals monitor all authorized and approved activities within the facility. These individuals are segregated from the rest of the employees and trained to detect numerous violations and threats from both patrons and employees alike. These individuals monitor gaming tables for potential cheating, slot machine or bingo areas for irregularities, and watch for other unwanted activities within the property.

The gaming and casino industry invests huge sums of money for state-of-the-art physical security equipment to protect property, human lives, and the overall assets of the organization. This equipment includes high-tech security centers which integrate and monitor CCTV systems and biometric access control systems, as well as advanced alarm, fire, and environmental control systems. The facilities may also incorporate state-of-the-art locking systems, internal and external lighting, computer systems monitoring electronic gaming devices, and physical building designs to control pedestrian and vehicular traffic.

The preventative and reactionary methods of gaming and casino venues are vital for the financial and business success of the organization. With the continued popularity of these gaming, entertainment, and lodging venues, the investment in security devices will continue to be valued by the owners of these facilities, organizations, and corporations.

National and International Sporting Events

For many people in the United States and around the world, sporting events are a source or entertainment, passion, and personal pride. Sporting events attract millions of people to stadiums and venues both small and large. While millions of people spend billions of dollars at these events, the protection of the facilities, athletes, employees, and spectators is a tremendous challenge. Owners of the stadium venues want to maintain safe and secure environments that will attract multitudes of loyal fans. These events are a continuous target for crime and violence. Working to protect these facilities literally takes a team approach to ensure the safety and well-being of all those within the fieldhouse, arena, or stadium.

Risks

The threat of "**fan-on-fan violence**" is a concern faced at many venues. The potential risks at sporting events can be greatly elevated based on the type of the event, the possible consumption of alcohol, and the aggressiveness of the fans in attendance. Many problems and issues are fueled by the consumption of alcohol, both before and during the game. For some fans, the overindulgence of alcohol can lead to violent outbursts such as verbal and physical confrontations. It should be noted that alcohol is not the only the source of misbehavior. Some attendees desire to initiate confrontations or intimidate others attending the event. In addition, most fans tend to be well behaved but the small percentage of those who wish to act out violently or aggressively are a regular concern to stadium owners and management.

Fans as well as venue employees may also desire to steal from others in attendance at the event. These crimes can include the theft of bags, backpacks, or purses; the theft of wallets, money, or electronic devices off a person's body (also referred to as "pick-pocketing"); the theft by patrons of food and goods; and fraudulent transactions where vendors overcharge patrons or give back the incorrect amount of change. These forms of larceny may take place so suddenly that victims may not realize what took place until after they leave the venue. Large crowds in a confined area may also allow for criminals to steal the data off of credit or debit cards. In these situations where a large number of people are congregated, individuals with small data readers can either extract the card user's information with a proximity reader or utilize an electronic magnetic strip reader during a transaction to illegally obtain the information. With the patron distracted by the events taking place, these criminals may easily obtain the card's data without the victim knowing.

The employees of these events are also at risk of becoming a victim of violence. When attempting to confront unruly or intoxicated fans, the employees could be assaulted. These potential altercations can take place anywhere within the stadium or arena. Fans may act violently against the employees when being denied entry due to carrying unauthorized or illegal items into the facility, when they are confronted for inappropriate behavior, or while being removed from the facility due to unwanted behavior. The employees must always be aware of the fan's behavior and be ready for verbal and physical outbursts from uncooperative fans.

The athletes involved in the game can also be at risk of violent acts from the fans. Unruly fans may throw items onto the playing field or surface, attempt to provoke physical confrontations with players, and attempt to enter the playing field or surface to disrupt the game's activities. These unwanted events can occur spontaneously and without notice. When they do occur, the players, the venue employees, and the instigating fans can sustain injuries.

In today's society, the threat of a terrorist act at a sporting event is a very real concern. With many sporting events receiving television, radio, and electronic coverage combined with a large group of people congregated in a single place, these occasions can be a valued target for a lone terrorist or a terrorist group. An attack at a highly popular sporting event will draw immediate attention to the terrorist group to promote their hateful ideologies, kill or injure countless people, and potentially create chaos and turmoil in society as a whole. The history of violence at athletic events illustrates the reality of these threats. Examples include the attacks at the 1972 Olympic Games in Munich, Germany, as well as the bombings at the 2013 marathon in Boston, Massachusetts. These threats by organized groups or individuals attempting to cause injuries or promote ideological causes is a very real concern for every type of event within every city.

Sporting events are intended to be a source of entertainment for the fans. The unfortunate reality is that even in a venue intended to entertain, unruly fans, parasitic criminals, and those promoting harmful ideological agendas can cause death, injuries, and loss of property.

Preventative Measures

As in the case of most security programs, written rules, policies, and procedures are the cornerstone for the process to protect lives and property. In the case of protecting sporting events, multiple sets of policies and procedures could be in place depending on the venue and the game taking place. Depending on the sport and its governing body or association, the specific league may develop rules for the team owners and the venues to abide by. These league policies and procedures may be general or specific. In some cases, the owners of the teams or the venues may develop additional guidelines which enhance the league's regulations as well as other security policies for non-sporting events.

Frequently, patrons at sporting events are subjected to a search of any bag entering into the facility (if bags are permitted). In addition, patrons may also be subjected to a search of outer garments for restricted items including food or alcoholic beverages. Finally, those entering an athletic stadium or arena may be required to either walk through a metal detector or be searched with a hand-held detector.

The use of physical security equipment may also be incorporated into the venue. Closed-circuit television systems may be installed to monitor concourses, corridors, and insolated areas. Access control systems may be used to restrict access in areas such as press boxes, locker rooms, stadium offices, executive/corporate suites, or equipment rooms. In some cases where team stores are available to sell merchandise, electronic article systems (EAS) are utilized to prevent moderate to high-priced items from being stolen. Physical security measures such as fencing, lighting, and locks may be incorporated to deter unwanted activities and keep patrons safe. Finally, stadiums and arenas may install burglar alarm systems to protect the facility from unwanted intrusion when activities are not taking place as well as deter theft or vandalism.

The issue of controlling the crowd incorporates multiple layers of personnel with varying degrees of authority. Security personnel may be hired to conduct the search of bags and patrons upon entering the facility. In many cases, **customer service personnel** (once referred to as ushers) are employed by the stadium to assist patrons to find their seats, offer direction to various areas of the facility, and act as the first line of defense when dealing with issues in the seating areas. The customer service personnel may be granted the authority and authorization to intervene when problems arise and order unruly patrons from the seating areas or from the venue. Frequently, uniformed police personnel are on hand to potentially arrest unruly fans in the case of fights or erratic behavior. These multiple layers of personnel protection must work with one another to ensure that policies and procedures are effectively enacted.

Depending on the magnitude of the event, additional personnel, equipment, and agencies may be incorporated to protect the facility and the people inside it. For example, major sporting events such as league playoffs and championships as well as international sporting events will also work to protect against large-scale crimes and terrorist acts. Local, state, and federal law enforcement agencies may be assembled to incorporate anti-terrorist strategies to limit or control access into the area around the stadium. In some cases, departments of the military may be asked to protect the air space or waterways around the facility. With these circumstances, state-of-the-art detection equipment is temporarily installed to search for bombs, toxic agents, and known or suspected terrorists. High-tech command and control centers are established to coordinate protective efforts and issue any orders on the occasion of an unwanted event. The cost for the protection of these major events could run into the thousands or even millions of dollars. With thousands of people in attendance and potentially millions watching or listening to the event, it is imperative to observe, detect, and prevent any unwanted events so the focus will be on the game and not the potential incident.

Concert Venues

Similarities exist between the risks and protection of stadiums or arenas and concert venues. Concerts can be held in small and intimate settings or moderate-sized venues, as well as large arenas or stadiums. Concerts are a multimillion-dollar source of entertainment to millions of people every year. To the entertainer, concerts are a great way to generate income, promote their talents, and feel connected to their fans.

Risks

The vetting of the audience and control of the crowd are major components of security at the concert venue. At many venues, the fans are subjected to similar searches to those found at athletic events. This can be a consistent practice if the facility also hosts athletic games. For locations which solely host music or entertainment shows, permanent policies for searching fans are established by the management of the venue. For temporary events or festivals, the managing or promotion company can establish policies and procedures to search patrons upon entry of the grounds. These policies can include searching all bags and rolled up blankets or tarps for unwanted items as well as scanning the patrons with metal detectors. The venue or promotional organization should establish consistent entry policies and procedures that can be used for all events and not develop special or biased search procedures based on the act or the potential crowd which may attend.

Controlling the crowd's movement into and out of the venue as well as their activities during the show is also a continuous concern. Many locations allow "general admission" either to the entire venue or to certain portions of the facility. In the past, tragic events have occurred with over-zealous fans rushing into the seating area, injuring or even killing other concert attendees. The organization hosting the event must work to ensure an orderly flow of fans takes place both in and out of the facility.

The activities of intoxicated and unruly fans must also be monitored and managed. Arguments and fights can be triggered for a variety of reasons. These altercations can be heightened and intensified by the consumption of alcohol or illegal drugs. When these events occur, other patrons and staff member can also be injured by the incident.

Concert attendees and staff members can also be victimized by theft similar to the illegal activities at a sporting event. Belongings can be easily taken while the victim is distracted by the concert activities. Large groups of people congregating in common areas, restrooms, and concession stands can also be victimized by people stealing wallets or using illegal electronic devices to copy data from credit and debit cards.

The protection of the performers is another major concern at these events. Crazed or inebriated fans may attempt to climb up on the stage to either get close to their favorite performer, attempt to hurt the individual, or simply gain attention. These incidents can happen at any time and with or without warning. The performer is potentially at risk from the rushing individual and the fan could get injured by the equipment used as part of the performance. At some events, this risk can be greatly elevated when the performer desires to either enter the area where the fans are located or walks onto an unprotected section of the stage where the patrons can come into physical contact with the performer. The size and demeanor of the crowd can influence the potential of harm to the performer. These considerations must be taken into account by the show's organizers as well as the management of the venue.

Preventative Measures

The preventative measures to protect concert venues are similar to those previously listed for sporting events. It is important for the concert promoters to work with the owners and managers of the venue to ensure safety and security for all in attendance. One notable exception is the actions taken to protect the performers. The amount of security needed to protect the acts will depend on the popularity of the performer and the size of the audience. For many extremely popular performers, the employment of **executive protection teams** may occur to ensure the safety and well-being of the act as they travel on tour. The team may be employed by the tour promoter or in some cases the performer or group. These **executive protection teams** may review the venue in advance of the performer's arrival for entry and exit points, ensure that proper barriers are in place to deter fans from rushing onto the stage, and be physically posted at the sides or in front of the stage. The team can also be responsible for physically escorting the performers to and from vehicles as well as into and out of all buildings. Finally, depending on the genre of the act and the potential for harm, some executive protection team members may be armed with either non-lethal or lethal weapons or trained for physical combat. For other performers that do not draw extremely large or aggressive crowds, their personal security may be the responsibility of the venue management. In these cases, members of the security or customer service teams may be designated to escort the performer and ensure his or her safety while on stage. Through the incorporation of the protection of the performers with the practices outlined for sporting venues, crowds can be controlled, unruly or intoxicated attendees can be confronted or removed, and the employees and the remaining fans in attendance can remain safe and enjoy the event.

Amusement Parks and Resorts

Today's amusement parks and their resorts provide various styles of entertainment for their guests. Rides, shows, educational exhibits, games, various places to eat, stores, waterparks, pools, and beaches are just some of the offerings found in these venues. The International Association of Amusement Parks and Attractions (IAAPA) estimates that in the United States alone there are over 400 amusement parks drawing over 290 million visitors, employing over 600,000 employees and generating 12 billion dollars in annual revenue (n.d.). With the popularity of these parks also comes the opportunity for crime, deviance, and personal harm. To keep these venues safe, concentrated and often unnoticed efforts continually take place. Effective security efforts in these parks combine exceptional customer service, covert physical security measures, and detailed policies and procedures.

Risks

The threat of crime, deviance, and unruly visitors is a continuous concern for the amusement park owners and managers. The large crowds of patrons seeking an enjoyable experience can also attract criminals seeking an easy opportunity. Theft and pilferage are a daily threat in these venues. Criminal opportunists enter the parks looking for the chance to steal unattended items from other visitors as well as gifts or food from the retail and restaurant establishments. Internal threats of theft come from employees seeking the same opportunities as the external criminals in addition to seeking chances to potentially overcharge visitors for food and goods or stealing credit cards or the personal identification of those in attendance.

The chance for violent acts to occur is also a continuous threat. Physical altercations between unruly guests, the abduction of children, sexual assaults, or acts of terrorism can occur if not properly deterred. These incidents may be crimes of opportunity or potentially planned in advance. If undetected and ignored, these threats can result in injuries and loss of lives. These violent acts can cause fear and concern in current or potential visitors, thus driving away potential guests from patronizing the venue.

Preventative Measures

Access into amusement parks should be controlled with the same effort and actions as sporting event venues. Patron's bags should be subjected to a search for unwanted or illegal items, and the use of metal detectors can be a solid preventative measure to intercept potential problems or problem visitors before they integrate into the park. In addition, any supplier or delivery person should be monitored for possible illegal or unwanted activities.

Like effective loss prevention programs used in the retail sector, amusement parks and resorts implement solid customer service models by well-trained employees to deter, prevent, and intercept unwanted criminal acts. The employees working in the park are the first line of defense and detection against violent, criminal, or disruptive behaviors. Through the use of a customer service model of protection, employees can interact with potential problem visitors while maintaining a pleasant and upbeat disposition. In the event the visitor continues to be disruptive or threatening, the front-line employee can contact the trained security staff to intervene. The security staff can also patrol in the parking lots and structures, the perimeter of the park property, and the non-public areas to deter or prevent unwanted acts. For moderate to larger parks, deputized police officers can be used to add another layer of protection and prevention. Deputized police officers can either be assigned by the local law enforcement department or be a part of a formal park police department. These trained individuals can immediately enforce criminal laws and place violators under arrest. Through the use of all employees working to maintain a safe and pleasant atmosphere, patrons of these establishments can remain safe and not notice the protective activities around them.

The use of integrated security systems can be a great benefit to these establishments. Security systems such as access control systems and covert security cameras can be monitored, recorded, and controlled at central locations staffed by trained security personnel. Additional integration of biometric identification systems, locking devices, and lights on the park property can also greatly assist in the monitoring, activation, and proper use of these protective measures. Many amusement parks and resorts work to incorporate these devices into the décor of the park. Devices such as closed-circuit television cameras can be installed in or on buildings where park guests are oblivious to their presence. As with any physical security system, proper monitoring and use is essential for its success. Employees must be trained in proper observation and communication techniques to detect and prevent potential events from taking place.

The overall integration of these policies and procedures are the responsibility of the park security management. As with any security program, all policies and procedures must be regularly reviewed and updated as well as trained to all appropriate personnel. The combination of personnel and physical security measures is critical for patrons to have a safe and pleasurable experience in the park or resort.

Hotels and Motels

Hotels and motels are establishments designed to provide lodging services to patrons on a temporary or short-term basis. Hotels offer broader services to guests such as meeting or conference rooms, saunas, formal exercise facilities, or swimming pools, day spas, restaurants, bars, and retail establishments. Hotels are typically located in populated areas such as cities or near airports. Conversely, motels (also known as motor lodges) offer lodging and ample parking with limited services such as swimming pools or exercise rooms. Motels tend to be located near major highways, servicing travelers driving through a particular area.

According to the American Hotel and Lodging Association, during the year 2013, there were over 52,000 lodging facilities (facilities with 15 or more rooms) which offered over 4.9 million rooms and generated an estimated 163 billion dollars in revenue (2014). With the continuous turnover in patrons and guests, these establishments face unique risks on a continuous basis. Because of these threats, hotels and motels typically employ different protection methods to ensure the safety and security for their guests, visitors, and employees.

Risks

The United States Bureau of Justice Statistics reports that during the years of 2004 to 2008, 7,840 violent crimes and 45,910 non-violent crimes took place at American hotels and motels. The data compiled through the National Crime Victimization Survey (NCVS) was a representation of those selected and surveyed regarding crimes suffered during that specific time frame. These numbers may only be a partial representation of all the crimes that take place at these establishments. Other criminal acts may be reported to the management of the hotel or motel, the local law enforcement authority, or go unreported to any organization. These statistics provide a glance into the risks faced by patrons of hotels and motels on a regular basis.

With a fairly transient population staying in hotels and motels, these facilities can become ample grounds for potential crime. Theft can be an ongoing issue in these businesses. Items can be appropriated from luggage and baggage entering and exiting the property, from rooms, and from retail shops and restaurants, and patrons can have wallets, electronics, and credit/debit card information stolen. In addition, robberies may also occur within these venues. Unsuspecting guests may be victimized in hallways, parking facilities, or areas with few people around. Robberies may also take place when guests are in their rooms. In these cases, people open their doors to criminals pretending to be room service, maintenance, housekeeping, or even perpetrators randomly knocking on doors for no announced reason. Along with robberies, assaults may occur in the same areas and under the same circumstances. Unsuspecting patrons or employees can be assaulted and forced to surrender personal property, or in some cases become victims of sexual assault.

Additional criminal encounters can also take place in these facilities. Vandalism can occur to unprotected or unmonitored property. This may include damage to rooms or hallways by unruly guests, destruction of the outer facilities or property, as well as damage or theft of guests' vehicles. Additional criminal activities can take place in rented rooms when hotel or motel employees are inattentive or disinterested in their surroundings. Rooms can be rented by drug dealers, operators of illegal gambling activities, and prostitutes. In some cases, the cover of the rented room can also house elaborate activities such as the production of counterfeit money or the production of illegal drugs. Without proper security and monitoring of the buildings and property, hotels and motels can become a "breeding ground" for criminal activity.

Camera in Business/Entertainment District © missisya via fotolia.com

Preventative Measures

Multiple devices can be utilized to help protect employees and patrons in hotels and motels. To avoid many potential criminal events, personal awareness can be a tremendous asset. Many people see hotels and motels as an extension of their homes, where they feel safe. Because of that mind-set, the guests do not expect or suspect that they may be victimized by a crime. Guests of the facility need to maintain a heightened sense of awareness of their surroundings. This means paying attention to those around them, avoiding leaving unsecured valuables in their rooms, and having a guarded mentality to question the activities and events around them.

Physical security measures are often utilized by hotels and motels to attempt to keep patrons and employees safe. The use of adequate lighting within areas such as parking lots or ramps, the exterior of the building, and in common hallways or corridors can greatly help to deter unwanted events. Closed-circuit television systems, which are strategically placed, well maintained, and properly used, can also help to prevent criminal activities. In a worst case scenario, if a crime does occur, the CCTV system's recordings of the events may assist to identify and potentially apprehend a criminal.

Many hotels and motels are now integrating card access systems for entry into guest rooms, the use of facility amenities such as exercise rooms, or after-hours entry into the exterior of the facility. The use of these systems can be a great cost benefit to the owners of the facilities. In the event of a lost card, another access card can be easily programmed for the client at a fraction of the cost of a physical key. When the card key is programmed, the access control system can be programmed to let the guest or employee into certain rooms or areas of the structure as well as the days and times to use the card. Physical locking devices are also available to the guests and frequently underutilized. Lever locks, lock bars, or window locks are available to provide extra security to the guest when they are in the room. These devices can deter unwanted entry into the room from a hallway or balcony. Also, programmable safes may be available in guest rooms. Typically found in closets or wardrobe cabinets, these devices may be large enough to store money, small valuable items, and even electronic equipment such as laptop computers or tablets. These safes allow the guest to program a personal code to open and close the safe. These items help to prevent the theft of items when the customer is not in the room.

Some travelers take extra precautions and bring personal security devices when they are in hotel or motels rooms. These items may include small door wedges (or door jams) what can be slid between the bottom of the door and the floor to prevent or slow the door from being opened. In addition, travelers may also use portable local alarms which can be activated either manually or by the opening of a door. These devices will emit a loud and piercing noise when activated. They are intended to scare any unwanted intruder away.

Finally, the use of security personnel can be a benefit to protecting the facility, its patrons, and its employees. Formal and highly trained security personnel or departments may be employed by mid- to upper-sized hotels. These security professionals may be highly trained to assist guests, protect the property, and deter unwanted events. Small hotels and motels tend to rely on the desk clerks or maintenance staffs to assist in security matters. Depending on the training and personal motivation of the employee, they may not act as a deterrent and only be instructed to call local law enforcement departments in the event of a problem.

For some travelers, hotels and motels are viewed as a "home away from home." In reality they can be facilities which potentially attract criminal activities. It is up to the management of the facility as well as guests to use every precaution available for their protection and to understand that this is not a home but rather a place of business.

Cruise Ships

Cruise ships (also known as passenger liners) combine transportation, entertainment, dining, tourism, and lodging. The vessels travel from various ports, both foreign and domestic, to numerous destinations around the world. According to the Cruise Lines International Association (2014), it was estimated that over 21.7 million people would travel and vacation on approximately 410 ships operated by 63 different cruise lines. These floating resorts offer a unique set of challenges to protect the passengers and employees on board. With regular passage into international waters, cruise ships adhere to maritime laws. The normal procedure for law enforcement on these vessels is to adhere to the laws the ocean liner "flies under" (the country it is registered). This means that if the ship is from the United States, the laws of the United States apply. To further complicate matters, the laws of each port must be taken into consideration and adhered to. These differing legal regulations can become very confusing in the event an incident takes place either while it is under way or in port. The perceived isolation of these vessels while at sail combined with the potentially confusing legal regulations creates a possible haven for criminal activities.

Risks

Cruise ships face similar risks to those of hotels. These include theft or fraud as well as violent crimes such as sexual assault, robbery, and aggravated assault. Additional possibilities for criminal encounters can take place when the ship docks at port to visit local areas. Local criminals wait at these port landings for opportunities to defraud, rob, or accost the passengers. When these unfortunate incidents occur, the passenger may not have the time to report the crime to the local authorities and remain awaiting an outcome. Depending on the country, the local law enforcement authorities may also be corrupt and part of the criminal enterprise, essentially offering no assistance to the victimized traveler.

Two other risks face the passengers and employees of the ships while they are in transit. Passengers face a risk of falling overboard from the ship if they are not cautious of their surroundings. Responsive methods are available for a passenger or employee who falls overboard but depending on the time of day or night in addition to the weather conditions, recovery of the fallen person can be difficult, if it is even detected. Another threat to cruise ships is the crime of **piracy**. In these circumstances, rogue criminals sail out in smaller and faster boats carrying small arms to intercept the larger vessel. In recent history, these criminals have been a part of loosely organized groups from underdeveloped countries. The pirates then force their way aboard the ship and either steal goods and money or can hold the ship and the passengers hostage. Although the threat of piracy is typically limited to certain geographic areas in the world, the ship's crew must remain alert for such attacks.

Preventative Measures

Passengers aboard a cruise ship need to maintain an awareness of their environment and its activities at all times. Like patrons in hotels, those sailing on cruise lines need to remain observant and vigilant for possible dangers, both aboard ship and in port. Many crimes against passengers are opportunistic in nature. When those traveling on these ocean liners fail to take advantage of locks on doors and the window(s) in their cabin, remain in well-lit and occupied spaces, and refrain from unsafe areas in port, the risk for crime elevates dramatically.

The formal safety and security of the cruise ships falls upon the organization that owns the vessel and the country that it refers to as home port. In the case of the United States, specific rules and regulations for the protection of cruise liners in domestic waters (around the U.S. and its territories) fall upon the responsibility of the United States Coast Guard. During peacetime, the Coast Guard is organizationally assigned as part of the Department of Homeland Security (during wartime, the Coast Guard is assigned to the United States Navy). In 2010, the **Cruise Vessel Security and Safety Act** was created, detailing guidelines for the protection of cruise ships. Under the jurisdiction and enforcement of the Coast Guard, this act defines protective measures such as the height of deck railings to prevent falls overboard and security measures, as well as responding to crimes, the preservation of criminal evidence, and the formal reporting of incidents (U.S. Government Publishing Office, 2015). It is always advised that travelers on cruise ships take the time to understand the rules, precautionary measures, and legal guidelines for the ship they are traveling upon. By doing so, the guest can help to avoid unwanted incidents and accidents when traveling on these vessels and visiting foreign ports.

Conclusion

The entertainment, vacation, and lodging industries draw millions of people into their venues or establishments each year. These companies and organizations create numerous jobs and generate billions of dollars for the economy. Patrons enjoying these events or using these services must be aware of the possible perils and risks that accompany venues. An unaware patron can be quickly victimized by opportunistic criminals waiting to take advantage of a situation. The owners and operators of these venues have responsibilities to maintain a safe environment but they cannot stop or deter all criminal activities. This is why it is essential for the traveler or event patron to maintain awareness of their environment and to be continuously on guard to prevent becoming the next victim of a criminal act. It is possible to enjoy an event, vacation, or traveling accommodation while still maintaining the proper proactive mind-set to protect lives and property.

Case Study — Terror at Sea

Over the past decade, loosely organized bands of pirates have sailed into waters attempting to take over any ships which may come close to their shores. The pirates attempt to board the ships and hold the crew and passengers hostage until a ransom is paid by the organization that owns the vessel. If you were part of the security management team for a cruise line (company), how would you answer the following questions:

1. What type of preventative measures and equipment would you recommend to protect the ship from pirates?
2. Do you believe that these preventative measures and equipment would distract the passengers from enjoying their trips or seem threatening?
3. What type of legal options do cruise lines have to prosecute these pirates when they attack?
4. Would you support recommending to senior management that the cruise line discontinue sailing in these waters and if so, what do you believe the organization's response would be to your proposal?

Discussion Topic — Customer Service or Security

Many entertainment venues have incorporated a "customer service" approach to personnel security efforts. The idea behind this concept is to offer positive and friendly interactions with people in the venue, while still enforcing the rules and regulations of the organization. After reading this chapter, answer the following questions:

1. What do you believe are the advantages of using as customer friendly approach to securing an entertainment venue?
2. What disadvantages to you believe could develop from using this type of customer service approach?
3. How could you integrate law enforcement or police personnel into these venues without disrupting the customer service model of protection?

Research Focus — The Protection of Casinos

The casino industry invests millions of dollars every year on state-of-the-art physical security devices. Logging onto the Internet, search the term "casino security," looking for references and articles on the physical devices used to protect lives, property, and investments. After finding some appropriate articles, answer the following questions:

1. What specific security devices do casinos use to protect their facilities?
2. Are these devices different or unique to only casinos and the gaming industry?
3. How often are devices replaced for new or upgraded technology?
4. What issues, problems, violations, or illegalities do these devices detect?

Key Terms

Gaming manipulation	Fan-on-fan violence	Customer service personnel
Executive protection teams	Piracy	Cruse Vessel Security and Safety Act

Sources

American Gaming Association. (n.d.). *2013 State of the states: The AGA survey of casino entertainment*. Retrieved from https://www.americangaming.org/sites/default/files/uploads/docs/aga_sos2013_fnl.pdf

American Hotel & Lodging Association. (2014). *2014 Lodging industry profile*. Retrieved from https://www.ahla.com/content.aspx?id=36332

Amusement Park and Attractions Industry Statistics. (n.d.). *The International association of amusement parks and attractions*. Retrieved from http://www.

iaapa.org/resources/by-park-type/amusement-parks-and-attractions/industry-statistics

Bureau of Justice Statistics. (n.d.). *Detailed place of occurrence for violent and property crimes, average annual 2004–2008*. Retrieved from http://www.bjs.gov/index.cfm?ty=tp&tid=44

Cruise Lines International Association, Inc. (2014). *The state of the cruise industry in 2014: Global growth in passenger numbers and product offerings*. Retrieved from http://www.cruising.org/vacation/news/press_releases/2014/01/state-cruise-industry-2014-global-growth-passenger-numbers-and-product-o

Get to Know Gaming. (n.d.). *National data*. Retrieved from http://www.gettoknowgaming.org/by-the-book

United States Department of Labor. (2014). *Consumer expenditures—2013*. Retrieved from http://www.bls.gov/news.release/cesan.nr0.htm

United States Government Publishing Office. (2015). *Cruise vessel security and safety act of 2010*. Retrieved from http://www.gpo.gov/fdsys/pkg/FR-2015-01-16/pdf/2015-00464.pdf

Chapter 14

"So, Now What?" The Future of the Security Industry

Introduction

As one of the oldest informal protective concepts known to the criminal justice system, people have been attempting to protect lives and property for centuries. Even though the practice of securing is very old, the evolution of the security industry into a trusted member of the criminal justice system only began to occur over the past few decades. As the industry continues to grow and prosper, this practice of "the business element of the criminal justice system" faces challenges in the future. In this concluding chapter, four specific areas are identified that will be important for the security industry to address in order to remain viable in the foreseeable future.

Continued Public/Private Sector Partnering

Despite the era of disrespect and misunderstanding between the security and law enforcement sectors having taken place in the past, misconceptions and bad feelings still linger between the two entities. Continued work and collaboration needs to take place between the security and law enforcement professions to benefit all of those individuals and organizations they serve. Members of each group must work to accept the abilities and strengths the other entity offers. Through a better understanding of the positive attributes these sectors of the criminal justice system have to offer, collaborative efforts to fight crime can and will continue to develop. The negative mind-set between security and law enforcement which plagued a large portion of the twentieth century must completely end in order to properly protect the public.

Computer Screen with Biometric Data © James Thew via fotolia.com

With an acceptance of the skills, knowledge, and positive attributes security and law enforcement have to offer, development of joint educational opportunities can continue to thrive. The efforts of organizations such as ASIS International can bring both groups together and collaborate with educational programs centered on mutual problems and issues. Even local and regional efforts to bring representatives from security and law enforcement together, creating a positive dialogue and sharing of information, will greatly assist both groups as well as the public as a whole.

When security and law enforcement understand each other's duties and responsibilities and then show a willingness to work together, a sharing of resources as well as critical information will take place. Some sharing of resources and knowledge currently exists, but in some of the cases the collaboration is forced by a governmental agency or occurs in the response to a tragic event. Some local and regional crime prevention groups have been established between security and law enforcement organizations but additional sharing of viable resources and knowledge is still needed. Legal limitations, contractual issues, and liability concerns can prevent the sharing of all resources and knowledge but a systemic effort must continue to join the forces together and use the available knowledge, data, and information to benefit both segments of the criminal justice society.

Finally, the egotistical and negative mind-sets between both groups must conclude. The two sectors of the criminal justice system must agree that mutually positive and professional efforts can and will help to protect the general public as a whole. As many retiring law enforcement officials enter into the security industry as a second career, these institutional transitions can help bridge the ideological gap between the two groups. Also, with the continued need for law enforcement organizations to invest in electronic security devices, additional lines of communication and cooperation will flourish. As previously stated in the Hallcrest Reports and by the 9-11 Commission, security and law enforcement must work together if the general public is to be protected from violence, harm, and the continued threat of terrorism.

The Global Fight against Terrorism

Within the content of this text, numerous direct and indirect examples have been presented to illustrate security's role in the fight against terrorism. Terrorism is a problem that has plagued our society for centuries and will not be slowing or departing in the future. Established terrorist organizations continue to work to recruit new members globally and develop sympathetic members to carry out atrocities when commanded. Regional or local terrorist groups, with radical ideologies, attempt to capitalize on public or private targets to inflict pain and promote their toxic agendas. Lone-wolf terrorists ingest or develop concepts of hatred and mistrust and use the radical thoughts to fuel their own destruction and hate. The harmful acts can occur at any time both physically or digitally. Nobody is insulated or immune from these atrocities in our global society. We are all at risk. This is reality—this is the world we now live in.

The security industry is a vital component in the fight against terrorism. Technological development of physical security measures can be used to detect, identify, and deter terrorist plots. Security personnel can be trained and educated to recognize these threats, initiate proactive protective actions, and work with the law enforcement sector to combat these terrorist elements. Cybersecurity professionals must continue their efforts to constantly develop electronic protective measures to fend off possible attacks on computer networks and electronic infrastructures. These are just a few of the broadly defined roles of the security sector as it applies to the war on terror. Above all, continued vigilance, dedication, and proactive efforts must continue by the security industry in order to protect lives and property. These efforts by the security industry are just a part of the overall and unified work to deter these ever-looming terrorist threats that plague our modern-day society.

Training and Education

As the need for quality security devices and practices continues, so should the need for quality education programs and the requirement of security managers and executives to earn advanced degrees. If the security industry is going to continue to "learn from their past," the industry must continue to embrace and advocate for more college and university security degree classes and programs. In the past, the Hallcrest Reports mentioned that professionalism within the security industry membership must improve. While there has been progress with this aspect of the industry, additional work is needed to educate and professionalize the occupation.

Reputable training programs will need continued development for new members joining the industry as well as the development of new training for emerging areas. For those individuals currently working within the security industry, training and educational programs must continue to be offered and attended to stay abreast to the ever-changing issues that impact this sector of the criminal justice system. It is obvious that the protective needs of our society have drastically changed in the last 20 years. It should be expected and anticipated that with the new threats facing the world today, additional educational seminars and training programs will also need to be developed for the industry to remain a proactive force in the protection of lives and property.

Continued emphasis must also remain on college and university programs to develop appropriate courses and programs pertaining to security management. With the duties and responsibilities of the security industry being a hybrid between the law enforcement and business sectors, appropriate classes need to be developed to educate the next generation of security managers. Quality security management programs need to include classes in criminal justice and security concepts, as well as business management. For specializations such as cybersecurity, programs must address the information technology aspect of the job but also include classes in general security practices. Security organizations and companies that employ management staff should require college degrees for these positions as well as graduate-level degrees for executive positions. With the appropriate balance of classes in security topics, management practices, theory, and research the aspiring security manager will have the proper educational foundation to lead the industry.

In addition to the education of security industry managers, an emphasis on the education and training opportunities must be presented for security employees. This concept of educating and training the entry-level or frontline employees is drastically lacking within the American security industry. Too many security officers and technicians are, at best, minimally educated. The security industry should follow the example of the law enforcement community with its added college degree programs for police officers. The same emphasis on education and training needs to be applied to security employees. These employees should be entering into post-high school vocational or college degree programs. The security industry has yet to fully embrace the need to train and educate their front-line employees. This lack of educational advocacy for these employees leads to poorly compensated positions and high employee turnover. If the security industry is to be properly trained to professionally protect lives and property, all members must be educated, not just the managers.

Finally, college and university criminal justice or criminology faculty and researchers must begin to embrace the issues facing the security industry for future research initiatives. The lack of academic security research by scholars is the result of misunderstandings or misperceptions on the roles, responsibilities, and issues facing the security industry today. The academic community must realize the importance the role of the security industry as it pertains to our global society today and the ongoing issues and concerns continually faced. With research support from the academic community, new protective concepts and practices can be developed, impacting physical, personnel, and informational security issues. If education is a key to success, then a greater effort must take place pertaining to the education of the security industry.

Adaptation to an Ever-Changing Environment

In the military, one of the first rules of warfare is to "adapt to your environment." This means that in order to battle and ultimately defeat the enemy, you must physically and mentally adjust to your surroundings. For the security industry, massive changes have taken place to our society and its protective needs. In today's world, the security industry now faces threats from white-collar and street crimes and domestic and international terrorists, as well as a deluge of crimes, scams, and heinous acts via electronic mediums.

In order to remain a successful, proactive, and relevant sector of the criminal justice system, the security industry must be able to adapt to combating new threats in addition to continuing fighting current risks and perils. Staying vigilant and proactive simultaneously can be a daunting task, but it is one that the security industry must continue to embrace for the future. In order to properly achieve these future protective goals, current industry professionals and educators must work to recruit, train, and mentor the next generation of security leaders. Too many young adults do not fully understand the roles and responsibilities of the security industry and the excellent career opportunities available. Far too many negative mental mind-sets exist pertaining to the security industry and the jobs types these professionals are employed to carry out. The current security leaders and educators must work to interact with our future professionals to promote all the positive attributes of the security industry. If a security professional is truly dedicated to a proactive role to deter unwanted incidents before they occur, he or she must also apply this same proactive mentality to develop the future security industry leaders. By accepting this challenge, today's current security professionals can truly leave a legacy exemplifying their desires to fully protect all lives and property.

Consilio et Animis

Index